Good Bounces
&
Bad Lies

Ben Wright

with

Michael Patrick Shiels

Sleeping Bear Press

Library of Congress Cataloging-in-Publication Data

Wright, Ben, 1932–
Good bounces & bad lies / by Ben Wright
with Michael Shiels.
p.   cm.
ISBN 1-886947-22-8
1. Wright, Ben, 1932– . 2. Sportscasters—Great Britain
Biography. 3. Sportswriters—Great Britain Biography. 4. Golf.
I. Shiels, Michael. II. Title.
GV742.42.W75W75   1999
070.4′49796′092—dc21
[B]
99-35754
CIP

All inquiries should be addressed to:

Sleeping Bear Press
121 South Main
P.O. Box 20
Chelsea, MI 48118

www.sleepingbearpress.com

Printed in the United States

10 9 8 7 6 5 4 3 2 1

Photograph of Ben and Vice President Quayle courtesy of the
George Bush Presidential Library.

Dedication

To my dear mother, my sister Susie, my daughter Margaret, and the love of my life, Eleni, who have brightened even the beautiful days, but more importantly, illuminated the darker moments.

Preface

When I finally sat down to tell these stories, it was fortunate that Michael Shiels's baby tape recorder made my old English quill pen seem redundant. In all truth, the venerable instrument was literally dripping acid from my bitterness. I even wanted to call this offering "Bad Bounces & Bad Lies."

But as I retold some of my experiences of nearly half a century of following and observing big-time golf, the bile and bitterness slowly ebbed out of my system. Gradually at first, then wholeheartedly, I came to realize how much the game and its strolling players had given me, and meant to me. It has, indeed, been a charmed life.

It matters not at all, from a playing-of-the-game point of view, that I peaked exactly 50 years ago—a two handicap in 1949, and never less than five thereafter. (I now languish in double figures, as Gary McCord loves to tell.) My own frailties on the links have been far, *far* outweighed by the deeds of all the magnificent people surrounding golf that I have been privileged to witness practicing their art and craft—amateurs and professionals, writers and broadcasters—during what I believe to have been golf's golden era. From Jones to Jacklin, from Thomson to Tiger, from Darwin to Chirkinian, I have marveled at the skills of these men, and—dare I say it—these women, from Zaharias to Lopez, and from Wethered to Carner.

If some of the wonderful people in golf that I have met and liked do not appear in this book, it is not for absence of appreciation. I have been fortunate in that there have been so many. As Jack Nicklaus so rightly entitled his best book, golf is indeed "The Greatest Game of All."

Read on.

—Ben Wright

Introduction

It was on the first of my many visits from Michigan to stay with Ben Wright at his North Carolina home and assist him with the writing of this book that Ben told me what I feared might be a most prophetic story:

"Michael, my lad, do you realize that the great golf writer Charles Price went to live with Walter Hagen in Michigan to assist him with the writing of his book? They lived together for 18 months with nary a single word written before they decided not to bother. They did, however, have one hell of a good time!"

John Bentley-Wright, now residing in western North Carolina, was born in England in 1932. He was educated at Felsted School in Essex, and at London University, where he graduated in English language, literature, and Russian. While in the British Army, he served as a Russian interpreter.

Wright then became a sportswriter, and then golf correspondent for *The Daily Dispatch* in Manchester and for *The Daily Mirror* in London before becoming a freelance writer and broadcaster in 1961.

Wright penned weekly columns for *The Observer* and *Sunday Times* national newspapers, contributed regularly to *Time* magazine and *Sports Illustrated,* and broadcast for BBC radio and television, and then ITV (the British commercial network).

The lively and studious Brit was a founder and associate editor of *Golf World* (UK), and joined *The Financial Times* as its first ever golf correspondent in 1966. He held that position until retiring in 1989.

In addition to serving as a television announcer for CBS Sports since 1972, Wright commented on golf for the BBC, ITV, Australian Television, and in New Zealand. From 1993–1996, he hosted the South African Broadcasting Corporation's and BBC's worldwide telecast of the *Sun City Million Dollar Challenge,* and broadcast the World Cup from Cape Town in 1996.

Wright was a member of the CBS TV golf commentary team that won an Emmy Award in 1980–1981 and the Peabody Award in 1992. A member of the Golf Writers Association of America, Wright was an award winner in the MacGregor golf writing contest in 1982 and 1989. He has authored books on golf, cricket, and soccer in Great Britain.

Wright has attended the world's major golf events since 1954, and has announced the Ryder Cup Matches in 1989, 1991, 1993, and 1995. His 1995 broadcast of the Masters was the 23rd in succession that Wright broadcast for CBS; he called the action from the 15th and 16th holes.

He continues as editor-at-large for *Links Magazine,* where he has worked since 1988.

In 1994, Wright designed his first golf course in America—Cliffs Valley Golf Club in Traveler's Rest, South Carolina, which opened to rave reviews on October 2, 1995.

Hitting the big screen in 1996, Wright appeared in Kevin Costner's golf film *Tin Cup,* directed by Ron Shelton and released worldwide.

Wright, single now but four times married, has one daughter, Margaret Fraser Wright, who was born on March 25, 1982. She has won seven United States National Championships as an Arabian Show Horse rider.

Wright continues to contribute to the world of golf with charitable activities, speaking engagements, and by hosting travel tours to golf destinations all over the world. He is a member of Bermuda's Mid Ocean Club, Loch Lomond Golf Club in Scotland, Champion Hills Golf Club in Hendersonville, North Carolina, and his own Cliff's Valley Golf Club in Traveler's Rest, South Carolina.

It has been an honor to work with a true journalist and individual who loves the game of golf as much as Ben Wright does.

—Michael Patrick Shiels

Contents

I Am...Ben Hogan

M y deep-rooted esteem for golf has been with me for as long as I can remember, but there is one defining moment, a beacon shining across the entire harbor of my experiences that guided my soul to the game.

During Britain's reconstruction period following World War II, I was obliged to complete a mandatory term in the British Army. As an officer cadet, I was stationed for a short spell at a little place called Crail, which is to say that I was in Scotland, a wee few miles south along the coast from St. Andrews. My duty in Crail was to complete a refresher course in Russian linguistics at the JSSL: the Joint Services School for Linguists. I found the studies to be a perfunctory task. Clothed in my civilian mufti, I reported for the daylong sessions and breezed through each class. Crail, one of the three oldest clubs in Scotland on the edge of the North Sea in the Kingdom of Fife, was famous for its very old little golf course, the Crail Golfing Society's links course at Balcomie. During stolen moments from Army studies, I came to learn that the Balcomie links were a stunning layout of holes that did their best to quench my thirst for the game during my service to His and Her Majesties.

The year was 1953, and the Open Championship was scheduled to return to Scotland and be contested at nearby Carnoustie. The Open hadn't been at Carnoustie in 15 years, since Henry Cotton lifted the Claret Jug there in 1937. Carnoustie's only other Open Championship was won by "the Silver Scot," Tommy Armour, in 1931.

Despite the novelty of a Carnoustie Open, and its temptingly reachable location, I may not have been as wildly keen on attending if it weren't for the buzz making its way through the British Isles: Ben Hogan was coming across the ocean to compete.

1

Hogan appearing, at last, in the Open Championship! I was enthralled at the thought. As a 21-year-old budding student of the game, I was acutely aware of Hogan's mystique. The stories of his intensity, and the sheer strength of will that brought him back from the car accident that many assumed had woefully ended his career, made me feel as if I was a disciple of Hogan. Indeed, as explained elsewhere in this book, I even adopted Ben's name as my own for lifelong use.

Word that Hogan had already won the 1953 Masters and United States Open Championship had come from America. Now, the coming proximity of the great Hogan was unnerving, and I couldn't imagine the Army keeping me from missing the opportunity to see him appear, finally, in Scotland, at the birthplace of the game, and see if his legend held up. I schemed and plotted, and found myself totally distracted.

When the day came, I still had not devised nor determined a way to secure proper relief from my duties as an officer in order to get to Carnoustie. I was in a near fit of madness. I sometimes can't believe the maneuver that I conceived.

We all bunked in Nissen huts made of corrugated steel with cement floors. Like a mischievous child, I placed all the pillows on my bed under the wool covers and downed the bed in such an arrangement that it looked as if there was a body in the bed. I got my buddies to attest that I was desperately ill and not to be bothered. I shamelessly, though without a trace of guilt, went AWOL...absent without leave.

By my accounting, the British Army owed me a debt anyway. The outbreak of the Second World War had come on a Sunday, exactly six days before my seventh birthday. My family lived in Luton, some 30 miles north of London, and within a week, a gentleman, swathed in a gray raincoat and a sinister looking homburg hat, came knocking at our front door.

"Are you Mr. Wright?" the gentleman asked my father.

"I am, sir."

"Is this your son?" he queried, motioning to me, while I watched and listened with the natural curiosity of a child.

My father answered him in the affirmative.

"Mr. Wright, it would seem certain that your son has plenty of toys. Is that correct?"

Popping out his chest, my father agreed.

"Well then," the man stated, without a trace of sympathy, "I've come to take them away and melt them down for scrap metal. So if your son has any lead toy soldiers, we'll need them for the war effort."

My eyes opened like saucers. Of course, I had battalions of lead toy soldiers! They were laid out on a large table, all perfectly lined up and perfectly positioned for the "trooping of the color" for the King. I watched in horror as they began to take my toys away. I protested mightily, to the point of kicking and screaming, as I was carried to a back room and detained under lock while they took everything away. Although I was spared having to view the dismantling of my prized collection of toys, it was the first of many times the war would touch me personally.

Fourteen years later in Crail, within striking distance of a golf legend, I would not again allow the Army to keep "my toys" from me. I set off for Carnoustie.

I crossed the Tay Bridge and covered the short jaunt in my little black buggy of an Austin Seven. I had never been to Carnoustie, and upon arrival quickly realized that it was a horrible town. It was really a scruffy, industrial place, and lacking in facilities. It was still soon after the war, and things were really rough. Carnoustie has always been a mean little town, but it was excessively so at that time because nothing had come back to normal after the war.

I could hardly wait to cheer my spirits by going down to the club. I abandoned my car and walked hastily down to the course. Several clubs play over the links, and they have their own neat clubhouses along the road beside the golf course. To view the links at Carnoustie was to be presented with 7,199 yards of jagged hillocks, snarling traps, and poorly manicured greens. The conditions were a perfect complement to the mood of the course. The weather was dreadful. It was gray and mean and awful—blowy and cold as it so often is in the United Kingdom. And it was July!

I was beginning to second-guess my scheme to come to Carnoustie when, just as I happened upon the golf course, there was Mr. Hogan getting out of his chauffeured car! For all of the buildup, I'm not certain I was prepared to come across him that quickly. But I fixed my gaze upon him. His usual trademark white cap crowned him, and he wore a very beautiful cashmere sweater, bundled over his white shirt. His outfit was fawn in color...very elegant. To a scruffy Brit—and most Brits at that time were excessively scruffy—to see this perfectly tailored gentleman in his perfectly pressed pants and sparkling shoes was eminently impressive and equally breathtaking. Hogan looked like he was a king. He had an aura of invincibility and superiority about him. He cast around with a baleful glare, looking over the land that he was surely intent to conquer. It was the mighty Hogan's legendary "game face." The risk of my journey to Carnoustie was suddenly and certainly now justified.

Not willing to let the mighty Hogan escape my gaze, I shadowed him when he went to practice. It was one of the most extraordinary experiences of my life. His caddie, dispatched with a bag to retrieve balls, barely moved, except when Hogan motioned to him to back up. Hogan would hit 2-irons that he would shape right to left, then left to right, and land them at the caddie's feet. I'm talking about shots in excess of 200 yards. The caddie, with the shag bag in one hand, would catch the ball on the hop and just pop it into the bag. He barely moved at any time, with any club Hogan drew from his bag. Of course, I'd never seen anything the equal of it. It was totally amazing, and the crowd of players who'd gathered around just to watch Hogan practice was equally impressed.

In addition to Hogan's necessary qualifying rounds, the Open Championship was contested over 72 holes, with the final 36 holes played on Friday. Hogan's opening rounds of 73 and 71 left him tied for third, two strokes out of the lead. However, many of the locals were expressing the opinion that as a result of his automobile crash, Hogan would have physical difficulty playing 36 long holes at Carnoustie on the final day. Locals in the bars were speculating that the attendant agonies that had transpired since Hogan's accident would hamper him from walking the final 36. They didn't fancy that Hogan could withstand the conditions and grueling demands, despite the incredible fact that Hogan had already won the first two legs of the modern Grand Slam.

It was also known that Hogan had spoken of Carnoustie with disdain after the early rounds, comparing the greens to putting on glue and even facetiously offering to have a lawn mower sent over from Texas.

Not deterred, I walked every inch of the way with Hogan. I shadowed him for all 36 holes, and even I was tired at the conclusion of that glorious march. The galleries were quite large, with Hogan taking the majority. I would guess the tattered and bundled crowd at about 20,000 in number. Most of them were swarming through the terrain, climbing hills, hopping ditches, and weathering rain to get a glimpse of Hogan. Curiously hidden amongst the teeming gallery was another giant of American culture, singer Frank Sinatra, though he attracted little attention aside from slight mentions in the press.

The people of Carnoustie showed that they were warming to Hogan by attaching to him the moniker: "Wee Ice Mon." His methodical, chilly approach went from being an annoyance to being admired by the Scots, who were mystified by the way Hogan expressed no emotion whatsoever. There was no way of telling how well or poorly he had hit the last shot because his reaction was always the same. Hogan was totally emotionless, and this all served to further my fascination with him. He seemed to drift, as might a glowing ghost, through Carnoustie. The mystique of Hogan was just compelling, and he had presence the likes of which I have never experienced. The aura of superiority was overwhelming.

In those days, the leaders were not the last to tee off, and there were no electronic leaderboards. If you wanted to know how a player was doing, you probably went and asked him. The modern day golfer has no idea how primitive it was. Hogan had no way of knowing where he stood, so all he did was just concentrate on playing each shot. Everything was compartmentalized. On careful inspection, I could almost see the cogs turning in his mind. It was such a thorough, military-type operation of silently stalking and playing the golf course, with total disregard of the blustery conditions and the rest of the field—ruthless, merciless execution coupled with precise strategy. Step by step he played the golf course with total authority...every shot was a different entity. He'd go into this cocoon of absolutely flawless concentration over every shot.

I'd not seen the like of it before, nor an equal of it since.

As for those who doubted Hogan's omniscience, he got better with each round. Suitably bundled, he ground out a 70 through the damp, dull morning in the penultimate round. I then watched the 40-year-old Hogan, legs weakened by his 1949 automobile crash, pale-faced and beginning to look worn, carve out a 68 in the final round.

A 68 'round Carnoustie, fending off an approaching bout with the flu through the suddenly still weather that even offered glimpses of the sun. For him to shoot 68 in the second round of the day…God, it was powerful stuff.

The doubters were few by this point, especially the massive crowd that watched him make birdie four at the 18th. He finally doffed his cap and allowed a tight, stoic smile. The crowd rooted for Hogan. They cheered openly in recognition and appreciation. Hogan, with little elation, claimed the championship with a 282, four shots and an eternity ahead of runners-up Frank Stranahan, the American amateur; Antonio Cerda of Argentina; Peter Thomson of Australia; and Dai Rees of Wales. Victorious over them all, Hogan bowed, and only impassively lifted his cap.

The Scots now revered Hogan, and his legend was only elevated in their eyes by the way the "Wee Ice Mon" dominated what was to be his only British Open appearance. Even British golf hero Henry Cotton referred to the occasion as "the Coronation Open," as Elizabeth II had just been crowned in 1953. He was now their conqueror, and mine as well. His victory, total and complete, made an immeasurably profound impression on me.

It wasn't easy to sneak back to my barracks in Crail because I was very nearly bursting with excitement and awe over the scene I had witnessed. There surely was a noticeable bounce in my step, and I so wanted to tell everyone I met about where I had been and what I had seen. Instead, I had to continue my unbridled joy in silent dreams. I quietly slipped into my bed, pushed the lumpy pillows aside and waited for the dark. My return to the barracks was only bearable because I now slept in the full and certain knowledge that at any risk, golf would be my life and my life would be golf.

My Moveable
Feast of Golf

———◆———

I don't think I'd ever given golf a single thought when, in 1942, my very elderly grandfather, Arthur Wright, gave me a hickory-shafted mashie for my tenth birthday. He'd cut it down to fit me, and I must say that I found the gift puzzling, since I had never expressed any interest in the game.

Arthur Wright was a very well-respected Coventry businessman who was at one time the secretary of Triumph Cars and Motorcycles. I now believe that my aged and wise grandfather may have been using the gift of a cut-down, hickory-shafted mashie to send a message, lift my spirit, and add a bit of civility and hope to my life.

You see, the war had turned my young friends and I into beastly little savages. Luton, the town in which I was born, is 30 miles north of London and was quickly in the thick of things in World War II. A Vauxhall factory (now a General Motors plant) had switched from making automobiles to becoming Britain's biggest producer of Churchill Tanks. The townspeople, therefore, experienced daylight raids of dive-bombing German Stukas early in the war. I learned as a young boy to recognize the frightening whine of a Stuka in full dive.

My lads and I had opportunities to view the occasional handiwork of the Royal Air Force when we would pedal our bikes to the crash sites and raid the downed German planes. We would always be in a hurry to reach the downed bombers, because if we got there before anyone else, we could canvas the wreckage for wallets, valuables, and gauges from the instrument panels. We'd grimly scavenge for anything we might be able to sell on the black market. We never ran into any pilots who were still alive, but I won't kid you, we *did* run into pilots who were still warm. It was a morbid hobby for a ten-year-old child to have.

7

We were very evil little children, shaped from the hardship of war. I recall vividly coming very quickly upon a downed Messerschmitt 110, which was a two-engined fighter-bomber. One of my friends and I were rooting around in the cabin, where we'd collected both pilots' wallets, when we noticed smoke billowing out of one of the engines.

"We'd better get out of here!" I shouted.

As we fled, the plane exploded and we were both blown into a nearby hedge. By the grace of God, we didn't suffer a scratch, but even we had more sense than to go back into downed aircraft after that awful experience.

My younger sister and I slept underground each night for six years in a very extensive air raid shelter that my father had built under his yard at 163 Old Bedford Road to protect his only two offspring. As we exited the kitchen we would hurry down a flight of stone steps to the lawn level, whereupon we came across the elegant rock garden. Beneath the beauty and elegance of that decorative rock garden was a stark and practical reminder of the ugliness of war. The sophisticated shelter was camouflaged by the rock garden. As we descended into the shelter, the rock steps made a 90-degree "L-shaped" turn to help deflect the blast. Behind a heavy metal door there was an electric space heater set into the wall and bunk beds for my sister and me. I'm certain that my parents had invested in this shelter fully expecting to hide there during what seemed like an inevitable German invasion. We fully expected to experience the fear and unthinkable reality of being under Nazi occupation.

Though "Jerry" never landed in Britain, it was this dark shelter that spared my sister and me from the wrath of many powerful attacks.

In November of 1941, my sister and I, away from the safety of our home shelter, hid in a cellar at 14 Grosvenor Road in Coventry. It was under the three-story townhouse of my maternal grandmother and it was where my sister and I experienced firsthand the infamous Coventry Blitz. As we shook in the subterranean darkness of that comparatively vulnerable cellar, my grandmother's home above us was razed to the ground by a land-mine. It was called a "land-mine" but it was basically a tub bomb that looked like an oil barrel full of explosives. In any case, it caused the entire three stories of her townhouse to collapse on top of us like a pack of cards. Nobody was upstairs when the bomb hit, as all of my adult relations were out serving as air wardens. Twenty-six steps below, my sister and I were trapped under the rubble in the wine cellar. Mortar blew out from between the bricks like puffs of smoke from the violence of the continued bombing.

My sister, at age six, was much more frightened than I was, so I talked to her as much as I could to keep her calm. She cried quite a bit, but to me it was like a game, so I was a little rough on her, imploring her to contain her emotions. There was plenty of oxygen, so we lit candles and listened to the sounds above from deep inside the beautiful wine cellar. Unfortunately, I hadn't gotten a taste for wine yet at that young age of eight. Otherwise, I could have had a party because we weren't freed from below for a couple of days. It is, indeed, a story much easier told now than experienced then.

From time to time, we would hear faint scrapings and dull noises from above. We comforted ourselves with the assumptions that these noises served as evidence that efforts indeed were being made to extract us from the cellar, below what must have been mounds of wreckage. The severity and impact of the explosion had not been lost on me, as it was more intense than any other I had experienced. My sister and I were at the mercy of the rescuers and their ability to dig through in a timely fashion. All we could do was wait, and wait we did, buoying our hopes with the vague sounds from above.

It was tough to ward off the dark thoughts, and we began to wonder if the rescuers would be able to get to us. Did they even know we were trapped below? Was it our names I heard the rescuers calling out, or was my imagination playing a cruel trick on me?

At last, the sight of blinding light shining through the rubble and invading our darkness meant that we were saved. Elation was soon replaced by a dull sense of shock as my father tried to shield my young sister and me from the scene around us. He quickly drove us out of town as darkness again began to creep over what was left of Coventry. To our horror, the entire row of terrace-linked Victorian townhouses had been gutted by bombs, and it became apparent that my sister and I were the only survivors. In this grim knowledge, we were spirited away through canyons of rubble piled higher than the car on either side. I caught a glimpse of St. Michael's Cathedral in Coventry—the place in which I was christened—burned and destroyed by the Nazis.

At that young, impressionable age, I was forced to learn to get used to this kind of violence and destruction. I survived the V-1 rockets and the V-2s, which were more lethal. The V-1s were little unmanned airplanes with a primitive, noisy jet engine on the tail. Flames came out of the engine, so they could always be spotted at night. I could hear their sound—a "chug-chug-chug"—as they flew over. The sound would stop when their engines cut out, and they would take about 45 seconds to fall from the sky and explode on impact. My sister and I would stand on the steps of the air raid shelter and watch them fly over. When the motor cut there was a very distinct silence, so we would run down into the shelter, slam shut the heavy door and brace for the explosion.

The sight of London burning, its skies orange with the glow of fire, became sort of ordinary to me and the others who were going to survive this horror. I became emotionally dead, and became this little beast. While I looked for ways to strike back, my sister, more mentally affected than I, definitely turned inward. I befriended the American soldiers as they prepared for the Normandy invasion. Their vehicles were parked outside the house as they gradually assembled their forces and got ready to move down to the coast. I hung around with the G.I.'s on the clear understanding that I needed candy and gum, which I would then sell on the black market. I was a very healthy little twelve-year-old black marketer. A product of war, I scrounged madly for candy and gum, which the Americans were very generous with. I didn't eat sugar because it was rationed. To this day, I have never been able to eat anything sweet. It's amazing what rationing can do to you in that respect.

We received all of our information huddled around the radio. As an intrepid radio listener, I heard Prime Minister Winston Churchill's declaration of war on September 3, 1939. Even when I was a young boy, Churchill's oratory abilities were not lost on me. His speaking skills were unbelievable, and he so fired me up that I believe I'd have run through a wall if he told me to do so. Churchill was my boyhood hero. I wanted to be like him, and some would say that my eventual broadcast delivery, like that of Henry Longhurst, was Churchillian in nature.

I even celebrated the war's end in 1945 in a mischievous manner. A big party was held at my home in Luton. Somehow, I got my hands on some rockets. Being this horrible little child, I launched these fireworks from my hip in a big lemonade bottle. I lit the rockets in celebration of the Allies' victory, but I ended up shooting one through the breakfast room window and into my parents' home, setting the drapes on fire. That action didn't make me a war hero. My parents' home had somehow withstood the war, and I nearly burned it down in a victory celebration.

B y now, it should be evident that my grandfather, by presenting me with the hickory-shafted mashie, was apparently attempting to inject some civility into the savagery the war had assisted me in embracing.

I soon thereafter began to wield the mashie in a very primitive way, smashing a bundle of rags or rocks around the garden at my home. My father had two acres (half of the property was lawn and half bore vegetables and fruit) and this was my first acquaintance with the game of golf.

I played my first round of golf at age 11. My father, on his way to work at 8 A.M., would drive me to the golf course at South Bedfordshire. I would walk 54 holes before he would stop at the course at day's end to collect me on his way home from the factory he managed. I was 13 years old when I put together my first full set of assorted clubs. My clubs were recruited from attics and dusty storerooms. There was just no equipment to be had in those days because of the war. There were no golf balls, either, so some of the balls I found to use looked like old pieces of furnace coke. Awful looking beat-up rocks, they were, but I was by then completely besotted by the game.

In 1946, I began my study at a very famous public boys' school called Felsted in Essex. I was very well educated there. However, lodging on campus, I found myself surrounded by interminable cricket fields. I was forced to hit golf shots from outside my study through the field hockey and rugby fields onto the beautifully manicured cricket pitches. I even daringly hit golf balls right over the top of the school buildings. I drew the ire of the cricket coach when he began to notice suspicious pitch marks and indentations on his cricket squares. From that day forward, I would enlist my schoolmates in matches in which we played from tree to tree all over the Felsted grounds, excluding the cricket fields. Eventually, the game was altogether banned by the school.

While studying at Felsted, I was fortunate to be named editor of the school magazine. My top sidekick and assistant was a guy named

Neil Allen, with whom I shared a study. Because the head of the school had elected not to live on campus, Allen and I managed the good fortune of inheriting the vacant study that was intended for the headmaster. It was spacious and elegant, occupying the corner of the red brick lodging building, with two large windows that provided a sweeping view of the lawns and landscape.

Though we were only students, Allen and I lived large, hiding booze under the floorboards of the study and planning to conquer the world. For my part, and with Neil's encouragement, I began by conquering a young assistant matron named Pam Baylis. We were red-blooded and youthful boys, making attempts at real machismo.

Neil and I were total Hemingway buffs. All we ever wanted was to be like "Papa," and we had complete delusions of grandeur. We were full of admiration for his masculine way and his lifestyle full of great adventure. Hemingway was a wild sportsman, and pugnacious. Neil and I were also determined to follow in Hemingway's footsteps and become colorful writers of active life. In my enthusiasm, I wrote and posted a letter to Hemingway, spelling out my appreciation for him and asking what advice he might have for me.

Imagine my excitement when I was delivered a letter from Hemingway in return. This larger than life character had actually taken the time to devise and send correspondence to me. The note was terse and wise.

> *I would never give any advice to a young writer other than to always be true to yourself.*
>
> —*Ernest Hemingway*

Felsted was a famous field hockey school, and Neil was a very talented field hockey goalkeeper. He was also a phenomenally good athlete who held the school record for the half-mile for some years after he left. Because of Neil, I maintained an interest in the field hockey goings-on.

England held a field hockey trial at Felsted to determine the makeup of their national team. A team of "probables" was to play against a team of "possibles." In other words, the first team would play the shadow squad. Now Felsted is set in the wilds of Essex, which is a near neighbor to Siberia. Siberia is across the North Sea, past Lithuania, and Estonia. When Essex gets bad weather in the winter, it is a fierce place to dwell because very often the winds come in due east from Siberia and just sweep across the fields of Felsted, taking no prisoners. On the particular day the national hockey trial was to be held, the weather was so bad that the reporters who were in Essex to cover the competition for the *Times Newspaper* and the *Sunday Times*, its Sunday sister, pulled a "no-show." Reports were that when they arrived at the local pub, they took one look at the weather and decided never to emerge until the weather passed.

Being an enterprising young Hemingway maven, I sent in unsolicited accounts of the hockey trials to both newspapers. To my delight, they were published under the byline "Special Correspondent." I got no name credit, but I was no less thrilled.

The sports editor of the *Sunday Times* was a guy named Pat Murphy, a huge one-eyed Irishman and a marvelous man. Murphy wrote a letter to me at Felsted after he published my submissions.

"I'm so impressed that a young schoolboy would have the guts to do what you've done. I want you to know that if you ever want a job in journalism, you must get in touch with me." I wouldn't forget it.

Though I more than thoroughly enjoyed my unforgettable time at Felsted, it naturally came to an end. My actual departure from Felsted in 1951 was a memorable example of our grandiose flailings.

"To hell with this place," I shouted to Neil as I climbed behind the wheel of my father's station wagon. "I'm out of here." I then stepped on the gas to make my grand exit. In my wild haste and exuberance, however, I embarrassed myself by accidentally smashing the car straight into the school gates.

"Lucky Jim strikes again!" Neil yelled, comparing me to the bumbling British Kingsley Amis antihero. "Oh, Lucky Jim, how I envy him," my pal mocked, quoting from the comic novel.

Following Felsted, I began my mandatory service term in the British Army. The Army sent me to study Russian Language at London University, where I also completed my degree in English. I completed the Russian course in 15 months, placing sixth amongst my classmates. From the 1,600 students that began the course, only 408 finished. As the Army had hoped, I made high marks. Therefore, I was sent to Berlin to interrogate Russian deserters.

Due to security reasons, I didn't see much of the city. It was instilled into our group of interrogators that one of every ten Russian deserters was, in fact, a spy planted by the Russians. Our task was to identify these "plants" and weed them out. Two of us would sit a deserter down and fire questions at him, trying to learn his life history, starting with his date of birth. Genuine deserters were all too happy to cooperate. Those that were plants were very savvy at attempting to ingratiate themselves to us.

If we were in doubt whether our subject was being evasive or not telling the truth, we'd send him up the corridor and someone would hit him upside the head a few times. Suddenly, the deserter would have total recall. It was a savage world, and we were in the height of the Cold War. In many cases, the plants would confess because they realized that they were better off being captured and interned by the Allies, rather than serving in the Russian Army where they would face bitter cold with inferior uniforms and footwear. It was during my involvement in these operations that I was sent to Crail in Scotland for the aforementioned Russian refresher course that led me to Hogan and the change in my life.

On October 4, 1953, I finished my term with the British Army. Allowing myself a little time to relax, I went to Paris for a weekend...and ended up staying for months.

The weekend of my arrival, I was intent upon attending the Prix de l'Arc de Triomphe, France's most important horse race. I wanted to back the English horse "Premonition," which had just won the St. Leger, the stamina race of the big three that dominate the English three-year-old season, similar to the American Triple Crown. I was very expert on horses, as I had run book in the Army (with the blessing of my company commander). Despite my expertise, the unthinkable and surprising results of the Prix de l'Arc de Triomphe cost me all of the money I'd brought with me from England. Brits were only allowed to take a certain amount of money out of England and my 40 pounds sterling vanished before my eyes with the surprising ignominy of "Premonition." I didn't have enough money to pay my initial bill at the Hotel Bedford on the Boulevard Haussmann. Just like that, I became a dishwasher at the hotel until I paid off the expense I had incurred.

I also masqueraded as an Australian student at the Cité Universitaire, which allowed me to lodge at an inexpensive student rate. Along with assorted friends, I partied like a boy relieved to be out of the service. Living the life of Riley, I laid waste to Paris. I was just as mad as could be.

During my time in Paris, I encountered some of the great American jazz musicians who were fugitives from the McCarthy era. I saw Lionel Hampton, Buck Clayton, Art Simmons, Sidney Bechet, and Stephane Grapelli. Jazz was king, and all of the greats were in Paris. To revel as I did and allow myself to hear this magnificent music, I became most adept at washing dishes. Sugar Ray Robinson had a club called "Ringside" near the Champs Elysees, and I washed many dishes there just to maintain my hedonistic lifestyle.

When I had enough money, I spent more than my share of time at "Harry's New York Bar" at V Rue Daunou. I was again attempting to follow in the sycophantic footsteps of Hemingway, whose pictures adorned the walls there because he'd been known to frequent the little red-curtained bar. *Sign me up*, I thought. *I'm Hemingway!*

My bravado and swagger wilted one day when I happened into "Harry's" and what to my wondering eyes did appear but "Papa" himself occupying the bar. My jaw hit the floor as I observed him in his legendary setting. I had always wanted to be Hemingway, and here he was, right in front of me. I was awed such that I was lacking the guts to approach him. I flunked talking to Hemingway at Harry's and have since kicked myself. I was startled to stumble across him in that manner, but observing him that night made my hero become more than a legendary literary giant. Previously seen to me only in print, photo, and in my imagination, he became decidedly real.

I knew then that it was time to leave Paris behind and try to make something of myself. There was work to be done if I were to measure up to the standards set by "Papa."

My months of living in the City of Light and behaving like a lunatic were over.

It was time to call in a chit and give journalism a try. I retrieved the tattered letter and phoned Pat Murphy at the *Sunday Times*. Murphy, however, had moved on to greater things as editor of the *Daily Dispatch* in Manchester, a newspaper owned by Viscount Kemsley. Therefore, I wrote to Mr. Murphy at the *Daily Dispatch* and he responded, good to his word:

Dear John Bentley,

> *Subject to your being accepted by the union, you may start here in February, 1954, with special reference to sport as your future once you have been put through your paces. I will second you to the sports department, where I know your heart truly lies.*

Signed,

Pat Murphy

I was absolutely over the moon about this! At four pounds per week, I rented lodgings in Manchester and toiled as a cub reporter. My first paycheck, which came in a brown envelope, amounted, after taxes, to eight pounds, sixteen shillings, and three pence. I felt as if I was a bloody millionaire. Good God, I felt like a king! This was the first money I'd ever earned for an honest day's toil.

These were incredibly happy days for me, even though I was given every dirty little job to be done. In Britain, just as it can be in the United States, Southerners and Northerners are wary of each other. I was a Southerner in a northern town, and so I was an easy target for prejudice.

My night news editor was Maurice Wigglesworth. No matter how hard I try, I shall never be able to purge the Dickensian sight of that man from my memory. He was an extraordinarily obese, totally bald, evil smelling, and truly disgusting creature. Wigglesworth, or "Mr. 5×5," as we used to call him—like an unhappy Buddha sweating from his every pore, coated with grease and dirt—was a very ugly man. When he sat on his stool, his buttocks hung over and virtually touched the floor on either side.

The River Trent divides Britain's north and south, and there is no love lost between those rivals hailing from opposing latitudes. Wigglesworth, being from the north, considered me to be a southern toff, and the tension between us was constantly palpable. I had little choice but to suffer him, and he did little to conceal his disdain for the very sight of me.

Wigglesworth hated me with a passion, and he would purposely give me ever-dirtier assignments. Wigglesworth would have me getting lists of prostitutes who had been arrested that evening and cover tenement fires in the slums. I interviewed people who kept coal in their bath. All of the dirty, filthy jobs were given to young Wright.

After two months of this abuse, Wigglesworth called me to his desk at around 7:00 one winter's evening.

"Wright," he gleefully grunted at me, "I am going to give you an assignment tonight that is absolutely vile, and totally befits you."

I swallowed hard.

"You see, Wright, what has happened is that on the moors, about an hour from here, where the wind is blowing the snow horizontally at 40 miles per hour, there has been an horrendous crash."

I listened intently to each blood-curdling word and the annoying sound of his whiny voice.

"A head-on crash, Wright, between a truckload of sugar and a coach-load of teenage mill workers. There is blood and guts and sugar and shit all over the highway. That's where you're bound, Wright, to write me a lead for page seven, with pictures, Wright. Your photographer will be Arthur Brooks, and he is waiting. Do well, and I'll consider actually giving you a byline. Now get the hell out of here."

Brooks and I arrived at the moors, and to say it was unpleasant would be a grave understatement. It was gory, and I threw up countless times. I rode with a girl to the hospital. She was lying on a gurney, and suddenly she sat bolt upright, mumbled some frantic gibberish, and keeled over dead. There were four killed and twenty-two seriously injured. That night was filled with horrible experiences. Eventually, I returned to the office, soaking wet and spent. I heaved down at my desk in the back of the newsroom to begin to diligently hammer out the hideous story on my clumsy typewriter. Awful as it was, I knew that this assignment was my first big break.

With some measure of triumph, I slammed the finished story down on the desk of Maurice Wigglesworth. He looked over the copy up and down, looked up at me, and looked back down at the copy. I began to wonder if he would indeed relent and give me what I felt would be a well-deserved byline. I stood at his desk trying to withstand his gagging stench.

"John Bentley hyphen-fuckin' Wright," he muttered without looking up at me. "Now there's a name to conjure with. Allow me to ask you one thing, Mr. John Bentley hyphen-fuckin' Wright. Do you think that we should run the columns of the newspaper horizontally to accommodate your pompously lengthy and self-important name? If so, you're going to remain in terrifying anonymity for the remainder of your mediocre career. The only alternative that I can suggest is that you go to your seat at the back of this miserable little space and shorten your name forthwith."

As he directed so eloquently, I repaired to my desk and began to think about how to shorten my given name. It was not an easy thing to do. My mind drifted to Ben Hogan and how viewing him at Carnoustie had convinced me beyond a shadow of a doubt that I should devote my life to golf. "Ben Wright" seemed fairly uncomplicated, and it allowed me to adopt the name of my golf idol. I had emulated Hogan, I tried to play like him, and I'd even taken to wearing a flat Hogan-style cap.

That evening, "Ben Wright" was born, and that's how my first byline appeared in the newspaper, page lead, page seven, the following day.

Having finally received a byline, and serving what I felt to be a more than adequate amount of time and toil in the hellish purgatory of Wigglesworth, I petitioned Murphy to fulfill his promise to shift my duties to the area of sport. You see, in my grandiose mind, I was on my way to joining the field of elite British golf writers. Pat Ward Thomas of *The Guardian*, Bernard Darwin and his successor Peter Ryde of *The Times of London,* Henry Longhurst of the *Sunday Times*, and Peter Dobereiner of the *Observer*. This was a closely knit group of people who prided themselves on the way they wrote. It was the golden age of the golf writer, and in golf circles, they were better respected than the players themselves. I made every effort to emulate them, and tried always to be as literate as possible.

I took careful note, as well, of the aplomb with which the golf writers lived. The enduring charm of Longhurst, for instance, who resided in two authentic windmills. One he named "Jack," the other, "Jill." "Jack" served as his sleeping quarters, and he kept his office in "Jill." Each morning he rose, dressed, and walked the 25 paces from "Jack" to "Jill" to begin work. Longhurst had collected a lot of money from wagers in soccer pools, and used every bit of it to purchase a lifetime supply of champagne splits. Longhurst would begin each workday at "Jill" by drinking one of these little half bottles of champagne. God, he was a character.

Longhurst was captain of the Cambridge golf team in the 1920s. He and I were members of the same golf club in Bedfordshire, England, called Aspley Guise and Woburn Sands. It was, curiously, a nine-hole golf course that straddled the boundary between two villages. My parents lived in Woburn Sands. I never knew Henry while growing up because he was over 20 years my senior, but came to know him while covering sporting events as an apprentice.

It was in the long room of the clubhouse at the Royal and Ancient Golf Club that I first came across Bernard Darwin, the doyen of British golf writers. Darwin, like I, was in St. Andrews to cover the 1958 Eisenhower Trophy competition, and I was allowed access to the R&A clubhouse during the event because of my little metal "Association of Golf Writers" badge. Darwin, though, was a member of the Royal and Ancient Golf Club. I had read each inch of every column that Darwin had ever written, and doted on his every rich word. He was the founder of his craft, a man who wrote what can only be described as great golfing literature. I had to meet him.

Quickly, I maneuvered over to my mentor Longhurst and grabbed his elbow.

"Henry, sir, would it be appropriate for me to ask you the favor of introducing me to Mr. Darwin?"

Longhurst could sense my excitement and nervousness. "That's quite easy, my boy," he droned. "Quite easy, indeed. I'll take you over and you'll buy him a scotch, and it'll be quite easy."

We walked over to Darwin's table near the tall windows at the front of the long room, and as Longhurst introduced me to the aloof and feebly crotchety elder statesman, I was further humbled by the realization that while I considered Longhurst to be my mentor, Darwin was indeed Longhurst's mentor. Henry was correct, though, in that a scotch bought me a ticket to Darwin's table, and a few moments of Darwin's company. I can assure you, though, that it was a one-way conversation, as I did little but sit and listen to Longhurst and Darwin. As an apprentice writer, I knew better than to start to pontificate about my views in front of these two learned and accomplished men. In this situation, I followed the old adage that "children should be seen and not heard."

In the middle of the conversation, Darwin, seemingly distracted and without explanation, rose and left Longhurst and me at the table. I assumed he was going to heed nature's call until I saw him toddle down past the window that looked out over the first tee. Puzzled, I watched him determinedly make his way down to the tee box. Once there, he began pointing and shaking his cane in an animated conversation with a golfer sporting a brightly colored sweater. Their dialogue was brief. Darwin reentered the esteemed and august clubhouse, returned to our table, and continued our conversation as if nothing had happened. My curiosity surpassed my manners, and with a youthful burst of foolhardy courage I stammered up the temerity to politely question Darwin.

"Mr. Darwin, if you don't mind me inquiring, would you see fit to let me in on the conversation you just had down there on the tee?"

"Oh well, just look at that man down there, in that silly attire," Darwin grumbled as the man was by now progressing down the first fairway. "That 'coat of many colors' he's wearing looks as if he's tugged the quilt from his bed and wrapped it 'round himself to play the Old Course."

"Yes, quite right, Mr. Darwin. But whatever did you say to him?"

"I walked up to him, examined his clothing, and asked him, 'Young man, are those the colors of your old school, or those of your own unfortunate choosing?'"

"How did he reply?" I asked, barely containing my grin.

"He didn't. After all, what could he say?"

Another character, though he could hardly be described as literate, was American golf writer Dan Jenkins. I recall vividly being in Rome with the crude and wily Jenkins. I was guiding him around the continent as he researched an article on the European Tour. We were standing together on one of the seven hills of Rome on our first evening, and there was a marvelous light as the sun was starting to set. Jenkins looked around at the vista that is Rome, took a big drag on his cigarette, and in his Texas drawl uttered, "You know, Ben, this could have been one helluva town if they had ever finished it."

In those days, golf writing was like a fraternity in that the writers were very close with the players. The Tour was in its infancy, far from the corporate hyperbole and garish entourages of today. Golf was, at that time, so much more intimate and charmingly antiquated.

In the early years, championships and tournaments in Britain finished on Friday nights because the contestants were club professionals who needed to scurry back to work in their professional shops on Saturday mornings. Otherwise, they might not have a job come Monday. One exception was Henry Cotton, one of the great figures in British golf. Cotton, like Walter Hagen in America, helped to elevate the status of a PGA professional from a serf-like position to that of a respected human being.

Growing up with an interest in the game, I was keenly aware of Cotton, who served as a hero to many when British heroes were in short supply. His Open Championship victories in 1934, 1937 and 1948 were cherished and celebrated. In fact, the Dunlop 65 ball was named after a score he shot in the second round while achieving his first victory at Royal St. George's. All this I knew as a youth, and now my aim was to report about him as an adult, which meant having a chance to get to know the man.

He was keen to help reporters because he knew the value of publicity. He was even an official of the Association of Golf Writers in Europe. I found him to be very accessible, as well as a man with a wild streak in him, something that I certainly might be considered to be an expert on.

Eschewing the life of a humble golf professional, Cotton refused to be subservient and was good and determined to live life. To ensure his aspiration, he married an Argentinian millionairess called "Toots" who allowed Cotton to enjoy the good things in life: fine dining, fancy American cars, tailored apparel, the finest hotels, and a magnificent residence in Eaton Square, which is among London's prized addresses. Cotton lived like a king.

His theory about the golf swing was that it was all in the hands. Pupils of Cotton would hit abandoned automobile tires to develop wrist strength. I got to know Cotton while he was competing in the 1950s, and it was fairly well-known that it was Toots and her financial resources that gave Cotton the opportunity to become the kind of golfer he was. I came to realize the downside of Cotton's arrangement at the British Open at Hoylake in 1956. Intent on interviewing Cotton as he headed for the car park, I caught up with him as he neared his car, where Toots was waiting for him.

"You played like an idiot!" she barked, slapping his face at the same time.

I ceased in my tracks and went no farther, avoiding further witness of the indignity he was suffering at the hands of his hot-blooded wife.

The first British Open I covered as a writer was in 1954 at Royal Birkdale. The press room was actually a Quonset hut left over from the war. Compared to today's modern, modem-filled, plush communications centers, they were primitive digs. The woman at the desk next to me was a golf writer named Betty Debenham for a Fleet Street tabloid called the *Daily Sketch.* She would come in to work and her fox terrier would sleep at her feet under the desk. If you brought a dog into the press room today they'd bloody well have you arrested.

There I was, a 22-year-old humble cub reporter with the Manchester *Daily Dispatch,* accompanying my sports editor Archie Ledbrooke to the Open. Ledbrooke wrote the main stories, and I was given the job of writing sidebars on the local pros and how they fared. Qualifying was on Monday and Tuesday, and the first round was Wednesday. By the second round's end on Thursday, however, none of the local Manchester pros were within 100 miles of the cut.

"What should I do in this case, Archie?" I asked Ledbrooke. "Should I head back to the office on Friday?"

"No, Ben. I want you to stay because after the final round on Friday, I have to leave as soon as possible. I want you to do an in-depth interview with the winner. See if you can get a really nice story."

Peter Thomson won his first of five Opens that day, and while there was little of the pomp and circumstance you'd find today, he did meet with the press. I crept up to Thomson once he'd finished with everyone else. He was cradling the Claret Jug and chatting with his buddies. I was out of my depth, and nervous beyond belief, but I plucked up the courage and approached Thomson, gasping and gulping for air.

"Excuse me, Mr. Thomson," I began, not knowing what terrible fate awaited me. "My sports editor, Mr. Archie Ledbrooke, would like me to do a in-depth article with you, and I wondered if you could spare me a few minutes of your valuable time?"

The new British Open Champion looked me over.

"What are you doing for dinner?" Thomson asked me.

"Huh? Uh, well, nothing," I stammered, caught completely off guard.

I ended up having dinner in the Prince of Wales Hotel in Southport with Peter Thomson, the Claret Jug between us.

Not an awful lot was known about Peter Thomson. He was the newcomer from Australia. Of course, he went on to become one of the great players of all time. I collected a great deal of information and insight during our splendid dinner. Thomson was very cerebral, and a man of real substance. He was a vividly intellectual person, and very well read. He was a qualified chemist, went on to write for the *Melbourne Age,* and even stood for Parliament at one point. On the golf course his method was so simple and repetitive, it could never go wrong. Nicknamed "the Melbourne Tiger," Thomson was ruthlessly competitive and would rather grind an opponent into the ground than look at him. He was a killer, and he went on to employ his tactics to win four more Open Championships—each of which I witnessed. In 1985, Thomson set a U.S. Senior Tour record by winning nine events in one calendar year. (The record was tied by Hale Irwin in 1997.)

Following our extended conversation and meal on this day in 1954, I rushed the 30 miles back to Manchester to write my piece. Since there was no Sunday edition, my story ran early Monday all over the whole of page one, along with a photo of Thomson and the Claret Jug. The paper gave me one hell of a showing.

Monday morning, I went into the office and prepared to go about my regular duties.

"Damned fine work, Wright." Ledbrooke's voice startled me. "Damned fine. Damned fine. You did an enormous job, Ben, and you are now my deputy sports editor."

At age 22, after that first fortuitous golf assignment, I suddenly went from cub reporter to assistant sports editor. I was grateful and excited to be granted a significant raise. The thought of my grandfather presenting me with that cut-down mashie, and the chance at dignity it triggered, flashed through my mind. Thanks to that gesture, I'd come a long way in a short time.

I can only guess that the reason Thomson generously afforded me such time and attention was that he could tell that, unlike some of my infamous British tabloid scribes, I was interested in and fascinated only by the game. I was not interested in the scandalous and salacious personal details the muckrakers from Fleet Street found so sensational. Thomson could see in my line of questioning and true curiosity that I was not out there to gather dirt.

That's not to say, especially as a young cub reporter, that I did not, from time to time, stumble across occurrences and information that were surprising, delicate, and indeed sensational.

The Canada Cup Golf Tournament, now known as the World Cup, was an international competition made up of two-man teams from countries around the world. In 1956, I covered the event in London, which featured the exciting American team of Ben Hogan and Sam Snead. As I stood outside the Savoy Hotel preparing to taxi over to the station to catch a train down to the golf course, I noticed that a young tournament official was directing each of the two-man teams toward their respective limousines to be driven to the tough, tree-lined Burma Road West Course at Wentworth.

As Hogan came out of the hotel and looked toward the waiting limousine, the tournament official greeted him excitedly.

"Good morning, Mr. Hogan," he said warmly. "Your car is right here waiting. Mr. Snead is already in the car, and so you'll be driven immediately."

Hogan responded quickly and sharply.

"I'll not be riding with Mr. Snead," he snapped.

"Oh, but Mr. Hogan, we've arranged it so that each team has their own car and are able to ride together.

"I'll not be riding with Mr. Snead," was Hogan's even firmer reply. Only Hogan would ever have the cold temerity to be so stubborn.

Realizing that no further discussion of the matter was to be tolerated by Hogan, the tournament official, now completely flustered, was scurrying around for a solution when his eyes inadvertently met mine. I'd been standing there observing this scene with great interest.

"Hogan refuses to ride with Snead," the official explained, nearly breathless. "How am I to remedy this? I mean, that's Ben Hogan, and he won't get in the car with Sam Snead!"

I looked at the official with a simple shrug and said, "Well then, I suppose you'd just better get yourself another bloody car."

I was cavalier about the fellow's problem, but, as a cub reporter of 23 years of age, I was indeed wide-eyed at Hogan being so stubborn as to refuse to ride with his American partner. Why would Hogan harbor so much enmity toward his teammate? Hogan and Snead were the most popular names in American golf. They were often mentioned in the same breath, and it was assumed that their time spent in proximity to each other would mean that some sense of camaraderie would exist, especially when teamed together away from home on foreign soil.

In later years, Hogan would confide in me the very personal reason for his ongoing contempt and enmity toward Snead. Unfortunately, I am sworn to secrecy on his feelings.

I was immensely pleased to have the opportunity to cover the golf world from the inside, and while it was certainly my forte, golf still was somewhat saddled by the opinion that it was a minor sport. Ledbrooke, therefore, felt confident enough in my overall ability to write that he assigned me to the gamut. I reported on football, cricket, boxing, motor racing, rugby (union and league), and horse racing.

The most prestigious sports assignment was the football beat, which is called soccer in some parts of the world. Football was like a religion in England and I was fortunate to begin traveling with the Manchester United football team. Manchester United was a superpower of football. Nicknamed "the Busby Babes," the team was a fine-tuned machine of strong and speedy players. In February of 1958, I was scheduled to make my first international trip to cover Manchester United. It was another sign of the paper's confidence in my abilities when Ledbrooke decided to send me with the team to Belgrade to cover a game they were to play against Red Star, the Yugoslavian Army team, in the semifinal game of the European Cup.

As I was walking out of the offices, excited to be finally on my way to an overseas assignment, my mentor Pat Murphy grabbed my arm.

"Where the hell are you going?" he asked me.

"I'm going to Belgrade."

"The hell you are. You're not even dry behind the ears, Wright. You're a cub reporter. You're not going to Belgrade to cover an important assignment like this. Tell Ledbrooke to get his fat ass over here!"

Crestfallen, my last hope was to tell Murphy that Ledbrooke couldn't be reached.

"I don't know how to get ahold of him, Mr. Murphy. He's playing in a bridge tournament on the outskirts of town in Stockport."

"Just get him, Wright," were the stern words that dashed my Belgrade aspirations.

Ledbrooke was found, summoned, made it to the team's charter flight, and covered the game, which was played to a 3-3 draw. On the return trip from Belgrade, the charter flight landed in Munich, Germany to refuel. The Manchester United team, along with the officials and journalists aboard, trooped back onto the plane for take-off. Speeding down the runway, the aircraft's brakes were suddenly applied and the liftoff aborted. As the passengers patiently waited, a second liftoff was attempted, but was aborted even sooner than the last.

Journalist Frank Swift, a reporter with the *News of the World,* unbuckled his seat belt and leapt to his feet.

"What the hell is going on here?" he shouted.

With that the passengers were told of a technical difficulty and returned to the terminal, where they deplaned and drank coffee through the delay before being sent back aboard the aircraft. Again, the engines surged as the plane sped down the runway. In a gruesome crash, the Elizabethan turbo-prop plane went down attempting another liftoff. I attended 14 funerals in 5 days, including that of Archie Ledbrooke, which, without the finger of fate, would have been *my* funeral. It was a very dreary and dreadful week going from funeral to funeral.

So moved by the terrible tragedy, I wrote an account of the circumstances surrounding the crash with Bill Foulkes, a defenseman who survived the crash. The best-seller was entitled *Back to the Top,* and in it were many ghastly horror stories, including the account of survivor Bobby Charlton, now Sir Bobby, a legendary English soccer player. Charlton told me how he was knocked unconscious and that his seat fell through the bottom of the aircraft. He awakened, still buckled in, bouncing on the springs of his seat on the runway. Coverage of the entire incident made an indelible impression on me, full in the knowledge that without luck and the continuing providence of my acquaintance with Murphy, I, too, certainly would have perished in that flight.

Not too many years after, I was on board a flight attempting to leave Ringway Airport in Manchester. When the second attempt to lift off was not the charm, I insisted on deplaning. It was, after all, the third attempt at a liftoff that brought down the Manchester United charter. Having been so close to that situation, I was not willing to push my luck, even in the face of what would have been a purely coincidental fate.

The other event of my early days that left a lifetime impression on me was viewing the homecoming of Bobby Jones to St. Andrews in October of 1958. Three times a British Open champion and golf's only Grand Slam winner, Jones was returning to St. Andrews to act as a nonplaying captain of the American team competing in the inaugural World Amateur Team Championship. The event's trophy was named for Dwight D. Eisenhower, Jones's great friend and a member of his Augusta National Golf Club.

While back in St. Andrews, the legendary Jones, through a historic ceremony, was to be invested with citizenship through an honor called the "Freedom of the City." Benjamin Franklin was the only other American ever accorded that singular honor, which was given to a scant few figures of literary and political accomplishment.

I would be lying if I said I was eager to attend the ceremony. In truth, I wanted no part of it, dismissing it as tedious pomp and circumstance. I was just too young and too green to know any better. Thankfully, the more established golf writers convinced me that I simply must attend. I feel very privileged when I recall walking to the ceremony through the tiny streets of St. Andrews with the likes of Henry Longhurst, Leonard Crawley, and American golf writer Herbert Warren Wind. These masters of the golf writing craft steered me to the hall, past the moving curtains of the jealous townspeople, who peered out of their windows to get a look at Jones and to see who was invited to the private ceremony that even they could not attend. Though thousands were in attendance, there was precious little space, considering the guest of honor inside the auditorium.

Thousands milled about outside the graduation hall at St. Andrews University as the ceremonies for the returning champion began with prayer and continued with Jones receiving the Freedom of the City. The scroll on which the honor was scripted was then placed in a sterling silver casket and presented to Jones by the university provost.

"We are here today to confer the Freedom of the City and Royal Burgh of St. Andrews on Mr. Robert Tyre Jones Jr. of Atlanta, Georgia," stated the provost. "Mr. Jones is recognized as the most distinguished golfer of this age—one might say of all time. As representatives of the community of St. Andrews, we wish to honor Mr. Jones because we feel drawn to him by ties of affection and personal regard of a particularly cordial nature and because we know that he himself has declared his own enduring affection for this place and its people."

The provost went on to recall Jones's initial contempt for the Old Course, then his Open Championship victory at St. Andrews in 1927, and then his glorious accomplishment in 1930, when Jones captured both the Open and Amateur Championships of Britain and America, a feat never accomplished before or since. His British Amateur victory came at the Old Course, and was acclaimed in St. Andrews almost as the triumph of a favorite son.

"At the height of his attainments, and still at the height of his powers, Mr. Jones retired from major competitive events," the provost continued, "to reign forever after in our hearts, as Mr. Bernard Darwin suggests, as the Champion of Champions to the end of his days."

The drama was high as an ailing Jones rose from his wheelchair, his legs gnarled by disease, and struggled to his feet. Eschewing assistance, Jones, in leg braces, slid himself to the podium by pushing his body along the table. Holding himself up, Jones slowly worked his way down the table by pushing off with clenched fists. Applause filled the hall as those assembled viewed this unbelievable display of Jones's immense mental power. He did, indeed, will himself to that podium unassisted, as he had once willed victories over Sarazen, Wethered, Hagen, Turnesa, and others. It was the same mental power and strength of character that served him during his victorious conquests in the game.

Once at the lectern, Jones steadied himself and addressed the spellbound audience with a speech he delivered without any notes.

"People of St. Andrews, I know that you are doing me a very high honor and I want you to know that I am grateful for it," Jones said. He then detailed the supreme joy he experienced on each of his visits to St. Andrews. "When I say now to you, 'Greetings my friends at St.

Andrews,' I know I am not presuming, because of what has passed between us. It is another element of the sensitivity that you people have—a wonderful warm relationship. I could take out of my life everything except my experiences at St. Andrews, and I'd still have a rich full life. I just want to say to you that this is the finest thing that has ever happened to me....Now I officially have the right to feel as much at home at St. Andrews as I have presumed to feel for a number of years."

With that, Jones ended his speech and deafening applause filled the hall, along with boisterous Scottish chants of "Hip, hip, hooray! Hip, hip, hooray!" When finally the cheering ended, Jones was escorted into the golf cart that had assisted him in reaching the stage. As he was driven down the center aisle, the entire crowd, which feared this was surely a farewell, listened as a lone, Scot broke into a mournful old Scottish ballad, and then joined him in singing: "Will Ye No Come Back Again?"

"Will ye no come back again?
Will ye no come back again?
Better loved ye 'canna be
Will ye no come back again?"

Jones exited to the strains of this prophetic sentiment. Not a dry eye remained—not even those of the tough Scots witnessing this historic, once-in-a-lifetime event. The scene prompted golfer Billy Joe Patton, after moments of speechless silence, to turn to Wind and utter, "He is the greatest Southerner that has ever lived."

Blubbering like a child, as well, I once again bore witness to the deep power that the game of golf could have over the lives of those who held it dear. I continued my esteem for the game, and my tireless efforts to report about its nuances in the *Daily Mirror*.

Viscount Kemsley eventually became of a mind to sell off the rights of his printing operations to the *Daily Mirror* from London so that the *Mirror* could publish their northern edition from Manchester and circulate it all over the north of England. The financial deal was so sweet that Kemsley was able to close down the *Daily Dispatch*. I feared my promising career was in danger until our union bosses cut a deal with the *Daily Mirror* that allowed us to retain gainful employment with the *Mirror*. Although I was politically at the other end of the spectrum from the *Mirror,* my personal tenet became "any port in a storm." Believe it or not, I soon became their golden boy.

Transferred to London, I was being groomed for stardom to take over for the veteran columnist Peter Wilson, who had been dubbed "the man they can't gag." I spent a great deal of time attending boxing matches with Wilson, who took the opportunity to enjoy himself while letting me do a lot of his work.

My status and ability to cover golf at the *Daily Mirror* were short-lived, however. The *Mirror* was a left wing newspaper and they covered golf only under protest, thinking of the game as the sport of the elite. I persistently attempted to promote golf and gain column inches for the sport I championed. I tried to explain to the powers that be at the *Mirror* that golf was the sport of the future, but my pleading fell upon deaf ears. My effort to promote golf was 20 years ahead of its time.

The Daily Mirror wanted me out and, unfortunately, I inadvertently gave them the reason they were looking for to dispense with me.

I was covering the 1961 Amateur Championship at Turnberry and observing Ronnie Shade, who was the son of golf professional John Shade and a fantastic amateur golfer. Shade was known by the initials "RDBM," which stood for "right down the bloody middle," because his drives so rarely rested anywhere but in the fairway. That was Ronnie Shade's trademark: RDBM.

Shade came from the east of Scotland, on the Edinburgh side, and his opponent in the amateur, Jimmy Walker, hailed from Irvine, on the western side. There was never any love lost between the East and the West Coast Scots, so the contest was a genuine grudge match.

Speaking with Walker after the result, I learned of a bit of gamesmanship that took place at a key moment. Apparently, Walker was looking at an 18-inch putt for the win and he presumed that Shade would call it "good" and let Walker pick it up without perfunctorily putting it. A voice from the crowd cried to Shade, "Gee him nothin', son!" The whispered aside from the gallery convinced Shade to make Walker complete the tap in, which he missed! Walker assumed that it was Ronnie's father who spoke from the gallery.

I wrote about this act of gamesmanship; how Ronnie Shade was told by his father not to concede the putt. Many considered John

Shade's encroaching admonition of "Gee him nothin', son" to be boorish, not sporting, and an unwelcome intrusion on the match.

The only problem was that it turned out that John Shade was not even present at the match. He was east of Edinburgh. The Shade family had me dead to rights for libel and defamation of character. The *Daily Mirror* released me ostensibly, to appease the Shade family.

It was the beginning of my freelance career.

I walked out of my office and drove home to tell my then wife Pat that I'd been fired, and that we were potentially on our uppers. We were forced to sell our fashionable home just outside London in St. Albans and go back into limited accommodation and pick up the pieces. We moved back near my wife's roots in Cheshire, which allowed me to toil as a night sub-editor at the *Daily Herald* in Manchester. I experienced five years of struggle working day and night, scrambling to write freelance spec articles, submitting them with the hope they might actually be published, and that I might then actually be compensated for them. I wrote about rugby, cricket, soccer, golf, and whatever else I could.

It was a difficult and stressful period. One evening, I left the press club quite late after a more than adequate number of pints. I drove home needing to get to bed and in the certain knowledge that I had very little time to sleep before having to leave again for the newspaper. The car reached the gate at the bottom of the driveway, which my wife would normally leave just barely on its latch so that I could nose it open with the front end of my car upon my normally late arrivals. I gingerly pushed on the gates with the car, and nothing happened. The gate would not open.

That stupid bitch, I thought, employing endearments induced by the drink. *What the hell has she done? She's forgotten to leave the gate open. Ahh, she wouldn't have done that.*

I decided to push the accelerator a bit firmer, when suddenly, *crash!* The gate broke into pieces and my car zoomed up the drive into the back of my next door neighbor's car. Every light in the sleeping neighborhood went on, and every occupant of every home was at his bedroom window peering at this bloody idiot!

Unfortunately, the instability of that period would cause the breakup of my first marriage, as Pat and I agreed to part rather than continue our daily rows. I suppose the stress that can accompany the highs and lows of a show business career led me in and out of three subsequent betrothals, culminating in the end of my 16-year marriage to my fourth wife Kitty in 1996.

The life I had chosen was rough on marriage and especially rough on my wives. The frequent absences, in my case, did not "make their hearts grow fonder." In 1976, for instance, I made 22 round-trip flights back and forth across the Atlantic and four round-trips from London to Australia, not to mention my frequent flights from London to cover the European Tour. When I would return home from these trips, I would be eager to just put my feet up and recharge my batteries. Of course, my wives, having been shut in alone during my journeys, were eager to go out, get some entertainment, and do some living. This was an immediate and constant quarrel point. My wives were keenly aware that I was living a "Five-Star" existence on the road, and wanted their turn to be wined and dined.

I was away from home when my only child Margaret was born in New York City in 1982. My then wife Kitty was overdue by two weeks and had experienced one "false start," during which I scurried with her to the hospital.

On March 25, 1982, I received permission from CBS producer Frank Chirkinian to remain in New York and miss my television rehearsal in Hilton Head because we felt that Kitty was about to deliver. Eventually, I stood by Kitty's side at the hospital during the epidural procedure—but not for long. I became wobbly in the knees at the sight of an eight-inch needle perforating my wife's spine and nearly fainted away.

Kitty's sister Margaret Brennan came to stay with her because I was to fly down to Hilton Head for the actual broadcast. While I was live on the air in my tower on the golf course, a call came into the production truck. The news was relayed to the broadcast anchor, Vin Scully, who announced on the air, and to me, that Kitty had indeed given birth to a girl...Margaret. I learned about the birth of my daughter from hundreds of miles away, on television, through Scully's announcement and a graphic superimposed over the screen.

Despite the end of my first marriage, and the bad career bounces along the way, at least my writing ambitions seemed to be moving forward and aimed in the right direction, at times with the help of fate.

Covering the 1964 British Open on a freelance assignment for *GolfWorld UK,* I participated in a draw with other writers as to which player each of us would be assigned to follow all week and write about. I drew the last pick, and had to watch helplessly as the other writers took their turns in front of me drawing all of the American stars.

My favorite choice would have been Arnold Palmer, but alas, he had been unable to make the trip to Britain on this occasion. It was a disappointment to the galleries, as it was to me because I had witnessed how Palmer had single-handedly rescued the Open Championship over the four years previously, beginning with his 1960 appearance at St. Andrews.

When Palmer agreed to play in the Centenary Open after his victorious final round charge at Cherry Hills that summer in the 1960 U.S. Open, the British crowds at St. Andrews were immense. Only one year previously, when Gary Player defeated Fred Bullock and the elegant Belgian golfer Flory van Donch at Muirfield in 1959, Bullock's clubs were toted by his daughter on a pull cart. That's how low the Open had sunk until Palmer competed in 1960.

Palmer's appearance in 1960 was celebrated by the British in much the same way Hogan's arrival was cherished in 1953 at Carnoustie and Jones's appearance in 1930 was cherished in St. Andrews. As much as the British rooted for their native players, there was no denying that the glamour of having Palmer was most attractive to the Brits. The charming and heroic Palmer won their respect, admiration, and especially affection in a way that even Hogan had not. Hogan crowds were reserved and respectful, while Palmer found his galleries— "Arnie's Armies"—to be boisterous and enthusiastic.

In 1960, the final two rounds of the Open were played on a Friday. After completion of the morning round, Palmer was lying second, in perfect position to repeat his Cherry Hills charge there at St. Andrews in the afternoon. The stage was set, and spectators, competitors, and Palmer all expected the inevitable charge over the final 18 holes that day.

As I interviewed him in the basement locker room between rounds, a freak thunderstorm hit the course. As Palmer was answering one of my questions, an announcement was made that the afternoon's golf would be cancelled and the final round would be rescheduled for the following morning. The look that came over Palmer's face was that of sheer and utter rage. Palmer was fit to be tied at hearing the news. He knew he had the rest of the field on the run and that they'd be looking over their shoulders in the heat of battle that afternoon. As far as Palmer was concerned, his pigeons were all lined up. He was younger, he was stronger, and the momentum and advantage that he'd gained would now be lost. Insisting that the R&A was hasty in their decision to cancel the day's play, Palmer went into a fit and began to throw clubs around the locker room.

That brought the interview to an awkward end, but Palmer's tirade itself was brought to a halt only when water from the rain overflow began rushing into the basement locker room. We scurried around scooping up everyone else's shoes off of the floor and out of danger of the tide.

To Palmer's chagrin, the rain cleared. With so many hours of light left in the Scottish day, he was of the opinion that play should be able to continue. Palmer's perception that the course would be playable so soon after a major storm may have been unrealistic, but by the same token the decision of the R&A to cancel the day's play may well have been hasty and premature.

When play resumed the next day, however, it was Kel Nagle who lifted the Claret Jug victorious in the 100th anniversary of the Open Championship after holding off a dampened Palmer charge by one shot.

The following year, Palmer cemented his legendary macho image with the Brits by defeating nature itself on his way to a one-shot victory at Royal Birkdale. A plaque remains to this day at the spot where Palmer's mighty swing at his ball in a gorse bush preserved his first Open championship. Of course, in an odd way, the plaque also commemorates the willow scrub bush, which ceased to exist the minute Palmer's thrashing club made its pass at the ball—a shot impossible for mere mortals.

It was a revival-like atmosphere at Troon in 1962 when the dashing Palmer forged an insurmountable lead and won the Open by six shots. I witnessed my *GolfWorld UK* editor Ken Bowden get trampled at the 18th by the mob trying to catch glimpses of Palmer and get close to him as he defended his title. Bowden showed me the actual spike marks that ran up and down his scarred back after the near riot. Palmer himself emerged from the mob hobbling and looking gleefully exasperated.

A las, though, back to 1964 where I awaited my turn to draw and learn which player it would be that I was assigned to shadow for *GolfWorld UK*. My fears were confirmed when Nicklaus, Player, and others were drawn by other writers. "Muggins" here, picking last, ended up drawing a player I'd never seen play—"Champagne" Tony Lema. I knew that he'd never played the Old Course before and would probably suffer the same fate that Jones did on his first visit.

I thought I'd make the best if it, and tried to remain positive, which was a keen attitude until I went to meet Lema as he arrived in town. Along with another pro named Doug Sanders, Lema had been driven into St. Andrews from Edinburgh early in the morning. My first sight of him was to see a man who'd traveled a long way, was unshaven, and had possibly overindulged himself along the way.

What the hell do we have here? I asked myself. They looked like a couple of ruffians. Two party animals like Lema and Sanders lodging together. I figured I had no chance.

I introduced myself anyway, and Lema was all too happy to agree to my request to shadow him since he was unfamiliar with the country and could use my help. "It helps me to relax to have someone to talk to," he admitted. I showed Lema around everywhere.

At the Old Course during a casual practice round that afternoon, I walked with Lema and gave him direction on where to hit his shots. Palmer's no-show allowed Lema to use the services of Arnold's regular Open caddie, Tip Anderson, and we forged a little three-man alliance over the storied links. Anderson and I did our best to advise Lema on the tricks and traps of the Old Course, steering him around the ancient track.

One could not fail to be impressed immediately by the sheer feline grace of the man, his wiry toughness, and his enormous ability. What astounded me most was that Lema, a man who'd partied his way over from the States and had never seen the Old Course, lipped out three full wedge shots and he didn't even finish all 18 holes. I was surprised because I had assumed he'd left himself far too little time to adjust to the time differential. I was also impressed; his steeple-high wedge shots were truly breathtaking. After witnessing this display, I said, "Tony, you know that even if you should win, they'll never forgive you here for using your wedge and not playing bump-and-run shots."

"To hell with that," Lema scoffed. "I'll play the game the way I know how."

Lema possessed as elegant a swing as I have ever seen. Although his method was one obviously impossible for most ordinary mortals to imitate, it was remarkable for its fluency and perfection of timing. Lema's driving was a joy to behold, even though he was plainly exhausted. His only intent was to loosen his aching limbs and make a cursory examination of the course.

His pivot was immensely deep, the shoulders turning so fully that only a superb athlete could achieve it. His left arm was stiff as a ramrod. The takeaway was very much on the inside, but a loop at the top took the hands high. A tremendously swift drop of the wrists on the downswing produced a very late hit. The knees were bent, and they slid forward as Lema's arms drove on and up through the ball in the accepted American manner. He was a spectacularly beautiful golfer.

I rushed out to make a wager on Lema, and backed him at 66-1. The papers were saying Lema couldn't possibly win, even though he'd just come off of a win at the Buick Open. They said he hadn't given himself enough time to prepare. Certainly no player could win on his first time on the Old Course, especially an American. The British boys and Scots at the Jigger Inn scoffed at my account of Lema's practice round and were further startled to hear that I'd dared to place a wager on the American.

"That round the American played is a fluke," the patrons taunted me from behind their pints. "If he dares hit those wedge shots in the Championship, the wind will blow them out to sea!"

I walked every step of all 72 holes of the Open with the lanky, slim-hipped Lema. Of course, everybody knows the happy ending. Tony defeated Jack Nicklaus by five shots. Lema got his Open Championship, I got my story for *GolfWorld UK*, I collected on the 66-1 bet on Lema, and Tony, true to his trademark, bought champagne for all of the assembled press.

Most importantly, I had a new friend. Lema was a lovely man, and just as wild as a March hare. He was a great guy to hang around with if you were a derelict like me. When you think that he had the panache to buy champagne for the press each time he won, you understand why a company like Moët & Chandon was willing to sponsor him and supply the bottles of White Star.

This was the great thing about Lema. Although golf had become a very serious business to him, he was determined that it should not rule his life to the exclusion of enjoyment. He held an irresistible fascination for the opposite sex, who were no doubt partly intrigued by his lingering reputation as a lady killer of monumental prowess. Men liked him for the same reason—here was a latter day Walter Hagen. Even when he'd given up the life of a playboy (which he had used to compensate himself in moments of despair during his early unsuccessful days on the Tour), few people guessed what turmoil of the soul this nervous, sensitive and self-conscious man was suffering, and the agonies of the ulcers those moments produced.

My spirits and career were lifted again in 1965, when the British Open once again came to nearby Southport. Lema was back in town, and we enjoyed a hilarious time at a cricket match, drinking and discussing the nuances of the game so foreign to Lema.

To put the real icing on the cake, 11 years after I had dinner with Peter Thomson to complete my first ever golf writing assignment, right before my eyes the Aussie won again at Royal Birkdale. He beat Nicklaus, Palmer, and everybody else into a cocked hat to collect his fifth (and final) British Open. Thomson particularly enjoyed beating high-profile Americans like Palmer and Nicklaus at the height of their powers because he despised everything American. In reality, he despised the big ball. Thomson was a real "picker" of the ball, which he could easily do with the British ball because it was 1.62 inches in diameter. With the American ball—which was 1.68 inches in diameter—he had a much harder time. To disguise this Achilles Heel, Thomson claimed to despise the slow way Americans played, their manners, their lack of culture, and their food.

"Ben," Thomson said to me after his victory, "since you were here with me for my first win at Birkdale, I suppose it's only fitting that you come on back to the room."

I went back to his room at the beautiful Prince of Wales Hotel again—11 years and four Open wins later. Thomson had now joined John H. Taylor and James Braid among the five-time winners.

Thomson had a rabbit hutch of a little room at the hotel with a tiny bathroom and a wash basin. We used the mugs from the wash basin to drink champagne. After a few toasts with Thomson's pals Bruce Devlin and Mike Wolveridge, the four of us enjoyed a princely dinner in the very same restaurant where we had eaten upon the occasion of his first Open victory and my first golf writing assignment.

Following dinner, we strolled down a big staircase that led from the dining room to the bar area and the lobby. Walking with the stride of a proud champion, Thomson gazed around and surveyed the room. Eventually, he peered into the bar. There he spied two of his competitors seated behind drinks at the bar, commiserating. Thomson paused to take in the scene of these two chaps, who looked as if they were consoling each other.

Finally, Thomson allowed himself a broad, seraphic smile of triumph, which crept over his face like a rushing tide. I then realized that Thomson's satisfaction was derived from the fact that the two men drowning their sorrows were Nicklaus and Palmer, side by side at the bar, shoulders slumped.

Palmer and Nicklaus, perhaps sensing a presence, casually turned back to see who was darkening the door of the bar. When they saw Thomson in full grin, they quickly and without any acknowledgment turned back to their drinks in synchronized self-annoyance.

His unbridled joy at conquering the pride of America was boundless. This made Thomson even more of a hero to the Brits, some of whom still had not forgiven Nicklaus for his debut in the United Kingdom at the 1959 Walker Cup at Muirfield. That occasion was the first time I'd ever seen Nicklaus, and I, too, can remember the fat lad offending British sensibilities by callously complaining about the lack of air conditioning and his inability to find what he considered to be a decent steak. Britain was still suffering from the horrors of WWII. The toll of victory had been high, and many amenities commonplace to an American were not yet available to all Brits. It was reminiscent of when Sam Snead, upon winning the 1946 Open at St. Andrews, likened traveling to Great Britain to "camping out." Typically, the British maintain a stiff upper lip and make do without whining and complaining as Nicklaus did, somewhat spoiling our first impression of him.

Never have I seen the British "stiff upper lip" challenged more than I did at what turned out to be one of the most important golf tournaments of my career. Since 1924 in Britain, a proud and magnificent golf event is held each spring at Easter. "The Halford Hewitt Tournament" includes 64 of the leading schools of Britain, which each sponsor a ten-man team, made up of five two-man alternate shot pairings. The schools face off, head to head, in match play. As an alumnus, I had become a regular member of the Felsted team. In fact, I was a member of the only Felsted team ever to reach the quarterfinals and the semifinals in consecutive years, a fact that I am rather proud of.

The Halford Hewitt Tournament is one of the great binges of all time. It is one of the great drinking weeks, as 640 players come into town from all over the land, along with assorted hangers-on and baggage masters and captains. It is a major social event on the British calendar, and in 1966 it proved to be a boon to my career.

The event is held at Royal Cinque Ports, in Deal, Kent, and Royal St. George's, in Sandwich, Kent, the latter being the site of several modern British Opens. As the teams prepared for play, including my Felsted team, we were hit with a force ten gale that completely surprised the weather forecasters. In typical British stiff upper lip fashion, the tournament organizers expected us to play into, and through, the menacing weather. Not only was a force ten gale blowing across the links, but it was blowing snow from out over the English Channel. The big flakes, which left the grass green by not hitting the ground, frosted the players and made them look like "Nanooks of the North!" The crazed competitors were going around the links in every bit of clothing they could lay their hands on. The conditions were not fit for animals, let alone human beings.

My Felsted partner's name was Tony Jackson, and we were playing against Richard McLean and Tony Hill representing Marlborough, which was another very famous school. Hill's father was president of the English Golf Union, and McLean was the advertising director of the *Financial Times*.

As luck would have it, now close to darkness in the afternoon, the wind fell to nothing—as it so often does when the tide changes. Therefore, within minutes, the snow that had been swirling in the wind began falling and blanketing the course to a depth of one inch.

A man came out, dressed like some Eskimo, walking up the fairway from the clubhouse, ringing a bell to alert players of the suspension of play. By the time the bell ringer had arrived, I must have been quite a sight myself. He found me sitting in the middle of the ninth fairway with my knees tucked up, quietly crying because I was so cold. I was freezing, soaked by the wicked snow. I was *very* pleased that we were being called in. It was wildly stupid to be playing in the first place. Three men who played that day suffered heart attacks within a month. Thankfully, none of them proved fatal.

I went to the car park to put my golf clubs away but was unable to open the trunk because the lock was iced up. Someone nearby lent me his cigarette lighter so that I could attempt to heat and thaw the lock, which I did. I then heaved my soaking wet bag of clubs into the trunk, hoping never to see them again.

I hurried into the warmth of the clubhouse, where half pints of scotch and brandy were being served in the club's solid silver tankards. The club had set them up on tables on either side of the door as frozen competitors stumbled in from the porch. I took my scotch, slugged it down, and continued to the locker room, where I began to peel off my layers of wet clothing. The other men in the locker room were suddenly startled to see me charging through the dressing area, laughing like an idiot. In an attempt to stay warm on the course, I had put on multicolored paisley pajamas underneath my clothes. The dye from these thoroughly soaked pajamas had run all over my skin, coloring me in red, green, yellow and blue swatches of dye! After I saw myself, I thought it was hilarious and ran wildly around the locker room. I'm sure everyone thought I'd gone mad.

The three men with whom I had been playing this arctic golf had agreed to meet in the bar downstairs to ward off the evil pneumonia. We got to talking, and hit it pretty hard. I thought I would never feel warm again, but eventually, aided by the imaginary assistance of spirits, I began to warm up. Many people around us were doing the same—drinking hard.

Finding it difficult to stand steadily by this stage, we adjourned to a table. We ordered another round of drinks as we got to know each other a little better. I began to tell long tales of my experiences covering golf. Richard McLean, the advertising director of the *Financial Times,* slurred to me: "Wright, you're a freelance writer about golf. Why don't you write a column for the *Financial Times*?"

"The *Financial Times*?" I drunkenly mumbled back. "Why would I write a golf column for the *Financial Times*? Isn't that a financial paper?"

This ridiculous, totally drunken conversation continued.

"I happen to be the advertising director of the *Financial Times,* and I would venture to say that 80 percent of our readers play golf. It seems like a natural that there should be a golf column in the *Financial Times.* There never has been a golf column, and I think you, Ben, should write it. I've enjoyed listening to you and your experiences."

"Well, Richard, if you are truly sincere, I've got to say that I am interested."

While I assumed it was merely his drunkenness doing the talking, McLean told me, "I'm going to take it up with the editor, Sir Gordon Newton, on Monday when I return to the office."

We resumed play at 8:30 the next morning and experienced dastardly cold again. I had to thaw the trunk lock again with flame just to get the clubs out, only to find that all of the zips on my golf bag were frozen as well, making it impossible to retrieve any of the bag's contents, including golf balls. It was blue sky, but brutal.

Quickly and mercifully knocked out of the matches, I went back to Manchester to defrost by the fireplace at home. Monday, at about 11:00 in the morning, I received a phone call from Richard McLean.

"Ben, I've seen the editor and he wants to see you tomorrow."

"Richard," I cried, "I've just driven back to Manchester!"

"The editor will pay your airfare down. Just fly down from Ringway Airport in Manchester. Be here at midday tomorrow."

I could tell he was quite serious, but still I remained somewhat skeptical.

Sure enough, the following day I was ushered into the office of Sir Gordon Newton, a very august gentleman who'd been knighted by the queen for his services to journalism.

"Wright," he said, "it's been brought to my notice that it might be a good idea if you wrote a golf column for this newspaper, and I think it would be a good idea. I see no reason why we shouldn't have a golf column."

I listened intently.

"I've got a proposal for you," Sir Newton continued, not pausing for me even to speak. "I want you to go down the corridor to meet my deputy, Mr. Bill Roger. He'll set you up in an office, and I want you to write a column for publication in this Tuesday's edition."

"What do you want me to write about, sir?"

"I want you to write about anything that you think pertains to the situation. If it's financial in nature, so much the better. If I like what you write, I will pay you what I think it's worth and then I'll want you to write for the rest of the month. That will be four columns. At the end of the month, you'll either like what I pay you, and I'll like what you write, or we'll part company. Obviously, if I don't like what you write, I won't ask you to go on. If you don't like the money I'm paying you, you won't go on anyhow."

"Sounds eminently fair to me, sir."

I went down the corridor and into an office, where I wrote an article entitled "A Test for Townsend," about a wonder boy golfer named Peter Townsend, who was a teenage boy who played in the 1965 Walker Cup. Townsend was preparing to play in the Brabazon Trophy—which is the English amateur stroke play championship at a place called Hunstanton in West Norfolk—that upcoming weekend. I forecast in the article that "although Townsend would be severely tested, he would win the tournament handily." I detailed Townsend's chief rivals and why he would be able to fend them off.

True to my column—word by word—Townsend won the tournament by seven shots.

Back in Manchester the following Monday, I received a telephone call from an impressed Sir Newton. "Wright, bloody good piece. When we come to the other major championships, I think you should go into the prediction business!"

While I may have preferred to rest a bit on my prediction laurels, Newton was calling my bluff to prove that it was no fluke.

A few weeks later, I wrote a column about the British Open. At this time in 1966, Jack Nicklaus had yet to win an Open Championship. Therefore, I forecast in the column that Nicklaus would finally break through at Muirfield and win the Open for the first time. I made this prediction even though I was training a player named Dave Thomas, a British Ryder Cup player, with the express intention of thwarting Nicklaus. I was trying to get Thomas in shape, running his overweight body ragged through the woodland, up in Cheshire, south of Manchester, where we both lived.

The 1966 British Open at Muirfield was, of course, won by Nicklaus, with Thomas and Doug Sanders one shot behind. I wrote a tournament recap article about Nicklaus's victory, which included all of the details, and many quotes from Nicklaus himself. A telegram then came from Sir Newton that read:

> *Another brilliant prediction, Wright, but, your recap article was really rather spoiled by your idiotic reliance on the words of Jack Nicklaus. He may be a splendid golfer, but we don't want to listen to him in this paper. We're paying you to express your opinions and to describe the action. I'm not interested in quotes, and if I see inverted commas in your column again, we may part company.*
>
> *—Newton*

Newton was like that. He was a baronet and he was a martinet. However, I never had to ask for a raise, and after a couple of months, when I inquired about foreign travel, Sir Newton's response was, "Wright, the world is your oyster. Go where you like, and send me the bill."

I could not have asked for a better arrangement. I traveled the world, sending columns in from everywhere under the sun. I was completely self-reliant, could literally go anywhere I wanted, and never had to wait long for a pay raise.

The relationship between Sir Newton and me grew nicely. I moved down to Surrey, the same county in which he lived. Newton and I would lunch together, and he would take me to his clubs. We'd play a day's golf every now and again, I became one of his protégés, and he seemed very proud of me. To his dying day, he only called me "Wright." I had total admiration for the man, so it was easy to work hard for him.

Newton recognized that I needed to phone in columns at odd hours from all over the world. Three o'clock in the morning from New Zealand was typical. From every tournament in the United States, I was forced to work against the clock due to the time change. The East Coast was at least five hours ahead, and if I was on the West Coast, I was eight hours ahead. A tournament that finished at 6:00 P.M.

Pacific Time, for instance, would have me phoning in results at 2:00 A.M. London time to try to file in time for the morning edition. In an age previous to the convenience of fax machines and instant e-mail, spoken dictation to a copywriter or editor was the only way to transfer the stories and columns, line by tedious line.

I covered the 1968 Alcan Tournament, for instance, from Portland, Oregon. Alcan staged qualifiers all around the globe for a world championship that was then golf's highest purse. Lee Trevino had a six-stroke lead with five holes to play. I phoned London, where a nervous copy-taker, eager to put the paper to bed, stressfully took my dictation of what surely was his final story of the night.

"Lee Trevino, the United States Open Champion who came from the woodwork earlier this year to win at Oak Hill, is strolling to victory in the Alcan qualifier for their world championship here at Portland Country Club this evening…"

By the time I had finished dictating the story, word by word to the copy-taker, Trevino had blown his insurmountable lead and lost to Billy Casper without even a playoff. For a player of his skill, it was unthinkable. Apparently, Trevino had a difference of opinion with his caddie during the final holes, and upon taking the caddie's club choice, under-clubbed himself on a par-three and landed in a bunker. Taking two to escape, and three-putting no doubt due to his rage at the caddie, Trevino's six matched against Casper's birdie two was the cornerstone of his collapse.

I was nearly finished signing off my column when the unbelievable numbers were posted in the press room. Looking at the numbers while in mid-sentence, the next words I dictated to the copy-taker on the phone were "Oh, hell…toss that all away because we'll have to start again now."

"Toss it away? Are you crazy, Ben? We're on a deadline!"

That is the only time I ad-libbed a story that was completely useless. I was very good at ad-libbing. I prided myself on it. I had the ability, without putting pen to paper, to simply dictate the article into the phone and tell the complete story, filling the needed copy length almost to the exact word count.

If the copy-taker didn't forgive me that mishap, Newton did, because I remained writing for the *Financial Times* for a total of 23 years. People say Newton knew nothing about journalism. He may not have, but he knew how to run a newspaper by appointing people who could do the job for him. He brought together a formidable staff of people and I was honored to be the first ever golf writer.

I was decidedly unhappy, however, when a meeting at Hoylake I was having with *Sports Illustrated* managing editor Andre La Guerre was interrupted. La Guerre and I were discussing *S.I.*'s interest in hiring me to string stories for their magazine from Europe. The urgent disruption came by way of a phone call from the *Financial Times*. It was July 24th, 1966, and the editor asked me to quickly write a story they needed immediately. It was to be the first obituary I would ever write. I was then deeply horrified to learn that the subject was my friend "Champagne" Tony Lema, who'd reached an untimely demise—along with his wife—in an air crash. He was 32.

This was no column to be ad-libbed, and putting that pen to paper was tough because the mere act made it all so real. I cried as I wrote the piece, and the world is much poorer without him. The tragic irony of the situation was that Lema was traveling because he'd packed in a one-day event between tournaments. Not long before, Lema had told me of his goal to relax and take life a bit easier.

"I hate traveling so much," he told me. "I log an awful lot of miles every year. I never bother to keep count but I'm constantly flying, at least twice a week. I don't hate the actual flying—that doesn't worry me. But all the tiresome business of checking your bags, getting a ticket, packing and unpacking becomes hard work."

Despite his wish for relaxation, Lema was playing a heavy schedule because of his humble economic beginnings. He was haunted by the necessity to capitalize on an enormous natural talent while he retained the ability to do so; before the hands began to shake a little, the eyes dimmed a little, or the ulcers that he once said "are like little corns in this game," got to him.

As Lema once told me, "I want to get out before the ulcers cripple me."

I was deeply saddened by my task of writing his obituary, but honored by the duty to properly eulogize him in the *Financial Times*.

It was as *FT's* golf writer that I also witnessed what I believe amounted to the demise of Ben Hogan's public competitive career. It was during a practice round at the 1970 PGA Championship that I followed Tony Jacklin and Hogan, who hadn't even entered the tournament, as they made their way around Southern Hills. A surprisingly tiny gallery watched with casual interest. Few seemed to know that Hogan was there, since he had not yet decided whether or not he would commit to compete in the championship. Hogan was testing whether his ailing body and weak knee would keep up with his willfully competitive mind throughout the practice round.

Shot after shot, Hogan maintained his legendary focus. Shortly after Jacklin and Hogan made the turn, Hogan found himself standing unsteadily over a hillside lie, with the ball below his feet. He eyed the ball, and then the target. He then deliberately took his time in setting up. He was obviously not comfortable in the stance the shot required. The hillside required a reach at the ball. Hogan positioned his club behind the ball, and prepared to execute his measured swing.

The clubhead slipped through the grass...and he shanked the ball down the hill and straight across the fairway.

Hogan, as usual, expressed no emotion at the sight of the result. He handed the iron to his caddie, said nothing, and began to walk. He marched on, even of pace, staring straight ahead. Hogan walked directly off the golf course and headed for the clubhouse.

I followed him as he abandoned the course, and competitive play. I watched every step of his silent, processional exit. When Hogan reached the clubhouse door, he sensed my presence, and halted. Turning back, he looked at me and thrust a $5 bill into my hand.

"Give this to Tony," were his only words before turning curtly and continuing to walk on.

In the late seventies, I was covering the World Match Play Championship at Wentworth in England for the *Financial Times*. After a walk of the course, I checked into the media center and saw a note for me tacked to the message board. It read:

Ben Wright, please meet Pam Baylis at the front door.

Pam Baylis! I thought. *Good lord, my old matron from Felsted!* It was a woman I'd had a boyhood affair with over twenty-five years before.

Nervous at the thought of encountering her, I followed the instructions and went to the front door, where I realized that I had been had. It was a practical joke, played by the man actually standing at the door waiting for me. I breathed both a sigh of embarrassment and a sigh of relief at the sight of Neil Allen.

During our reunion, Neil warmly related to me the details of his career path. It was an impressive line of experiences that eventually found him writing for the *London Evening Standard,* the *Stratford Express, The Times of London,* and the *New York Times* while covering glamorous prizefights and fourteen Olympic Games.

My continued travels for the *Financial Times* found me in Buenos Aires for the Eisenhower Cup in the late seventies. It was sadly not the golf, however, that made that trip to South America memorable. As I stood outside of the Sheraton Hotel waiting for a taxi, a terrorist bomb exploded in the floors above me, blowing out two stories of the corner of the building. As I recovered from the shock of the sound of the blast and scurried for cover, debris fell from above and landed directly in front of me on the sidewalk. It also turns out that British golfer and eventual R&A Secretary, Michael Bonallack, had actually been sitting on the balcony of the hotel when the bomb went off one floor above him. He escaped without injury, but two people were, in fact, killed that day.

There was an uncertain and nervous edge permeating the entire event. As Ben Crenshaw and I taxied to the golf course one day, Crenshaw became increasingly disturbed by the erratic, speedy, and dangerous manner in which the driver was steering the car. The bouncing, braking, swerving, sharp turns, and rabbit-like acceleration continued on the way to the golf course.

"Stop!" Crenshaw finally blurted out. "Stop right here! I can't take it any more. Open up the trunk!"

The driver opened the trunk, and Crenshaw bid me good luck, choosing rather to walk the last quarter-mile of the way to the golf course, with his clubs slung over his shoulder.

Time passes, things inevitably changed, and Sir Gordon Newton went on to become a director of the Pearson Group, the big international conglomerate that owned the *Financial Times.* His replacement was a man named Geoffrey Owen. Owen hated golf, so he gave me a hard time from the moment he succeeded Sir Gordon. Owen, if interested in sport at all, was preoccupied by tennis, a sport in which he excelled.

The final straw for me at the *Financial Times* came in 1989, as I prepared to cover The Ryder Cup Matches at the Belfry. The sports editor contacted me to tell me that he found my golf columns to be boring.

"You're too reverential to the game of golf," the sports editor claimed. "I want some dirt on golf," he stated, symptomatic of the direction of the modern media game. "There must be some financial corruption in golf, Ben."

At this point in the conversation, I began to think about the reasons the now late Henry Longhurst had given for quitting his *Sunday Times* column after a magnificent unbroken 25-year run. His weekly works were examples of great golfing literature, but a youth movement at the *Times* decided they'd shift the traditional location of his column from the prominent center of the back page to a less desirable location on the interior pages of the newspaper. This mortally insulted Longhurst. Then, while inspecting his column one Sunday morning, Longhurst noticed the slang word "shit" printed in another article on the same page as his column. That was enough for an outraged Longhurst, who was discouraged that his formerly esteemed newspaper would stoop to such a level, and embarrassed that his wife and daughter could read a word like "shit" during their Sunday breakfast. He wanted no part of it, and so he phoned his editor that Sunday morning and summarily relinquished his status with the newspaper.

Feeling now what I suspect was a similar contempt for the sports editor and pity for the state of modern journalism, I was wary to dignify his ridiculous opinion and direction with a response but was compelled to do so.

"Just because you live in a city where corruption is a byword doesn't mean that it is everywhere. I'm sorry, but that's not my attitude toward the game I love. You've got the wrong man. Good-bye."

It was the end of a great relationship with the *Financial Times*, but continued devotion and loyalty toward the love of my life. For golf is truly a moveable feast.

When in Doubt,
Tease the Brit

My father was bringing home a television set. Nobody in the neighborhood owned a television set, but my father was fairly wealthy because he had managed industrial factories before the war. He had 30,000 employees under his aegis at the SKF ball bearing factory, and usually, little time for me. He then went behind enemy lines to supervise German industrial activities in an attempt to prevent the Germans from sabotaging their own factories as they retreated. My father, Reg Wright, practiced counterespionage against a Third Reich "scorched earth" policy, for which he was decorated with the Order of the British Empire. My family would be considered the privileged class in England in 1953 because we would be able to own a television, which we never had before.

My father specifically wanted to give his family the opportunity to view the coronation of Queen Elizabeth II, so he brought home an eight-inch black and white television. My mother Gwen, sister Susie, and I gathered around the little box peering at the fuzzy and grainy black and white images.

I thought it was a miracle. I was amazed. I must also tell you that I never for one single second ever came near imagining that my image and voice would someday appear on television. In fact, my father, the first to introduce me to a television set, never wanted me to be in television and never supported such a move.

My television debut with the British Broadcasting Corporation was an important milestone for me. Although I had dabbled some in televised golf, and had filed reports for BBC radio, my bread was buttered as a freelance golf writer. The value of a chance to be seen and heard on the BBC was not to be underestimated.

I drove down from my residence in Cheshire to Long Ashton, Bristol, where I was to commentate on the 1965 Martini Tournament. My assignment would be to interview players as they came off of the 18th green.

Upon my arrival, I met the BBC crew for lunch. The legendary writer and announcer Henry Longhurst was seated at the table, and I was excited about the opportunity to work on the broadcast with such an esteemed literary giant and television performer.

As we began to discuss the plan for the day's telecast, I noticed three bottles of red wine sitting on the table. Throughout the course of the lunch, Longhurst proceeded to inhale glass after glass of Bordeaux. It was getting close to the time that we were to go out to the course and begin the broadcast and I couldn't see how Longhurst was going to be able to get a word out edgeways and straight. He was fairly chirpy by now, slurring his words and plainly half cut. More than half cut, to be honest—he was half in the bag! At that point, I was filled with all kinds of fear and dread that my debut with the BBC was going to be a disaster.

With the bottles emptied we left the restaurant, whereupon Longhurst and I headed toward our positions at the 18th green. Attached to the television tower was a fireman's lift—a pulley device with a canvas sling used to hoist the heavy, old-fashioned television cameras up the scaffold to the platform. Not allowing him to dare try the ladder, the technicians guided the tipsy Longhurst into the sling and hoisted him up to the tower.

Oh my God, I thought. *What is this going to be like?*

The program opened, and Longhurst began to speak. His delivery was word perfect. No slur, no stumble, nothing. He introduced me with warmth and wit, and performed the most exquisite broadcast.

When it came to broadcasting, Longhurst had a great deal of genius, and a tremendous command of the English language. He used silence to a wonderful degree to heighten the drama rather than employing too many words. These perfectly timed moments without words were effective because Longhurst always seemed to place his microphone in such a way that viewers could hear the wind blowing.

I recall his 1958 British Open broadcast at Royal Lytham as a splendid example of his wit and wisdom. In the afternoon round of a 36-hole playoff, Peter Thomson deftly pulled away from his challenger, the young Welshman Dave Thomas. Longhurst, never at a loss for words, came as near to struggling as I had ever heard him. With no commercial breaks, and virtually alone on the broadcast, he needed to fill the time while Thomson and Thomas walked to their drives on the par-five 11ᵗʰ hole.

To understand my paraphrase of Longhurst's commentary, imagine him directing his cameraman to aim the camera toward the outside edge of the golf course. Longhurst showed the viewers one of the last of British Rail's steam locomotives, belching forth clouds of steam and billowing dark smoke as it tugged six incredibly dirty and decrepit passenger coaches out of the local station.

"You fortunate people in your armchairs at home are now able to feast your eyes on one of the last, ill-fated Leviathans of the once formidable British rail system, shortly to be sent, without ceremony, to the knacker's yard and replaced by one of those infernal and evil smelling diesels," he droned. "Oh, the shame of it all! This wonderful giant is better known to train buffs as the 4-6-2. Isn't that a magnificent sight? Take it all in while you can, because you are watching the splendor of a dying breed, even as she is condemned to pulling the 4:10 P.M. stopping train from Lytham North to Manchester Central, calling at…" Longhurst then proceeded to name each and every stop that the train was destined to make.

"You can see the sweat on the brow of the fireman and the coal dust on his strong hands and forearms as he shovels fuel into the mouth of the monster, which has such a relentless appetite. Now, if our cameraman can pan a little right, we can read the number on the tender of this noble beast. Let me see now—2-3-2-3-2-4. My word! If only our man Thomas could reel off figures like those over the next few holes, we might have a contest yet! By the way, neither player has reached the green with their second shot…"

It was sheer brilliance and a far cry from today's sometimes robotic announcers.

Now deem him eccentric if you must, but the man was such a character. In fact, so brilliant was Longhurst that he served as a Member of Parliament for the Conservative Party in Cambridge. Such were his oratory skills that the party even considered grooming him to be Prime Minister. Upon learning this news Longhurst responded by saying, "No, no, I don't think we need that. We're having too much fun out on the golf tour."

Fun he did have, of that you can be assured. Covering the 1972 PGA Championship at Oakland Hills in Michigan, Longhurst enjoyed the chance to watch Gary Player achieve victory. He always revered Player because the South African was small in stature and comparatively low in talent, but high in work ethic. Longhurst liked the idea of the little man triumphing against the odds. Longhurst, to his death bed, was always referred to by Player as "Mister Longhurst," which was another thing Henry liked about him. Player was inordinately polite and well-mannered, and that impressed Longhurst.

Full of joy over Player's victory, Longhurst announced that he was going on a bender that night to celebrate his little pal's win.

Golf writer Dan Jenkins and I were to meet Longhurst at a quarter 'til midday the following morning in the coffee shop of the Kingsley Inn, the hotel in which we were staying. The idea was that I was to drive Longhurst to the airport so that he could fly back to London and courier the film of the PGA Championship to be aired in England. We had planned to leave a little early because Longhurst wanted to look at downtown Detroit, a desire which was quite beyond me since it was then largely blighted, burned down, and derelict.

At a quarter to noon, Jenkins and I, who'd also been known to hang it on and had been doing so, were having our remedial breakfast in the coffee shop. As we grumbled through our eggs and coffee, we began to worry because there was no sign of Longhurst. At 10 minutes to noon, however, a pitiful figure was seen trying to make his way through the swing doors, mumbling and moaning, looking like an unmade bed. It was Henry. His tie was all over the place and his collar was sticking up. He'd plainly slept in his clothes and had not bothered to clean himself up.

Longhurst plunked himself down at our table, and summoned the miniskirted waitress to pour him a cup of coffee. He had not yet spoken to Jenkins nor I when he attempted to lift the cup to his dry lips. His hands were shaking so badly that the coffee spilled onto his shirt. After the waitress wiped him up and brought him another, Longhurst gave it another attempt, this time recognizing that it was indeed a task that required two hands—a "two-hander" if you will—to hold the cup steady. Alas, poor Henry again suffered the fate of spilling coffee all over himself.

"Yes...yes...I'll be back in a moment," Longhurst muttered as he rose and shuffled toward the door.

"You've got to follow him," insisted Jenkins. "Go see where the hell he is going. You've got to get him on that flight."

I agreed and proceeded to shadow Henry out the door of the coffee shop, down through the winding corridors of the hotel and into the bar. Within earshot, I could see that the bartender was just preparing things for the day's opening when Longhurst managed to climb onto a stool and addressed the bartender.

"Paul, my dear boy," he said to the attentive barkeep, "you've looked after me fantastically well in the week that I have been here. Now, however, is a time for desperate measures...and I shall have three of them."

What a wonderful line! I then watched the bartender prepare three glasses of gin on the rocks with little dashes of soda. Henry drank them down...one...two...three.

Wide-eyed, I went rushing back to the coffee shop to report to Jenkins what I had seen transpire. We then waited innocently for Henry to resume his seat. Once back at the table, he again summoned the skeptical waitress, who poured him yet another cup of coffee, which he drank without even the suggestion of a shake.

It was Longhurst that I would eventually replace at CBS for the Masters broadcasts when he became too ill to travel and broadcast in the United States. The CBS crew considered my "candidacy" by "putting me through my paces." Announcer Pat Summerall, writer Bob Drum, public relations man Bill Brendle, announcer Jack Whitaker, and CBS Sports president Bill McPhail decided they needed to test my stamina and determine if I could handle my drink. Their test consisted of cocktails, lunch with wine, more cocktails, and then, the drink of choice after all of that was always "stingers." A stinger is brandy mixed with white crème de menthe—very good for the digestion, and also very lethal. Stingers were served to us in pitchers.

They wanted to make certain that I was not a liability and that I would not have to be scraped off of the floor at an early stage at some public appearance or event. I passed their test, and felt as if I had been accepted as a member of a very exclusive men's club. Of course, each of these fellows was a member of the infamous "5:42 Club" at Mike Manuche's Sports Bar on 52nd Street in Manhattan, so named for the precise time that network employees would arrive each afternoon. It was a brisk 12-minute walk for the network staffers after they abandoned their offices for the evening at 5:30. A plaque was placed in that bar in honor of the club.

My debut tournament on the air with CBS was the United States Match Play Championship at the Country Club of North Carolina in August of 1972, which was held concurrently with the Liggett & Meyers Open. Nicklaus defeated Frank Beard 2 and 1 in the finals, and Lou Graham won the Liggett & Meyers stroke play portion of the event, which, because of slow play, didn't even finish until after we went off the air. The event was to serve as a warm-up for me, and a de facto rehearsal for my first full Tour season, which would begin in 1973.

During my week at the U.S. Match Play, golf writer Bob Drum recognized that I was a long way from home and new to America, so he therefore invited me out to dinner to celebrate my CBS tryout. Drum was a grizzly curmudgeon with a wild streak and a bold way of living. Despite his ungainly and bear-like appearance, he became a part of the CBS television team by hosting wry and comical segments called "The Drummer's Beat" in which he would cast about his cynical opinions.

Drum and his wife M.J. suggested an enjoyable dinner at a nearby establishment called the Grey Fox Pub. Enjoying their company and appreciating the thoughtful invitation, I insisted on paying the check following the dinner. The Drums resisted, but I refused their protests and paid the bill, allowing the waiter what in Britain is regarded as a very adequate tip of ten percent.

I was startled when the waiter, apparently offended, threw the tip back on the table in front of me, pronouncing, "I don't want your money if you need it so badly that you cannot give me a better tip than this."

Upon hearing this, Drum, a 300-pound, former University of Alabama Hall of Fame basketball player, sprung from his chair and glared at the waiter.

"You idiot! You dare insult my guest from the United Kingdom, a guest in our country! You get your ass outside," he growled, "and I'll see you in two minutes."

Drum went out the door after the waiter but the kid had climbed up a tree from which he jumped and landed on Drum, wrestling him to the ground. The skirmish went on, but Drum, because of his size and strength, soon began to prevail. M.J. and I watched in horror as

Drum positioned himself on top of the waiter and clutched his head in his massive hands.

"You rotten son of a bitch," Drum howled. "I'm gonna bust your head open!"

Now I was really worried because Drum was in a certifiable rage.

"M.J., we have to get him off before he kills this guy!" I shouted.

M.J. was also in a frightful panic. "His hair, Ben, his hair!" she cried. "Bob hates to have his hair pulled!"

Before I could understand what she meant, M.J. had climbed up onto Drum's back and clutched at a fistful of her husband's stringy hair. Drum let out a noise of total agony and thankfully jumped off of the waiter, who scurried off into the darkness.

The next evening, I had dinner again at the Grey Fox Pub—this time without the imposing figure of Drum (he'd been ordered not to return). Across the room, there were over a dozen people in attendance at a long table, including golf writer Dan Jenkins and his wife June, and announcer Jack Whitaker with his wife Bert. I could overhear their conversation. Their host, the tournament director of the Liggett & Meyers Open, was apparently late to arrive. But what an entrance he made. I could scarcely believe my eyes.

Sweeping in the front door with a mad look in his eye, the man, who'd obviously been drinking, climbed up on top of the hostess stand and did a swan dive off of the lectern straight down the middle of their table. The women went flying backward off of their chairs, drinks were spilled all over the place, and the table was in shambles. It is beyond me how nobody was injured, most of all the tournament director.

As they all tried to pick themselves up and dust off, the tournament director, in a craze, climbed off of the table and ran into the minstrels' gallery to play darts. As they settled back into their seats, announcer Bob Beattie told me that he wasn't surprised to see the man pull a stunt like that.

"That's nothing for that guy," Beattie said. "He visited my home in Boulder for a party, arrived very drunk, and collapsed unconscious on the edge of the coals of a bonfire we had built. It was the opinion of the gathered," Beattie continued, "that we allow him to cook a bit, until he was finally awakened by the heat. He got up screaming with his coat smoldering, and ran hollering right into a fence, knocking himself unconscious again!"

At this point, I was beginning to learn why my British mentor Henry Longhurst refused to bemoan a defeat for a second term in England's Parliament because he was "having too much fun on the golf tour."

Having been put through my paces by the 5:42 Club and the dreadful L&M Match Play, I was set to broadcast my first full season with CBS. I was to travel to the United States for the leadoff tournament of 1973: The Los Angeles Open. It was a nightmarish journey.

I had spent a late New Year's Eve partying in Cornwall, and so on New Year's Day I made the woozy eight-hour drive over twisting, bumpy, small roads from Cornwall to Heathrow Airport in London. Once at the airport, I learned that my Pan Am flight over the pole to Los Angeles had been delayed. After an eight-hour wait in the airport, we finally lifted off and completed the long and arduous flight to California. Having never been to Los Angeles, I fetched a cab to take me to the Bel Air Hotel, a healthy drive from LAX. I checked in at half-past four in the morning, and the bellman, who happened to be an Englishman, said, "Ahh, I take it you are Mr. Wright?—by process of elimination, since you are the only guest that has not yet checked in."

I confirmed his suspicion with the moan of a worn-out man who had been traveling for well over 24 hours.

"I understand you're from London," he said. "Being so far from home I'm certain that you might appreciate a spot of tea, and so here's a pot I've prepared for you."

How civilized, I thought, accepting the gesture with gratitude. I then set out for my bed, seeking to collapse. As I turned to make my way toward my room, the desk clerk interrupted my near sleepwalk.

"Uh, Mr. Wright," he said, "I've got a bit of bad news for you, I'm afraid. It's a message here, sir, which reads that you must be at the Riviera Country Club this morning for rehearsal...at 10:00 A.M., sir."

The news was further deflating. Due to the time difference between the east and west coasts of the United States, the rehearsal was scheduled three hours earlier than it normally would have been. Not having the slightest idea how to get to Riviera, I asked the desk clerk to arrange a taxi pickup for 9:00 A.M., and went to bed for what literally would seem like 40 winks.

After my brief somnolent recharge, I somehow made it to my feet and down to the taxi stand at the appointed time, only to find no taxi. Finally, when a taxi did pull up, I was hopelessly late. Fatigued beyond belief, I dozed off in the taxi, which finally set out to deliver me to my rehearsal.

At about eight minutes after the hour of 10:00 A.M., I climbed out of the cab at Riviera in a panic. Upon making my way to the CBS trailer, I first encountered CBS associate producer Chuck Will, who looked at me and shook his head from behind his desk. His greeting was considerably less sympathetic than that of the desk clerk at the Bel Air Hotel.

"You'd better get your ass down to 16, where you should have been a half an hour ago. Rehearsal has started without you."

With no time to secure a golf cart, I got directions from Will and took off running. If you know Riviera, you know that the longest possible run is from the clubhouse down to the 16th green at the other end of the golf course.

After my panicked full sprint, I climbed into the tower and plopped myself down, breathlessly sticking on my earphones. Before I could even adjust the volume, the voice of producer/director Frank Chirkinian filled my ears, and the ears of all of the other announcers on the headphone system:

"Well, well. Isn't this nice? You goddamned limey son of a bitch! You finally agreed to join us for our rehearsal, although that started some time ago. One of my inflexible rules is that every announcer must be in his seat 15 minutes before rehearsal is due to begin!"

"Sorry, Frank," was the start of my only response, "I've just come over the pole all the way from London and—"

"I don't give a damn whether you've come from Timbuktu sliding on your ass! If you're not in your seat 15 minutes before time, you're late! If you need extra time to get to rehearsal, take extra time. But be on fucking time! Now...roll tape!"

Chirkinian's command to "roll tape" at the end of his tirade instructed CBS producers to pop up video on the monitor, a video they'd secretly shot of me running through the golf course trying to get to my tower. The tape was sped up so that I looked clownish in full sprint. I could hear the entire crew giggling into their headsets, and despite being the subject of their amusement, I was thankful for a moment of levity because I was very nearly in tears. My trip had been daunting, I was severely tired, and I was already on edge and nervous due to Chirkinian's reputation as a perfectionist. Now, in my debut rehearsal for my first full season with CBS, Chirkinian had mercilessly dressed me down in front of my new colleagues.

The rehearsal, which was conducted while the early play was going on, continued, and I struggled to get into a rhythm and groove. Bruce Devlin, in the lead at the time, reached my hole and I was commentating when he hit a poor tee shot into a greenside bunker. Devlin then proceeded to flash his next shot into the bunker on the other side of the green and ended up making a triple-bogey 6 on the hole, which moved him from the lead to back in the pack.

"Well, now it's a whole new ball game," I announced.

Immediately, Chirkinian piped into my earphones. *"What the hell are you talking about, you limey ass? 'Now it's a whole new ball game?' Where the did you get that damned expression?"*

"Frank, I got it from you Americans."

"You got it from 'we Americans?' Don't you realize what you're here for? You're a limey, and you talk like a limey, which means that you say everything as if you had a plum in your mouth. Waa waa waa, so no one understands a word you say. Come to think of it, if I ever understand another word you say, you're fired!"

By this point, I was wondering what I was even doing there and why I was putting myself through this. *Let me out of here*, I thought to myself. *Let me go back home.*

The Chirkinian-induced homesickness prompted me to phone my mother back in England from the hotel later that day for a dose of comfort and sympathy. Suddenly, she interrupted my account of my first-day rehearsal.

"Bentley," she said, "I have to tell you that you've only been over there one day and already you talk like one of them." I got no sympathy from my proper mother.

Later, I learned that my cameraman had revealed to Chirkinian that I had been reduced to tears. "And a good thing that is, too," Chirkinian huffed. "The son of a bitch should have been in tears." Not a vestige of sympathy from Chirkinian, who was put off that I had been hired above his head by Bill McPhail.

Chirkinian eventually cooled off and my relationship with him warmed up over time. I came to learn that Chirkinian was not only a professional genius and a master of his craft, but also a very loyal leader. If imitation is indeed the sincerest form of flattery, then Chirkinian can justly be called the father of golf television in America.

To his loyal, if irreverent CBS troops, he was known simply as "The Ayatollah." Would you believe the "real" Ayatollah Khomeini passed away on Chirkinian's 63rd birthday, an ironical coincidence that was *very* far from lost on our esteemed leader.

Quite simply put, Chirkinian has had many imitators but no equals in my decades of worldwide experience in the field of televised golf production and direction. But golf is not the only sport in which Chirkinian invented and established techniques that have become the accepted and much-copied norm.

For instance, Chirkinian was the first producer/director to use a television camera underwater at a swimming and diving meet at his native Philadelphia's Fairmount Park in 1956. At the same gala, for the first time ever, he ran a camera on a poolside track to follow the swimmers' every stroke.

In 1960, at the Orange Bowl, Chirkinian put a television camera in the Goodyear Blimp for the first time ever, spawning a breed of blimps over the next 30 years that have become an integral part of most major sports productions on television. In the same year, he put a camera on a 100-foot-high crane atop the Orange Bowl Regatta, a previously unheard of innovation that—like most of Chirkinian's brainchildren—have become commonplace devices that have so greatly enhanced our viewing pleasure.

For three years Chirkinian produced and directed the Indianapolis 500. True to form, he put a camera in the wall on the renowned track's fourth turn. Unfortunately for him, no cameraman at CBS would volunteer for such a perilous assignment, so Chirkinian had to completely enclose the camera in a foam-padded box to stop it from shaking as the cars hammered by.

In horse racing, Chirkinian revolutionized television coverage by putting a camera on a 110-foot scaffold in the infield at Belmont Park. The camera turned as the Belmont Stakes progressed. As Chirkinian explained, "There is no better way to capture the image and reality of speed than by panning across stationary objects as a backcloth."

For those of us who have come to expect—but nevertheless detest—that apparently unavoidable cliché of television sports announcers: "Just a few moments ago...", heralding as it does more and more the prevalent videotaped replay, it might be interesting to note that Chirkinian was the director of the first horse racing program on which videotape was utilized for such replays.

Another Chirkinian invention was the program interrupt system, which enables the director in the truck to talk directly to his announcers on their headsets. Those of us who have been controlled, cajoled, cheered, consoled, and often cruelly cackled at by Chirkinian through the years, almost never with any increase in his decibel level, might cynically observe that Frank's invention never gives us announcers the chance to answer back, which I am convinced was most certainly his intention.

When Chirkinian produced and directed the first live coverage of the Winter Olympic Games in 1960 at Squaw Valley, California, co-axial camera cables had an effective range of about 1,000 feet. But Chirkinian wanted to station a camera on the top of the 80-meter ski jump to, as it were, peep over each skier's shoulder as he launched himself on his daunting mission. The CBS engineers promptly developed for him a little black box to induce the necessary voltage to survive a 3,000-foot-long camera run, and yet another breakthrough in television's development had been chalked up to Chirkinian and his minions.

It was about this time that Chirkinian realized that golf was the supreme challenge of his powers of invention as a producer and director because golf, alone amongst the most popular sports, is not confined by its own boundaries. There is no court, pool, track, rink, field or stadium, just a limitless and photogenic rural panorama that even fanatical opponents of golf grudgingly admit makes for beautiful, restful viewing when presented with panache. Is it surprising that the Masters, which Chirkinian had produced from 1958 until 1996, has become America's spring sporting rite?

Chirkinian's first major venture into golf outside Augusta had been to produce the 1958 PGA Championship for CBS from Llanerch Country Club on the outskirts of Philadelphia in the year the event reverted from match play to stroke play. Two years later, Chirkinian changed the scoring system from a cumulative total to a much more easily comprehensible hole-by-hole relationship to par, another first that was quickly and universally accepted.

At an exhibition match of Scotch foursomes (alternate shot) that pitted the legendary Sam Snead and actor Ray Milland against the

1958 PGA champion Dow Finsterwald and Philadelphia Phillies pitcher Robin Roberts, Chirkinian became the first producer/director to "eavesdrop" on players' conversations, albeit slightly crudely, mounting a "shotgun" microphone on the back of a station wagon.

Later, when Chirkinian produced the incredibly popular CBS Golf Classic on videotape for eleven years, featuring a four-ball, best-ball match play knockout formula, he recorded another first when using the split screen technique. The Classic became, in time, the forerunner of the original Skins Game and was remarkable in its final year for Lanny Wadkins's extraordinary plundering of his hapless peers. Contrary to many subsequent boasts from his jealous rivals and imitators, Chirkinian staged the original Skins Game to commemorate the opening of Muirfield Village Golf Club, featuring the course's architect Jack Nicklaus, fellow Ohioan Tom Weiskopf, Lee Trevino, and Johnny Miller.

As an example of Chirkinian's fantastic flair for invention and innovation, Firestone Country Club, venue for the 1960 PGA Championship, presented limited access to cameras, particularly in the vital area around the 18th tee. So Chirkinian persuaded Firestone's Scotty Brubaker to erect a scaffold on which was mounted a huge mirror alongside the 18th tee, which the intrepid Chirkinian shot with a reversed image from his camera at the 17th green. Alas, this was one of Chirkinian's few unsuccessful innovations, because the wind caused the mirror to oscillate too severely.

Chirkinian and associate producer Chuck Will were so wise as to employ the use of out-of-work caddies to serve as spotters and scorers on the weekend CBS telecasts. This allowed the caddies to earn some sorely needed extra money, and ensured that the spotters and scorers were knowledgeable in the game of golf. Whenever possible, Will arranged for golf-minded part-timers—ranging from State Amateur Champions to young LPGA players—to fill those positions on a weekly basis. Helen Alfredsson even once worked with CBS in that role.

It was also Chirkinian who must take great credit for introducing Henry Longhurst to the American golfing public. It was at the old Carling World Open—which Clifford Roberts always referred to as "that beer event"—at Pleasant Valley Country Club in Massachusetts in 1965. The brewery's advertising agency was anxious for Chirkinian to give the telecast an international flavor, despite the fact that in those sad old days most, if not all, of the foreigners were destined to miss the cut.

Chirkinian was lunching with Paul Warren, the tournament director, when Warren first introduced him to Longhurst. Chirkinian quickly conceived the idea that Longhurst could very adequately provide that "international flavor" on the weekend, and asked him to do the broadcast. Longhurst accepted with alacrity and—despite Chirkinian's misgivings about his being able to ascend a 40-foot tower—Longhurst scurried up the vertical ladder just as he did regularly back home in Great Britain with the BBC. Bill McPhail, then president of CBS Sports, and his deputy, the late Jack Dolph, ironically told Chirkinian after that Friday afternoon rehearsal that he should not use Longhurst because "he talks too much," which was no doubt due to the fact that he broadcast solo at many of the BBC broadcasts, which also had no commercial breaks. But Chirkinian was not to be denied, and told Longhurst to be economical with his words because he was in the picture business, and the rest is history. Longhurst used even more than his usual brevity and silence to better effect than any other sports broadcaster I have ever known. He broadcast only one CBS tournament a year—the Masters—during his long tenure with ABC.

Chirkinian got his start in television in 1946 as an assistant director at a local television station, WCAU. This CBS affiliate in Philadelphia produced—amongst other giants of the broadcasting business—Dolph, Jack Whitaker, Ed McMahon, and Richard Lester. The last named became Chirkinian's own associate director until becoming famous as the director of the Beatles' highly successful films.

In less than a year, Chirkinian was directing news and weather bulletins and variety shows, including "Candy Carnival," a weekly circus show put out across the entire CBS network. In 1956, Chirkinian made the jump to CBS in New York, and directed mainly football and baseball until turning to golf, at which he became and remains an accomplished player and typically fierce competitor with a single-figure handicap.

He serves as godfather to my child Margaret, and my 25 years of knowing the man have been wonderful. I did, however, suitably pay Chirkinian back for the abuse he gave me by naming my dog "Frank" after him. Finally, with the dog having that name, I could freely utter the pent-up words I so often wanted to speak: "Come here, Frank, you miserable bastard! Sit, roll over, shut up!"

In 1999, Chirkinian finally sought suitable revenge, and named his new Jack Russell Terrier puppy "Bentley." I can only imagine the things he must say to that poor dog.

Frank Chirkinian's bark was infinitely worse than his bite, but at the same time, he could scare the daylights out of you. He demanded that we pay attention to business, and Chirkinian never allowed anyone's ego to get in the way or grow too large. He encouraged unity among us by becoming our "common enemy"—although we really did appreciate the way he fostered the team concept for CBS golf and its crew.

The Ayatollah could be unbearably demanding, and there were very few "atta-boy's" handed out by him. When he mercilessly dressed down a cameraman or staffer, you would get no excuses from Chirkinian for his actions, and there would be no apologies from him, either. What Frank would do, however, is very quietly and anonymously make up for his harshness with small gestures like sending over a bottle of wine to the scolded person's table.

For as hard as Chirkinian could be on me, I shall never forget the way he went to bat for me during my career. I went through thirteen presidents during my tenure at CBS, some effective and some less than effective. In this instance Van Gordon Sauter was the divisional president and a tough, tough man. He came into his leadership position at CBS Sports pronouncing that he didn't like golf because he didn't understand why it should be played in silence. He was seriously of the verbalized opinion that golf should be played in an atmosphere like a baseball stadium!

Sauter began to deal away the rights for tournaments that CBS typically broadcast, including the Andy Williams San Diego Open, which was a good event for CBS because we were able to broadcast bright, sunny ocean scenery back to the snowed-in Midwest and cold, gray Northeast.

At one point, Sauter called for a meeting with Chirkinian and me at CBS headquarters in Manhattan, called "Black Rock" because it is made of Canadian black marble. Chirkinian went into Sauter's office first as I waited in an anteroom. I was startled to hear a loud banging sound, which I correctly assumed was Chirkinian pounding on Sauter's desk.

"What in the world was going on in there?" I asked as Chirkinian exited the office.

"C'mon, lets go," Frank said. "Your meeting is cancelled. Sauter decided we didn't need an Englishman on the broadcast, and was going to can you. Don't worry, though. I told him in no uncertain terms that if the limey goes, I go."

As the father of televised golf, Chirkinian wielded a great deal of power, and ran his golf broadcasts with an iron hand. One famous example of Chirkinian's stubbornness was his aversion in the early days to putting any player on camera who was wearing a hat emblazoned with the "Amana" logo. Amana was the first company to recognize the value of having televised players wearing their logo. I believe Amana only paid players $50 per week to wear the logo caps, but to a young player trying to make it on tour, $50 was worth it.

J.C. Snead once complained to Chirkinian about not getting on television.

"Stop wearing that stupid hat and you can go on television," Chirkinian unabashedly pronounced. J.C. then tried to wear a broad brimmed straw hat with the Amana logo, but Chirkinian still wouldn't put him on television.

The logo business soon snowballed after that, and Chirkinian was the last to give in, but only because logos turned up everywhere. Greg Norman, in fact, became a walking billboard, with logos on his sleeves, pants, shoes, and golf bag, topped only recently by Tiger Woods, who even sported logos on the bottoms of his shoes.

Regardless of logos, though, if Chirkinian didn't like a player, said player would have a quite difficult time getting on television. If he liked a player, that player would be on most of the hours that God sent.

Chirkinian would encourage his announcers to behave themselves on the road, but he was always fighting a losing battle. He frequently tried to keep us under control, so we rather avoided him when we wanted a good night out. When we did go out with Frank, though, it would be for a civilized dinner and a very nice, early bedtime. The announcers had some of the most civilized dinners and fine wines a man can drink thanks to his incredible generosity...he always picked up the tab and expensed it to CBS. I don't think Frank ever bought a bottle of wine that cost less than $100. With Frank, it was always Chateau Lafite or Opus One. For those expensive tabs, we nicknamed Chirkinian "the American Express Card." We'd put our arms around him and say, "Don't leave home without him."

Producing four genuine live telecasts a week could get very stressful. No other sport has the particular telecast demands that golf does. After all, a hockey or basketball game is confined to one court, and each game is played in identical dimensions. Golf, spread over acres and acres of varying terrain, with simultaneous action spread out all over, is more difficult to cover.

Chirkinian recognized that we needed to be treated well to ward off the accompanying stress and tension week after week. After all, Chirkinian was honest enough to realize that without personalities, a golf telecast could be dreadfully boring. He needed his announcers to provide peak performances every time because it can be tough to keep it interesting. Chirkinian made no bones about the fact that his announcers were not journalists reporting on the action, but rather entertainers in place to enhance the show. When we produced telecasts on Thursday or Friday, for instance, there was no guarantee that any player we showed would even be remotely near to the top of the leader board. If all the best players had shot their leading scores early in the day before the telecast, we would be caught flashing up a leader board full of players who were already finished, while the audience at home was forced to watch the back end of the field.

In the worst case scenario, for instance, at the 1974 Houston Open, rain delayed the tournament, and players were teeing off from 1 and 10 to try to finish before dark. Lee Elder won the tournament, but finished on the 9th hole. Since there were no cameras positioned on the front nine, CBS's live, final round coverage of Elder's win at the Houston Open aired without even one shot of Elder's play, except for his last putt.

Our challenge as announcers was to somehow try to make these potential circumstances interesting to the viewer, as well as maintain our own interest. The PGA Tour would at least make some attempt to pad the leader board and stack the pairings draw so that we might have name players during our broadcast, but Chirkinian knew that name players were not always enough.

"Okay, boys, sing to me, you bastards," he would encourage us at the beginning of each telecast. "Make it sing."

After the nightmare of my debut at Riviera I began to settle in, and despite the jocular nature of covering golf, took my job very seriously. I would go to the tournament press rooms and collect any information that I thought was pertinent to the broadcast. More importantly, I would wander the practice tee, where most of my information was gleaned. If a player had a sore finger, he'd tell me so. If a player was hampered by a blister on his heel, I'd learn that, and know why the guy was limping when he came to my hole.

I would look into the players' bags and see what kind of equipment they were carrying, and whether or not they had changed brands. At the 1976 Masters, for instance, Raymond Floyd put a 5-wood in his bag for the first time and hit 5-woods at every par five that week. Floyd blistered the field by nine shots, and tied Nicklaus's record of 271.

Players would relate personal matters as well, and tell me what else might be on their minds, like a sick relative or a new swing thought. I would always collect more of these nuggets than I could possibly use, making certain to talk to the players I knew would be appearing on the telecast.

My first bit of recognition came after broadcasting the 1973 Jackie Gleason Inverrary National Airlines Classic in Lauderhill, Florida. The late sports writer Pete Axthelm wrote this item in the March 12 issue of *Newsweek:*

"In addition to providing the competitive highlights of the winner, the Gleason offered an omen for the coming months: The performance of Ben Wright, the British writer, amateur golfer, and bon vivant. From his position at the sixteenth green, which was near a water hazard, Wright offered a series of wry and dramatic bons mots. Some shots 'found dry land,' others were 'consigned to the deep,' and in one somber moment after a shot had gone astray, Wright intoned: 'The ripples tell the story.'

"Hopefully, CBS producers will not only continue to use Wright, but will keep him as close to the water holes as possible."

For most of my career, I was fortunate to enjoy supportive and flattering criticism from writers who seemed to enjoy my on-air performance. In the April 13, 1993 issue of the *New York Times,* Richard Sandomir wrote the following:

"You can't blame CBS for the dullness of Sunday's final round of the Masters. The only reason worth watching was the work of the wordsmith from England, reporter Ben Wright.

"On Chip Beck's lame layup shot on the 15th: 'When you lay up and don't hit the 15th green, you really look foolish.'

"On a shot by Seve Ballesteros into a pond: 'The hole has dealt scurvily with him.'

"On Beck's weak putt on the 16th: 'That's a very tentative prod. I think Chip Beck has been looking at too many leader boards.'

'On winner Bernhard Langer: 'The imperturbable, phlegmatic one.'

"On Langer walking to the 16th green: 'Once again, the green jacket is for export.'"

M ichigan golf writer Terry Moore once even penned a complete column in *Michigan Golfer* comprised of my on-air phrases during the 1983 Masters, which he referred to as "quotable gems":

During the final round: *"The sands of time have run out. Seve is watching while Watson is failing with monotonous regularity."*

On a ball creeping in from the side of the cup: *"It made a quick tour of the house and went in by the back door, the trademan's entrance."*

On the 15th hole at Augusta National: *"It's a compellingly dramatic hole guarded by the dreaded pond."*

On Tommy Nakajima: *"Plainly destined for stardom."*

On Palmer's strong showing: *"Palmer is compensating for Nicklaus's demise."*

On Gil Morgan's par-saving putt following back-to-back bogeys: *"He needs this little putt to stop the rot."*

On Tom Kite's missed putt at 15: *"He may rue that tomorrow night."*

On Jim Hallet, the low amateur of the tournament: *"The fearlessness of youth."*

On Nick Faldo's up-and-down round: *"His has been a strange round, a mixture of absolute brilliance and casual untidiness."*

On Isao Aoki: *"Not even that genius with his wand standing on its heel can negotiate this soggy surface."*

On the 15th hole: *"It's fraught with danger."*

On Tom Watson hitting the 15th in two shots: *"Played with the utmost bravery and considerable skill."*

On going for the 15th green in two: *"The heartbeat tends to increase at this moment, faced in this agony of indecision."*

On Seve Ballesteros's laying up at 15: *"He's eminently safe. In the old days, he might have had a dash at it. He's learned reason at the tender age of 26."*

None of the turns of phrase for which I received attention were ever scripted or planned, as my entire on-air delivery was always spontaneous.

Spontaneity was always a word with which one could describe the social antics and behavioral tactics of the CBS Sports golf team. It was quite a different era, and as I've mentioned, the group was like an exclusive men's club, traveling together, and enjoying ourselves to the fullest. Upon occasion, I believe the show off the air was more entertaining than the broadcasts.

Set to catch a 6:30 A.M. flight from Los Angeles to New York City after the L.A. Open one year, Summerall and I left the Bel Air Hotel each armed with a Bloody Mary. Once on board the aircraft, we drank our way across America, surely driving the stewardesses mad with our flirtatious jokes and belly laughter.

After we completed the tedious flight and subsequent trek into Manhattan, Summerall and I joined announcer Tom Brookshier for dinner at the Palm Restaurant. The Palm management encouraged our rowdy group to move on when dinner was over, and the marathon day continued with after dinner drinks at P.J. Clarke's Bar. I didn't think it was possible at Clarke's, but we were eventually asked, or rather commanded, to leave the premises.

Once on the street, Summerall, Brookshier, and I commandeered a horse-drawn carriage to carry us to our lodgings at the Wyndham Hotel. As we sang our way through the streets of Manhattan from the open-air carriage, Brookshier, who was riding shotgun, fell off the top of the carriage. Summerall and I implored the horseman to drive on, leaving Brookshier to pick himself up and stumble back to the Wyndham.

The driver was a big, splendid Irishman named Ryan, who sported a top hat and tails. When he pulled the carriage up in front of the hotel, we commanded him to come to our suite for a drink.

"Thank ye kindly, gentlemen," he shrugged, "but though I'd love to come up with you for a nip, I've no one to watch me horse while I'm up there."

Summerall and I then began a preposterous effort to convince Ryan that he could unhitch his horse, walk it through the lobby, and bring it up to the suite with him. It took no arm-twisting to persuade the thirsty lad to give it a try. He unhitched the horse, and to the horror of the doorman, the three of us began to try to coax the horse through the front entrance of the hotel. Alas, the jarring nature of the automatic doors sliding open startled the horse on each attempt, and the giant animal reared up and backed away every time we tried to walk him in. A crowd gathered, and the Wyndham management howled and begged that we please come to our senses.

By the time a battered and dirtied Brookshier came trudging up the sidewalk, we'd given up on having our drink with Ryan, and the Irishman and his nag were on their way.

While in Texas for the Colonial Tournament, a large group of guys from CBS went out for a night at Joe T. Garcia's, a Mexican restaurant in Fort Worth that featured a decorative swimming pool. In the spirit of our location and the theme of the establishment, we drank margaritas, pitcher after pitcher, mixed with Everclear, which is about 150 proof liquor. The pitchers seemed never to empty and when we finally walked away from that big rowdy table, we all went into the courtyard by the swimming pool, where Summerall and I climbed a tree that hung over the pool. I am deathly afraid of heights, but was encouraged by Summerall and the large quantities of margarita to jump fully dressed from the tree into the pool. We were creating havoc.

Summerall and I then tried to throw Bob Dailey—our #2 unit director—into the pool, but he deftly pushed us back in. Not to be denied, Summerall finally wrestled Dailey into the water. Once Dailey emerged, he began to chase Summerall.

Summerall sought to escape Dailey by dashing back into the hotel corridors and rushing through the kitchen, where he came around the corner and collided with a Mexican waiter carrying a tray. Pat flew ass over tip, landing hard and severely cutting his leg on the broken glasses.

Luckily, there was "a doctor in the house," and he told us that Summerall's cuts, which were bleeding heavily, were serious and that he should be taken posthaste to the hospital for stitches.

"I don't have to go anywhere," Summerall forcefully and drunkenly pronounced with his hand over the cuts, "I'm an American and I'm tough!"

Summerall did submit to the hospital trip once Chirkinian insisted, and we all climbed in two cars to accompany our fallen mate to the hospital. Chirkinian and Ken Venturi were in one car, while I occupied the passenger seat of the other, with Dailey driving and Summerall and his hastily bandaged leg in the backseat.

These two cars motored their way down the road, rushing Summerall to the hospital, while passing drinks from car to car at 70 miles per hour, seemingly without spilling a drop!

"I need another drink," Summerall claimed on the way. Somehow I tried to pass him the margarita pitcher back over my head, but tipped it and spilled it all over myself.

Once we returned from the hospital with Summerall, the boys started playing football in the hotel lobby with one of the glass pitchers. They were throwing the pitcher at each other with great force. How someone didn't get killed that night is amazing.

Joe T. Garcia's remained a popular haunt each time we returned to Fort Worth to broadcast the Colonial. On another occasion, Summerall and I were bunkered in there when a man, trying to curry favor with the "big time" CBS people and perhaps gain some tournament badges, brought two healthy looking young women around to introduce them to announcer Vin Scully. Scully wasn't interested, but Summerall and I took advantage of the situation, and escorted the women back to our hotel. According to my usual luck, I later heard rumors that the young woman I paired off with was involved in untoward and illegal substances.

Knowing that I was horrified that I'd been with a woman of such dubious distinction, I took a fair amount of ribbing from the CBS crew. The crewmembers, seizing upon my embarrassment, found someone who closely resembled the young woman the following year at Fort Worth. She approached me as I came down from my tower following the broadcast and threw her arms around me. I was flabbergasted as she told me how she'd been to prison and escaped and asked me for a cart ride back to the clubhouse.

My God! I thought to myself. *The rumors were true!* I made pained small talk with her and begged off giving her a cart ride, making one excuse after another and trying not to let her cause a scene.

When I thought I'd safely returned to the confines of the CBS trailer, one of the technicians shouted, "Roll tape!" and I was forced to view a videotape of myself talking with the imposter. The crew-members secretly had me on camera, and the woman was wired for sound, so everything I said was audible to these tricksters. Once again, I was the subject of an elaborate joke. It seems the CBS rule was: "When in doubt, tease the Brit." Chirkinian gave me the sobriquet "God's Toy," explaining that I would live forever, because God had so much fun tormenting me every day. "God wakes up every day and rubs his hands, wondering what he can do to you today," Chirkinian told me.

One of the CBS crew's favorite pranks was to steal and hide my briefcase, and watch me go frantic searching for it. It was not funny to me because inside that briefcase were all of my notes and research for the broadcast. I'll never forget one beautiful briefcase made of leather with beautiful brass corners, which I'd purchased in Madrid for a premium amount of money. I looked all evening for this prized possession, high and low, until the next morning Summerall gave in and told me where it was—in the freezer! Beautiful leather... completely ruined.

I knew the gag was out of hand when, at the Memorial Tournament, even Barbara Nicklaus got into the act, delighting in joining the hooliganism by hiding my briefcase. Later that season, I recognized that it was time for me to strike back and return the favor. While the entire crew was sitting at lunch in the clubhouse at Glen Abbey, discussing our plans for broadcasting the Canadian Open, I realized it was my chance. I deftly fingered announcer Frank Glieber's briefcase, and slipped away from the table. I carried it out the door of the clubhouse, and, noticing the low clubhouse roof stretched out over the balcony, I reached up and propped Glieber's briefcase up onto the roof. Giggling, I tiptoed away, subtly slipping back to the lunch table to listen to more of the conversation. I could barely contain my glee as I waited for the lunch to end and for Glieber to go into a panic trying to figure out where he might have left his briefcase.

"Okay," said Chirkinian, wrapping up the lunch, "let's go to rehearsal."

The group stood, and Glieber walked directly out the door, around the front of the building, and reached up to pull down his briefcase. With my eyes like saucers, the group began to laugh at me. It seems the tinted one-way windows on the clubhouse allowed everyone at the table to watch me perpetrate the entire crime, while I could not see them watching me through the glass. They decided to let me think I was getting away with something, and again I'd been had.

Perhaps it was boredom, perhaps it was a manner in which to alleviate stress, or perhaps it was, as Chirkinian suggested, the work of God that motivated the CBS crew to perpetrate what I consider to have been their finest and most elaborate prank.

Summerall, Gary McCord, Ken Venturi, Jim Nantz, and the others wrote to my mother in England, and requested that she ship to them my "Edward Bear," the stuffed teddy bear I had prized since babyhood, which remained safely in my mother's care.

Unbeknownst to me, these devils duped my wonderful, kindly, and trusting mother into airmailing the bear into their devious hands. One day, during a telecast, I looked into the monitor, and damn me if *there* wasn't Edward Bear in the background! I demanded to know how this had happened, and insisted on the safe return of my Edward Bear.

I was not allowed to know where the bear was, but week after week he kept turning up, very subtly, in the visible background of the telecasts. One week, they placed Edward Bear on a lawn chair wearing dark glasses. Another week, he'd be seated behind a green, or next to a tee. It was maddening, and at the same time, admittedly ingenious.

Word leaked out as the crew solicited the assistance of the galleries to place the bear in camera range, and I began to receive teddy bears in the mail with notes from viewers and spectators.

Finally, after our season-ending broadcast at the World Series of Golf in Akron, I was shown a videotape of the fate of my Edward Bear. I watched the monitors in horror as I saw footage of what appeared to be a Viking funeral in the pond at the 16th green on Firestone's south course. They'd crafted a small wooden box into a sailboat, and placed Edward Bear into the boat. Then, after setting the boat ablaze, pushed it away from the edge of the water into the center of the pond, where it burned. Sad music was dubbed over, and shots of Venturi and the gathered weeping were interspersed. I was aghast that the crew would bring this long joke to such a cruel and mean-spirited end!

Then suddenly the "mourners" on the tape all looked skyward as Handel's Messiah was dubbed onto the tape. The camera tilted up, and there was Edward Bear, dressed in an angel outfit replete with halo, floating down from the sky on a tiny parachute, reincarnated. The burned-up bear had obviously been a stunt double.

Ultimately, I was presented with Edward Bear, to my relief, and the crew and announcers laughed long into the evening's partying at my expense. Blessedly, I still have Edward Bear safely in my possession to this day.

On some occasions, the CBS crew was required to attend certain receptions or cocktail parties.

"Okay, boys, tonight is mandatory," Chirkinian would say, "you are to stay around and mingle with the clients and be nice to everybody.

Some of the receptions were billed "walk-throughs," which meant we could show up, make an appearance, and literally walk through. It was a "walk-through" that Summerall and I attended at the home of PGA Tour Commissioner Deane Beman in Ponte Vedra during the week of what was then called the Tournament Players Championship. We'd had a few drinks before we went to the party, and once we arrived, we found that it was just another mob scene. We could barely move in the crowded home, but had a couple more drinks before Pat decided he was bored, and agreed to accompany me in my drive to the Jacksonville airport. That evening, I was to pick up my wife Kitty and a friend of hers, a flight attendant for Air New Zealand who was interested in meeting Summerall.

We poured ourselves very large plastic cups full of vodka and I set out for the airport, driving down J. Turner Butler Boulevard with Summerall in the passenger seat. Flashing blue lights appeared in my rearview mirror in a manner of minutes. I was getting pulled over for the first time in America.

"Oh, hell, Pat, what do I do now?"

"What you do now," Summerall advised, "is you get this car over on the hard shoulder and then put on your best British accent and try to talk your way out of this."

I handed Summerall my vodka, and he attempted to hide the two great cups behind his knees. The imposing officer approached the car. It was dark, and he was wearing sunglasses. In a very local southern accent and drawl he bellowed, "Well, what have we here?"

Fearing my effort might be futile, I nonetheless put on my best English accent. "Well, officer, to be terribly honest, we are late, sir, making our way to the greater Jacksonville International Airport."

I felt the policeman stare at me through his intimidating mirrored sunglasses.

"Judging by how you talk, I know you ain't from here."

"No, officer, you're correct. I am from England."

"Hmm. Well, how about showing me your driver's license?"

Fumbling around and remembering I didn't have it, I shrugged and explained that I had left it back in my room.

"You left it back in your room, eh? You obviously don't know the rules."

"No officer, I really don't because in England, if you don't happen to have your driver's license with you when you're apprehended, you are given five days to produce it at the police station of your choice."

The policeman began to get irritable. "Even if I didn't know you wasn't in your country, I would know that you don't live by the same rules as everyone else. In this country, boy, we carry the driver's license at all times."

"Well, how about this?" I said, tugging out and handing over my American Express card. Upon seeing this, Summerall, still hiding the vodka, began to laugh out loud.

"You, in the passenger seat, you're very quick to laugh, but if you were in the predicament that this boy from England is in, wouldn't you expect him not to laugh and maybe even say something in your favor?"

"No," Summerall replied.

By now, another officer had walked around to Summerall's side of the car and shined a flashlight through the window and onto Summerall's face. The second officer then made a gesture to the first, and they met at the back of the car for a conference. I flashed Summerall an exasperated look as we awaited the result.

"Well, now look at what we got ourselves here," the officer gloated when he returned to my window. "Big time CBS announcers here for the golf tournament. That where you been, boys?"

"Yes, sir."

"Well, boys, we're gonna let you off this time, but I want you to know that my partner and I are going to sneak out to the golf tournament on Friday. Don't you put our faces on the TV cameras, or we'll come and throw you in jail for fleeing the scene."

I gave a knowing wink to the officer, and with that, he gave me back my American Express card and Summerall and I drove off into the night. Of course, the officers never appeared on screen and we never went to jail...although I think we probably deserved to.

One man I know who definitely should have received his share of speeding tickets and jail time is Greg Norman. At the World Series of Golf in Akron one Saturday night, Norman and a few of us decided to drive down to Canton for dinner. We took two cars, and on the way got stuck in some awesome traffic. Just as I'd resigned myself to a tedious and slow drive, I looked in the rearview mirror and saw Norman roaring up from behind like a race car driver. With Ian Baker-Finch in the passenger seat, Norman veered off into the median, and then rocketed back all the way across onto the hard shoulder, dodging cars and traffic along the route. I rejected the idea of following him because he was driving so wildly that any policeman would have locked him up and thrown away the key!

Perhaps my present-day quest for speed is similar to Norman's in that I think we both aspired to be race car drivers. In fact, I had a very short and undistinguished racing career in England when I was 18 years old. I raced a Silverstone Healey, which was an open-wheel sports car with a 2.5-liter Riley engine. My career—and life—nearly ended at Borehm in Essex, on a circuit that has now become a Ford Motor Company test track. Striking a slower-moving car, my car flipped into the air. On the fifth or sixth somersault, I was thrown from the vehicle and took a header into something that knocked me out and broke both of my cheekbones. My upper bridge was knocked out, and my nose was thrust down through the roof of my mouth.

It was great providence that the ambulance drivers had been brewing tea, and so the emergency doctor improvised by using their teaspoon handles to pull my nostrils out of my face, otherwise I would have choked. My mother was summoned, and fainted cold the moment she laid her eyes on me.

Plastic surgery followed, which involved taking skin from the back of my arm to patch me up. The English plastic surgeon must have slipped a bit, because he placed some skin on my nose that had hair in it. To the CBS crew, this was a big joke, and they would often sneak a very tight, up-close camera shot of my nose to see if I'd recently shaven it. Thanks to the plastic surgery, I have been forced, all of my life, to literally shave my nose three times a week.

The sharp wit and lunacy of the rotund Bob Drum always inspired the CBS crew to top themselves—or rather, lower themselves—again and again. The aforementioned Drum, a physically giant man, was born in Brooklyn, and had been a basketball star at the University of Alabama before being hired to a newspaper position in Pittsburgh, where he really made his mark.

Early in his journalistic career, Drum was writing hockey reports and covering the Pittsburgh Penguins. The cold weather in Pittsburgh during hockey season can be pretty rough, and so Drum's father presented him with a most magnificent bearskin overcoat to stay warm on those evenings covering hockey.

On many nights Drum would file his hockey game recaps with the newspaper offices via courier from some bar, where he'd written his story on odd scraps of paper and napkins. One evening, as the game went on into the night, Tom Place, Drum's night editor who went on to become communications director for the PGA Tour, received copy written on scraps of paper, matchboxes, and cigarette papers gleaned out of the various bars that Drum was moving to and writing in. After that late game, Place got worried because he didn't hear from Drum for two or three days.

It seems that Drum and his wife had just moved into a new home. The house was the first home in a new development on the outskirts of Pittsburgh. Drum caught the bus home very late that night and had to walk a quarter of a mile the rest of the way from the bus stop to his home. Trudging home through inches of fallen show, protected by his warm coat, Drum was minding his own business when a car came around the bend and sideswiped him, sending Drum through the air and into the roadside ditch. Drum was badly hurt by the collision but somehow managed to literally crawl home in his bearskin coat. Withered in a heap on his porch, he was unable to reach the doorbell.

Drum kicked in futility at the door until his wife M.J. came out to the porch and saw him lying there in a heap.

"You drunken swine," she charged. "I'm not letting you in this house." With that she slammed the door and returned to bed.

Eventually, Drum passed out. In time, his wife returned to the door to inspect him. Thinking perhaps that Drum might be in need of a stomach pump, M.J. woke him and helped him into the house, noticing blood on his bearskin coat. As Drum warmed in the house, he began to tell her that he'd been struck by a car, cursing the driver and muttering in anger.

"You drunken ass," M.J. replied. "You're not going to try to tell me that nonsense." She was certain that he had fallen over in the street or lost his drunken balance, and the scene led to a serious disagreement between Drum and his wife, who was staunchly unwilling to believe his tale.

Drum was lucky to be alive, but he couldn't move for days. Once he recovered, Drum returned to work covering the Penguins. After a few years, his subdivision had experienced construction growth and had been suitably built up. One of the neighbors hosted a cocktail party to give the many new neighbors a chance to meet each other. The Drums attended, and were engaging in idle conversation with another couple who had built a home there. They discussed the building process, the area, and the other details.

"You know, it's amazing," the neighbor remarked. "When I was first looking at this property a few years ago, there was only one house in the development."

"Yeah, that was mine," said Drum.

"I was a bit leery to buy the lot," the neighbor continued. "It seemed so remote. In fact, one night I was driving around looking at the area and considering the purchase, when I actually hit a huge bear on the side of the road with the car and sent that sucker bolting into the ditch. It scared me to death."

Drum stared at the man, and his wife fell meekly silent. While the neighbor giggled at his anecdote, the Drums were stony, until Drum finally spoke up.

"Well, now, I've got to tell you that that was no fucking bear, that was me! My wife didn't believe that I'd been knocked over that night. Now, in one fell swoop, I've got you, and I've got her...and I don't know who to kill first!"

Drum was really a remarkable character. Rough and gruff, and funny just to look at. One year, the Arkansas Razorback basketball team was to play the Duke Blue Devils in the NCAA Tournament semifinals. Drum supported Duke since he then lived in Pinehurst, North Carolina, and Summerall had graduated from Arkansas, so they decided to place a large wager on the game. It was then agreed between Drum and Summerall that the loser would provide the winner with a fine dinner and drinks. The winner could bring any family members or friends along as well.

Duke won the game, making Drum the winner of the bet, which would be settled at the Hofbrau Haus in Hilton Head, where we were broadcasting the Heritage Classic. In addition to his buddies at CBS, including Jack Whitaker and myself, Drum brought along almost every living relation he had, and I would swear a couple of dead ones as well. We all sat around a huge table at the Hofbrau Haus and had one hell of a party.

In South Carolina, liquor is served only in the miniature "airport type" bottles. So Drum, planning to have himself a night on Summerall, started by telling the waitress, "Bring me 15 bottles of Smirnoff." After drinking the first 15, Drum ordered 15 more, and 10 more after that.

At the end of the evening when we all stood up to leave, Drum stood upright, wobbled, and sunk back down to the floor, crashing in the corner of the room, totally unconscious. Whitaker and I each took one of Drum's legs, and Summerall grabbed him under his arms and walked backward as we carried him out of the restaurant. Drum was some big son-of-a-bitch and we were working hard to get him out of there.

Across the room, some wag yelled, "Well, well, there goes the CBS Golf team on just another Saturday night out."

Once in the parking lot, Drum's daughter drove her car up to the door to make it easier to load him into it. Trying to fit Drum into her two-door Honda Civic was like trying to get an oyster into the shell. Drum kept falling and bits of him were falling out of the car. Eventually we jammed him in there and slammed the door.

As his daughter was driving him away, she rolled down the window and yelled, "This is the last time I ever go out on a blind date!" With everyone laughing, she sped out of the parking lot.

With wild endings such as that one, we naturally had occasional bets being tossed around among the CBS Golf team. One year, certain members of the crew attended the CBS affiliates meeting in Los Angeles. We were all pretty well primed one evening in a restaurant that former tennis player Tony Trabert owned a stake in.

At one stage, Jack Whitaker did one of his table-thumping epics. Occasionally when Whitaker was in drink, he'd get mad with the world and go into vocal rages. This time, he was pronouncing that "Anwar Sadat should be made President of the United States. He's the greatest man in the history of civilization!" He then went on with a diatribe about the tenuous and ongoing Middle East peace efforts, and successfully cleared half of the restaurant. While Whitaker was raging on, I noticed that Summerall and Tom Brookshier were deeply involved in some devious conversation. I just got the feeling that they were plotting something because they continually kept peering across the table at Trabert and me as they talked.

"I think these two asses are plotting something," I warned Trabert.

"Okay," Trabert said. "If they are, you're the captain, and I'll go along with anything you say. You don't even have to consult me," he said.

Brookshier and Summerall got up and came around the table to Trabert and me.

"Look," said Summerall in his deep voice, "in our opinion, you two are a couple of nonathletic wimps. A tennis player and a British pouf. We're going to beat your asses tomorrow in a better ball match at Bel Air Country Club, and we're going to play for $100 per hole. Brookshier and Summerall versus Trabert and Wright."

"The match is on," I immediately answered. "That's all there is to it. We'll play you for anything you want; $100 per hole is just fine."

Due to a football injury, Summerall had a steel plate in his arm that ran from his right wrist to his right elbow, which meant that his putting never varied. He was a wonderful putter, but I knew that he also shanked the ball quite a bit. I was excited about our chances in the match.

All four contestants arrived the next morning at Bel Air suffering vicious hangovers. We were even in that department. Brookshier and Trabert had their own clubs, but Summerall and I had not brought clubs to L.A. The Bel Air golf professional Eddie Merrins leant Summerall and me UCLA rental sets in pipe bags. The borrowed Hogan clubs didn't suit Summerall, so I knew he was in for a long day. On the par-five first hole, our foursome was all over the place. Trabert and I lost it because the best score between us was a double-bogey 7.

After their opening hole default victory, the team of Summerall and Brookshier deteriorated rapidly. Summerall got a case of the terminal shanks, and shanked every shot forward from the second hole, blaming the clubs all of the way. Brookshier had a leg injury flare up on him, and was limping all over the course like the walking wounded. On a 210-yard par-three on the back nine, Brookshier hobbled to the green only to find that his errant drive sat out of bounds in some film star's backyard. He proposed dropping a ball at the spot.

"What are you talking about?" I asked incredulously. "You don't drop a ball when you're out of bounds! You put another bloody tee in the ground and hit another tee shot from the spot you last hit!"

I shamed Brookshier into hobbling from just next to the green all the way back up the hill to the tee. I knew the sight of this poor limping figure meant that we had destroyed them. It was an absolute travesty.

Summerall and Brookshier started having another one of their devious and furtive conversations on the 18th tee. Trabert whispered to me "It's the same as before, Ben. You're the captain. Anything they propose, you just make your deal."

Summerall and Brookshier—these two who had branded Trabert and me "nonathletic wimps"—proposed that we play for double or nothing on the 18th hole.

"Are you kidding?" I fumed. "You two haven't hit your hat for 16 holes now, and you dare to challenge two players who have absolutely whipped your asses? You think we're going to wager our $1,500 winnings on one hole, which you might be able to fluke-win by one of you *maybe* finishing the hole? We'll play you for a beer and that's all."

"You miserable, rotten bastards," they charged, obviously disappointed that their gamesmanship would give them no chance to win back the $1,500 they'd already lost. They muttered and moaned, and sure enough, neither one of them played well enough to even finish the hole, which meant they had to buy us the beer *and* pay us $1,600!

I shot 73 that day, and Summerall and Brookshier thirsted for a return match for a long time. But Trabert and I would always refuse. "No," we'd say, "you two were so pathetic that you've got to go through a qualifying school before we'll even play you again."

Alas, not all of my CBS golf matches were that easy. In the mid-1980s, Drum organized an event that he dubbed "The CBS World Championship Two Man Scramble" at Knollwood Country Club outside Chicago. Some of the CBS announcers were professionals, like Ken Venturi, and Steve Melnyk. I was double digits from being a professional, but nonetheless was paired with a 16-handicap fellow who was a pro basketball announcer. I ranted and raved about the unfairness of this event, but my complaints fell on deaf ears. We were paired with assistant producer Chuck Will and Jim Foley, the public relations manager for the Houston Rockets.

The day before this grandiose "CBS World Championship Two Man Scramble," I'd driven from Flint, Michigan to the Chicago area, stopping in Lansing to get a hamburger. That was an ill-fated lunch stop, because I contracted an evil case of food poisoning. Gamely, yet weakened, I agreed to employ my British stiff upper lip and play in spite of my condition. My efforts to beg off were largely ignored anyway.

By some good fortune, the third hole at Knollwood Country Club returns to the clubhouse. Just after my second shot on that third hole, I knew that I had to get to that clubhouse, and a bathroom, in a hurry. I shoved my partner out of the cart and told him that he'd have to finish the hole solo. I was never so pleased to see porcelain in all of my life, and believe me, was never more in need of it.

By the time I returned to the fourth tee, there was a three-group backup because my team had decided to wait for me. What a sight I was. Ashen, sweaty, and drained.

"Mr. Wright, you're looking at a 175-yard par-three," said my young Evans Scholar caddie. "It's a hard 6-iron or an easy 5-iron."

"Young man," I replied with annoyance, "don't you see the condition I am in? I'll take a bloody 4-iron."

Standing over the ball in front of the others waiting to play, I was dreadfully afraid to upset my constitution with a hard swing, and also fearful that I might lose my balance and fall over. I took a very smooth and measured swing with that borrowed Hogan Radial 4-iron, and watched the ball flutter in front of the hole, hop twice, and jump in!

My partners were jubilant, and we exchanged high fives. As if I had taken a swig of magic elixir, I began to forget my illness.

On the very next hole, the par-four fifth, I pushed my drive into the woods on the right. Spotting a tiny opening in the trees, I gave it a go, and the ball soared through the gap, up to the green, and into the hole for an eagle 2! By that point, I was completely cured! Just as golf had rescued my troubled childhood, it had now cured what ailed me.

Not too many scramble teams get to write 1-2 on their scorecards. That two-hole miracle propelled us to victory with a 68, and flooded the clubhouse with victory champagne.

My only other hole-in-one occurred at age 18, when I carried a 2-handicap. I was making my debut in representing the county of Bedfordshire in a tournament against our rivals from Hertfordshire. The alternate shot event was contested at South Bedfordshire Golf Club on the outskirts of Luton.

My partner and I were two holes down with three to play when we came to the 127-yard, par-three 16th hole. My opponent hit an utterly perfect shot to three feet from the pin on the hillside hole. I began to regret that it was my turn to tee off in the alternate shot match, because my partner was a 13-time county champion, and there I stood with only my inexperience and my inadequate equipment, staring elimination in the face.

I stone cold topped a 7-iron, which bounded down the pathway, hopped through a shallow pot bunker, slammed into the flagstick, and fell into the hole! Bewildered and yet inspired, my partner and I beat our stunned opponents from Hertfordshire on the next two holes and sent them in a rage directly to the car park without so much as a handshake.

Not to worry, there were 50 to 60 people in the clubhouse awaiting my appearance and obligation to buy the house a round due to my ace. I was only 18 years old, and was forced to secretly phone my father and have him bail me out by paying the bar bill.

Call my two holes-in-one flukes, if you will, but at least they reached their intended target. While playing golf in Blairgowrie, Scotland with Jack Whitaker, I witnessed a shot that deserved commemoration. Whitaker muffed his drive, and the tee shot smashed into the red plastic ball that marked the teeing area for the ladies' tee. The plastic marker shattered in all directions. When we stopped laughing at Whitaker's misfire, we began a diligent search for the ball amongst the wreckage. We actually found the ball inside what remained of the red plastic marker, and Whitaker called it an unplayable lie. To Whitaker's delight and secret chagrin, I took the ball and the balance of the destroyed tee marker and had them mounted on a plaque for posterity.

I was delighted that, for once, I didn't have to be the foil for a joke. If anyone deserved to be a foil, it was Whitaker, not me. In fact, I took to nicknaming Whitaker "Inspector Clouseau," since, at times, his actions could only be compared to the bumbling, incompetent ways of the Peter Sellers movie character.

For a very erudite, clever man, Whitaker was inordinately impractical and clueless. For instance, on the road, he would repeatedly, week after week, send his slacks out to the dry cleaner with his rental car keys still in the pocket. One could find him very often in the lobbies of hotels tearing his hair out because he'd sent away another set of keys. Keys were really one of "Clouseau's" weaknesses.

During my early years in the United States, before I had moved to America, Jack was very gracious in that he allowed me to stay with him in the weeks between CBS tournaments at his Bridgehampton, Long Island home.

Very early on my first morning at Whitaker's home, I awakened to the realization that something had gone terribly wrong. It sounded as if a buffalo had been let loose in the living room beside my bedroom. Suddenly startled awake, I jumped out of bed and ran into the living room, where I encountered Whitaker, who is given to ungovernable rages, having a terrible seizure.

"What appears to be the problem, Jack?" I gently asked.

"I cannot believe this," he answered. "I've lost the keys to my Mercedes."

"That's no problem, Jack. The keys to my rental car are right here. Go ahead and use it. Do whatever you need to do."

"No, you don't understand," Whitaker whined. "I wanted to slip out and get you the *New York Times* and bring back a nice breakfast, and now I've messed it all up, and you're awake and damn the whole idea now." His rage continued.

"Jack, what you'd better do is phone your Mercedes dealer in New York as soon as they open shop," I suggested. "Why don't you do yourself a favor and request, say, six sets of keys for your model, and what we'll do is position them around the house so that you'll always know where a backup is because, Jack, you do seem to have a habit of losing..."

"I know, I know," Whitaker interrupted. "I don't need to be told that, thank you very much."

I backed off, and at 9:00 A.M. sharp, overheard him on the telephone with the Mercedes dealer, ordering six sets of keys.

"Five bloody weeks?" I heard Whitaker exclaim.

I ran out to calm him and reminded him that if he just patiently awaited the arrival of the keys, he would never have this problem again.

I happened to be staying with Whitaker again when the keys arrived nearly a month later. Together, he and I began the business of positioning the spare keys around the house. One set went in the bedside table, one set in the garage, one in the kitchen, and so forth.

After returning to England the following week, I got a phone call.

"Jack Whitaker here."

"Well, hello Jack. To what do I owe the pleasure of your call?"

"Ben, I hate to bother you, but, where did we put those blasted keys?"

"Which set, Jack, are you referring to?"

"The whole lot, Ben," Whitaker painfully admitted. "I can't find a single set of those hidden keys!"

I'm sure my laughter didn't help much to settle "Clouseau."

I had the opportunity to return Whitaker's graciousness when he was scheduled to take a trip to London to interview Lord Killanin, who was then head of the International Olympic Committee. Lord Killanin was not available until after the weekend, so Whitaker decided that he'd come in early and drive down to my farm in Wiltshire, which was about 90 miles outside London. We planned to play a little golf, drink a little beer, and have a nice time.

Whitaker can never find his way anywhere, so I gave him exact, detailed directions. Right on time, he arrives absolutely flushed with joy, leaping out of his car.

"Ben, I didn't make a single wrong turn! This is a major triumph!"

"Yes, Jack, it is," I laughed, shaking his hand. "I really didn't expect you for another half of a day!"

I got Whitaker a nice cold beer, and we began to stroll around the farm. I was showing Whitaker where everything was when my then wife, the late Judy Wright, yelled to Jack from the porch that he had an important phone call from London. Whitaker went in to take the call.

"Damn, damn, this is too ridiculous for words!" he shouted, coming out of the house. He'd been recalled to London because Lord Killanin had decided that he would prefer to see Whitaker for the interview on Saturday instead of Monday after all. Jack was powerless to complain, and went into a total rage. He swigged down the rest of his beer, and it was then he disappeared in a mist of red rage.

Many times I have seen him, in a rage, jump into his car, put his hands on the steering wheel, and rest his head there until he composed himself and got into some kind of condition to safely drive the car. This time, Whitaker said good-bye to my wife and me, rushed out to his car, jumped in, put his hands out...and smashed his head on the dashboard! In his rage, "Clouseau" had forgotten that the car was right-hand drive in England. There was no steering wheel on the side he'd jumped into out of habit!

I stayed with Whitaker and his first wife Alberta on another occasion at their lovely home in Pelham, New York. Whitaker had to drive off very early one morning to cover the stables at Belmont Raceway, which was not far away. Still, he awakened pissed off, grumbling and muttering about the task, and put his briefcase on top of his car to unlock the door and climb in. In a mad rage, he drove off without removing his briefcase from the roof, and it flew off of the car into the bushes. Upon seeing this, I ran out into the drive yelling and waving, but Whitaker was so angry he was driving like mad and was gone.

Once Whitaker arrived at Belmont, he telephoned back to the house.

"Ben," he asked, "did you happen to see me go out of the house with my briefcase this morning?"

"Yes, Jack."

"I've lost it, then."

"No, you haven't, Clouseau. I retrieved it from the bushes on your driveway because you left it on the roof of your car when you drove off in a huff."

"Damn. I'll be back in a few minutes."

Whitaker's first wife Alberta, known affectionately as "Bert," was born in Pottsville, Pennsylvania. As Jack's career developed, Bert really didn't want to leave Philadelphia, where Jack was employed by WCAU TV. Bert's objections to Whitaker going big-time were a source of stress on their marriage.

Never was the stress more obvious than the occasion on which he was honored as "Sportscaster of the Month" at an elegant banquet at Luchow's Restaurant, to which Whitaker was allowed to invite 20 people. With myself, Dan and June Jenkins, and other close friends and associates of Whitaker present to see him accept his award in front of the banquet crowd, Bert got up and harangued him publicly. She belittled him with private issues and unfair personal charges, and the scene was tough to watch. The whole place fell silent as she berated him. It was an awful experience, and one that I'm sure led to their decision to divorce, a decision made more painful due to the fact that Jack and Bert were both devout Irish Catholics.

Some time later, Whitaker began to date professional golfer Suzy McAllister. At Pebble Beach, I was walking with Summerall from the lodge over to the CBS trailers for rehearsal when we spotted Whitaker and McAllister ahead. They were apparently involved in a serious argument, because they were literally squared off like the followers of the Marquis of Queensberry. It looked like a boxing film.

As Summerall and I watched from a distance, McAllister slugged Whitaker in the chest, and Whitaker threw his room key and hit her in the back of the head. Knowing the indignity and turmoil Whitaker suffered in his first marriage, Summerall shook his head and uttered, "Poor ol' Whitaker...bunkered again!"

During Whitaker's courtship with McAllister, we worked the Australian Open together in Sydney in 1978. Sitting at dinner with the fine television director Mac Hemion, Whitaker pondered phoning McAllister. He wanted to speak with her, but didn't want to ring her phone at an unreasonable hour. McAllister lived on the West Coast of the United States. Whitaker lived on the East Coast, and I lived in the

United Kingdom. The various time zones became confusing. There we were, after numerous drinks, sitting across the dateline in Australia, in total futility, trying to work out the math and figure out what time it was in California. It was like a trio of monkeys attempting to organize a moon shot.

Whitaker eventually married Nancy Kiner, who was the ex-wife of baseball player Ralph Kiner. Chaffee was Nancy's maiden name, and she was a world-class tennis player. It has been a very good marriage for Whitaker, who is talented and irascible, but a gentle soul. He and Nancy now divide their time between Palm Desert and Bridgehampton, where he built a lovely home called "Sparrow Hall." It was there that he asked me to design a par-three hole for him, which he built on the grounds of his home.

Whitaker is a member at both Winged Foot Golf Club and Shinnecock Hills Golf Club. Our friendship so warmed that we decided to form a tradition in which we would play against one another each year for a piece of silver. We staged a head to head, match play competition that we called the "Real Ryder Cup," and played each year only at venues that had, or should have, hosted major championships or, in the Bobby Jones tradition, amateur championships. Great courses like Winged Foot, Shinnecock Hills, Maidstone, and the National Golf Links of America.

Every few holes during the match, we would pause and issue "bulletins to the press," laughing and creating spoof headlines:

Bonfires rage in England to celebrate early lead of British captain.

British captain faces recall after appalling performance over first nine holes.

Whitaker won the first time we played, and asked that his prize be a sterling silver cocktail shaker, which I secured, had engraved, and presented to him. I am glad he enjoyed the prize, because he never won again. I now have countless pieces of silver in my trophy case. A solid silver tray to serve drinks on, a silver Scottish whiskey measure, my own cocktail shaker, and more, all engraved with the memorable words: "The Real Ryder Cup."

Jack eventually left CBS to work for ABC. At CBS, he occasionally manned the key 18th hole broadcast position. Whitaker didn't mind being supplanted on the prestigious 18th hole by Pat Summerall, but he could not tolerate being replaced there by Vin Scully, for whom he felt disdain because of the latter's cliché-ridden delivery. Therefore, in a rage, "Clouseau" bolted from the network, and has since sealed his reputation as a performer of beautifully done spontaneous summations of sporting events.

Just as I was very close with Whitaker, Summerall and I were also like brothers. I have a huge regard for his accomplishments as a sportsman, and an equally huge regard for his work on the air. He is the consummate "traffic cop," moving the broadcasts in and out of commercial breaks, and smoothly handling any transition thrown his way. Summerall is totally unselfish with the microphone, and always eager to defer to the experts on the team. Whether it was John Madden on National Football League broadcasts or Ken Venturi on golf telecasts, Summerall knows his place, and knows how to bring out the best in those around him, a talent very few have.

For many years, Summerall and I shared a house each April at the Masters. I'd come down for breakfast at 7:30 each morning and Pat would be hunched over the kitchen table with a big cup full of liquid that he claimed was grapefruit juice. Of course, although he would deny it, I knew there was vodka in that mixture.

The years of road life and partying were beginning to catch up with us as we aged. By the mid-1990s, Summerall was drinking very heavily and was beginning to do serious damage to himself physically and mentally. In fact, he nearly bled to death internally on a flight from Atlanta to Jacksonville, and was rushed to the hospital upon landing.

Summerall arrived for the 1994 Masters drunk, having been driven up on a Tuesday from his home in Ponte Vedra, Florida. On Wednesday night, I hosted a syndicated television show for InterSport called "The Green Jacket Show," which was taped at the now defunct "Green Jacket Restaurant" across the street from the entrance to the Augusta National Golf Club. InterSport would always provide a little dinner and drinks in a private room following the broadcast, for which I stayed and mingled with the guests and crew. I myself have been face down in that restaurant before, but on this occasion I returned fairly early to the house, and found Summerall very drunk.

"Where the hell have you been?" he demanded.

"Well, Pat, I stayed after the show for a bite to eat and some drinks with the crew."

"Yeah," Summerall growled, "you left me alone to sit here and drink on my own."

It was an unsettling scene, and to make matters worse, Summerall appeared haggard and worn on the air. That week Venturi, who sat right next to Summerall in the booth, told me that Summerall had not made eye contact with him through the entire broadcast and seemed slumped, nearly dozing during the telecast.

CBS president Neal Pilson warned Summerall that this must never happen again, but it was too late for Summerall. Following that Masters telecast, he headed north to Philadelphia to perform a voice-over for NFL Films. Summerall planned to return to Hilton Head for the next CBS Tour stop, but on Tuesday morning in Philadelphia, he was intervened upon. Tom Brookshier, who also worked with Summerall on NFL football, was a Philadelphia resident. Brookshier organized the intervention, asking many of Summerall's closest friends and family to surprise Summerall at his hotel room, pledge their concern and support, and send him to the Betty Ford Clinic.

Chirkinian attended the intervention, but I was not allowed to go. "If you go to this thing," Chirkinian told me, "the two of you will walk out when it's over and find the nearest bar."

Brookshier was given the responsibility of delivering Summerall to the Betty Ford Clinic in Palm Springs, and Summerall has not touched another drop since undergoing that terribly agonizing intervention and five-week clinic stay. Of course, Summerall was a prime mover in my own intervention, which came not long after, in 1996.

When the Fox Network landed the NFL contract in 1995, Summerall left CBS to continue his NFL work with Fox. It was thought by some that Summerall would be able to continue to work with the CBS Golf team, because Fox, which had little use for Summerall outside the football season, promised him that they would be willing to allow him to do so. CBS, however, in an unfortunate show of sour grapes mentality, denied Summerall that possibility and refused his services. I know that really hurt Pat, and that he misses golf more than anyone can tell.

At the 1995 Masters, Summerall's final CBS telecast, Augusta National chairman Jack Stevens made a presentation of a beautiful rose bowl to Pat, with an inscription of appreciation for over 20 years of

Masters telecasts. At this particular little ceremony, held at Stevens's villa in Augusta, Stevens also named Summerall and Chris Schenkel "broadcasters emeritus," and presented them with gold badges, which allowed them total access to the tournament. Summerall and Schenkel were also to be arbiters of the quality of the broadcasts, and would be asked to report their opinions each year to the Masters committee.

We were all indeed sorry to see Summerall go, but I wish that many of our relationships with Pat hadn't suffered such serious strain during the months and years since he left.

A scurrilous rumor reached Chirkinian that Summerall, in his official role as Masters "broadcaster emeritus," had reported to the Masters committee that he felt Chirkinian's performance as a director was slipping, and that perhaps he was no longer fit to properly produce the telecast. Thanks to Chirkinian, CBS had maintained those rights throughout the televised history of the Masters. In fact, Summerall's alleged condemnation may ultimately have helped to hurry Chirkinian's premature exit from CBS.

In 1996, a power play to maneuver Chirkinian out and replace him with former production assistant Lance Barrow was undertaken. In my opinion, Chirkinian's vehement defense of my employment status throughout my ill-fated bout with political correctness and the aggressiveness of ambitious corporate climbers became a potent combination. Suddenly, the coup was complete. Frank Chirkinian, "The Ayatollah," was quietly ousted. The father of golf television was sent into the sunset with his unparalleled talent and the balance of his lucrative contract.

A nnouncer Steve Melnyk was known by many to be an ambitious climber. I've known Melnyk since 1971, when he won the British Amateur at Carnoustie. Because he had played in the Walker Cup and the British Amateur, he'd played in two consecutive weeks of 36-hole matches, which was one hell of an achievement.

I took the young Melnyk to dinner on the night between the Amateur semifinals and finals, which was the evening before he beat Jim Simons 3-and-2. There was an entrée of a half a duckling on the menu. I ordered the duckling, and knowing that Melnyk was a husky trencherman, I whispered to the waiter not to mess around with the duckling but rather to bring Melnyk a full-grown duck.

I want to tell you, young Melnyk wolfed his dinner down. He absolutely field-stripped this duck until there were only bones left on the plate. I must say, I liked the kid as an amateur golfer. But I learned that he could be a devious manipulator as an announcer.

While injured during his playing career, Melnyk came to Summerall and me and begged us to convince Chirkinian to give him a shot at a broadcasting position. Summerall and I did go to Chirkinian on his behalf. Melnyk was given the break he wanted and, frankly, needed. Once on board at CBS, Melnyk set his sights on advancement, bypassing Chirkinian and socializing rather with CBS Sports presidents Pilson and Peter Lund. Eventually, though, Pilson left the network and Lund was promoted from Sports to the position of CBS Network president. Melnyk then found that his contract with CBS would not be renewed, and was left to convince ABC to hire him, which they did in 1992.

During my broadcast career I have ventured, from time to time, into commentating non-golf sporting events. But I clearly belong in a tower behind a green and not in a stadium press box.

I served as color analyst for a CBS telecast of Pele's debut with the New York Cosmos. Frank Glieber called the play-by-play. Ironically, even though Glieber didn't know much about soccer, I still had trouble getting a word in edgewise.

I provided color commentary for the 1981 America's Cup, in which Dennis Connor sailed *Freedom* through the last America's Cup sailing races staged on the storied Newport Course.

I hosted a segment from Milan, Italy during CBS's 1987 Super Bowl pregame show, explaining the differences between American and European "football."

In 1975, I appeared on a show called "CBS Sports Spectacular," so that Summerall could draw upon my past experience as an auto racer. I had just come from covering the 1975 British Grand Prix at Silverstone, where a surprise squall of rain had caused a multi-car pile-up due to suddenly slippery conditions. Without time to change the tires, the race cars smashed into each other even at the tentative speed of 20 miles per hour. Indeed, the sight of cars crashing at that slow of a pace appeared silly to Summerall and the television viewers, until I explained that without treads the high-speed tires were utterly useless in the surprise wet conditions.

I also announced the 1975 Irish Derby with Jack Whitaker. I forecasted the winner to be a horse called Grundy, and predicted the next three finishers. I even told Whitaker to copy my bet and back those four horses each way, but he chose only to bet King Pellinore to win. When the first four horses finished precisely in the positions I picked, many people accused me of having watched the Derby run before making my selections, therefore suspecting that the broadcast was tape-delayed, which indeed it was. To ensure the credibility of the broadcast, I was not used again on any horse racing telecasts. As consolation, I left the Curragh that day with pockets bulging with thousands of punts!

I belonged in a golf tower anyway, and was sometimes, perhaps, even a bit too visible there for golf's own good. Warwick Hills, for instance, was like golf nowhere else. It was the site of the Buick Open in Grand Blanc, Michigan. The gallery consisted of, along with others, a great deal of blue-collar automotive workers who enjoyed their beer on a Sunday afternoon. The 17th hole at Warwick Hills is a par-three with bleachers set behind the green and plenty of viewing areas around the hole. The Grand Blanc crowd at 17 developed a reputation for being the loudest hole on the Tour. Cheers erupted from the gallery at 17 that were more suitable for a football game. Indeed, this crowd even stood and raised their hands to create a "wave" cheer.

Some of the players thought the crowds were too noisy and unruly, particularly when they would roar with rousing approval over a three-inch tap-in. The crowds would only get angry with a player when the player refused to tip his cap or acknowledge them. Boos would rain down on players who were poor sports by refusing to give even a simple wave. Eventually, a totally unjustified witch-hunt was perpetrated by the officials of the Buick Open, and a large police presence began to arrest people and haul them out of the gallery in an attempt to quiet down the furor.

The 17th hole at the Greater Greensboro Open was similar in that it was a par-three that had a tendency to get rowdy. One year, GGO officials mounted a bit of a purge at 17. A crew went into the bleachers immediately after play, where they found 96 empty liquor bottles and hundreds of beer cans. That purge, in my opinion, was justified in that I wouldn't think it is necessary for a golf fan to take a Jack Daniels bottle into the stands with him. One or two beers are harmless enough, but turning the event into a real booze-up was not right. Liquor was banned at Greensboro, but the enthusiasm barely diminished.

The cheering was all in good fun, however, and from time to time at the Buick Open, the gallery, minds clearly idled between shots, would turn around to the booth and begin to chant, "Ben... Ben...Ben..." I was forced to stand and acknowledge them because they would scream and cheer until I waved or took a bow. Some officials accused me of riling up the crowd, but in fact, I was responding to them only to quell the charging bull.

"Hey, Ben," they would sometimes shout, "would you like a beer?"

Like it or not, a can of beer was coming into the booth, and I had to be sure to catch it or I might have gotten hit in the head! Beer cans were being hurled over the window on a regular basis.

Lest anyone think I drank those beers, I knew better. Trust me when I tell you that a golf tower during a live telecast is no place to put beer into your belly and bladder. That is a lesson I learned early in my career while providing commentary on a golf broadcast for the BBC in the early 1960s. Peter Thomson was seated next to me in the booth, when suddenly I heard the insistent call of nature. In a whispered aside, I informed the production assistant that very soon I would have to leave the booth for a spell.

The production assistant consulted with director Alan Mouncer, and came back with news.

"Mr. Mouncer says to tell you that you cannot leave the tower," the assistant whispered. "He suggests instead that you pee down into the top of the scaffolding pipe."

Any imagined ideals of the glamour of working in television were erased with the tinkling sound made as I stood on the side of the tower away from the crowd, carefully gauging the wind, relieving myself down into the scaffolding pipe.

Once, when I was working on a marathon 10-hour, live Australian golf broadcast, the situation was bound to occur again. To my relief and amazement, the first-class production staff there was prepared and had obviously considered the urgency of such situations. A man was employed to make a continuous route to each tower, and climb up the scaffolding with a plastic bucket, offering announcers the opportunity to relieve themselves. An undignified duty, to say the least, but I believe that man was the most appreciated fellow on the course that day, and the sight of him heading toward my tower was most welcome, and a very civilized gesture.

Another very civilized and appreciated gesture was perhaps the biggest surprise of my tenure at CBS. Early in my career at CBS, I was positioned in the 15th tower at the Augusta National Golf Club to broadcast during the Masters. The 15th was a very popular tower amongst CBS executives because you could see both of the pivotal 15th and 16th holes. CBS vice presidents, salespeople, clients, and hangers-on would load the booth during the broadcast, making it very difficult to work.

Through his earphones, my cameraman, Stan Gould, was given a command from Chirkinian to swing his camera around to catch a shot at 16. Gould, however, was unable to swivel the camera around in time because there were so many bodies packed into the tower.

Because Chirkinian directs the broadcast from a truck nowhere near the towers, Chirkinian had no idea of Gould's plight. When Gould missed the shot, Chirkinian lit into him with a barrage of criticism through Gould's earphones. Gould, nearly in tears, took his dressing-down like a man since he knew he could hardly cause a scene in front of the CBS brass and their clients.

After the broadcast, I went to Chirkinian and explained what a terrible working environment the tower had become, and that Gould was hampered by the crowd pushing its way into the tower, crawling all over us. Frank was upset about the situation, and immediately approached CBS Network president Bob Wood to complain. Wood agreed with Chirkinian wholeheartedly, and decreed that no one, other than Wood himself, should occupy that tower during the broadcasts. Gould and I were most pleased to hear this news.

The following day, I made my way to the tower after jump-starting my system with a few too many cups of coffee. Chirkinian, still angry about the previous day's sloppy broadcast, rehearsed us until only 10 minutes before the actual broadcast time. The announcers were left with only a few minutes to climb down from the tower and use the restroom before our two-hour live broadcast.

From my position at 15, it would have been impossible for me to climb down and find a restroom in time to return for the live telecast.

I had little choice but to grin and bear it as the broadcast began. During the first few minutes of the telecast, Wood, eager to be sure that his decree was followed and that our tower was empty, climbed up and made an appearance behind me. He then decided to observe the broadcast and began to look at me sideways when he could see me grimacing and performing the uncomfortable gestures of a man trying foolishly to ignore the call of nature.

With Wood behind me, and the action in front of me, I began to panic. Finally, during a commercial break, I had no choice but to confess.

"Mr. Wood," I said, "welcome to the 15th tower. I am Ben Wright."

He shook my hand suspiciously.

"Mr. Wood," I urgently continued, "I know that we have never met, but I need you to help me out with a favor. Do you see all of those discarded green paper 'Masters' cups down there in that waste basket?"

He nodded yes as if awaiting further instruction, and I could scarcely believe I was asking the network president to complete this task.

"Can you go down the ladder and gather as many of those as you can and bring them up to me in a hurry?"

With that, Wood was on his way down, and then up the ladder, with an armful of cups. With all pretense gone, I sat at my position and relieved myself below the desk into as many of them as was necessary. I was thoroughly embarrassed to have to resort to this in front of the network president, and gingerly sat each of the full cups down by the edge of the tower platform as I filled each one.

It was a sight that I'll never forget—Wood, in his jacket and tie, standing by the filled cups, trying to look inconspicuous while nudging them over the side, one-by-one, with his foot.

A much more serious problem occurred one autumn in Massachusetts, when we were broadcasting the United States Industries Classic at Pleasant Valley Country Club. On Friday afternoon, we were beginning the second-round rehearsal. I was positioned at the 215-yard par-three 16th hole when a player named Jim King arrived at my hole just a shot or two off the lead. A PGA Tour official named Pete Sesso was walking along monitoring King's group for slow play. King was showing some signs of irritation with Sesso when he came to the tee. He was plainly not happy about being monitored for slow play.

Having honors on the tee, King cold-shanked a five-iron into the evergreens, where it rattled around and came to rest under a hemlock tree. He then marched down to his ball and looked at it from all angles. King had considered all of his options before finally getting on his knees, choking way down on the metal shaft of the club, and chopping the ball out, sending it bounding into a greenside bunker. King then stormed into the bunker, and without any compunction, played a careless slap at the ball, knocking it onto the green before smacking the sand in the bunker and thrashing about in anger.

King then spotted Sesso across the green, sitting in his cart, writing King's misdemeanors down in a book. At the sight of this King turned purple, and huffed his way through a two-putt double bogey before going straight over to Sesso. King was a 6-foot-3, rawboned, ex-heavyweight boxer.

"Put your camera on King," I advised Chirkinian through my headset, "this might get ugly."

With that, King picked all 200 pounds of Sesso up out of his cart with one hand, and shoves his fist into Sesso's face before slamming him back down into the cart.

King moved on to play the par-four 17th and the long par-five 18th uphill to the clubhouse, absent of the monitoring eyes of Sesso. By the time King made his way off of the 18th green, though, Jack Tuthill, a former FBI agent and then head of the PGA Tour's field staff, intercepted King.

"You don't need to sign your card, Jim," Tuthill told him. "You're out of here. First of all, you've assaulted a PGA Tour official. You've beat up a bunker, and were guilty of slow play in the first place. You don't need to submit a score, and I'm recommending your immediate suspension from the Tour."

King, a bully but a coward, walked away with his tail between his legs.

To the surprise of everyone, King showed up at the golf course the next day and appeared at the CBS hospitality tent, ranging about in search of me.

"You, you're the guy who put me out of this tournament," King growled at me. "You're the one who had those cameras on me. You're the guy who is messing with my career, and I'm going to kill you, Wright!"

King was then asked to leave the tent, and I was hustled away. CBS had clients and sponsors in the tent, and was wary of a scene. I, on the other hand, could see in the man's eyes that he was sincere about his threat.

The following day at the tournament, King showed up again looking for me. CBS then decided to make his threats a police matter, and I was given a police escort. I found it somewhat unreal that as I went to the water closet [bathroom] before the telecast, there was an officer standing back to back with me as I stood at the urinal!

I finished the tournament and flew back home to England, planning not to return to the United States until the new golf season. Thinking over the incident at home, I realized how unsettled I was by King, considered the lunacy of it, and pondered not returning to the United States. Someone had threatened to kill me, and it was not an idle threat.

The only other time my commentary would have that kind of effect on a player was while broadcasting the Heritage Classic at Hilton Head, when Greer Jones had a putt at 17 that stopped on the lip and hung as if suspended over the hole. Jones then took an unconscionable amount of time to walk up and around the putt, hoping it would fall in.

"I think that's rather more than a reasonable amount of time that he's waited," I said on the air, as it seemed longer than the alotted 10 seconds.

The PGA Tour then reviewed the tape and disqualified Greer in retrospect. It was an expensive mistake for Greer, and he was rightly upset, but at least he didn't threaten to kill me as King had quite seriously done.

I was threatened with violence only once before. I wrote a pointed story in the *Daily Mirror* warning that the gambling element would ruin the sport of boxing and should be eliminated from the sport wherever possible. The next morning, a man known as "One-Armed Lou" darkened the door of the newspaper's London office.

"Is Ben Wright here?" he asked the receptionist.

She quickly told the sinister character that I was not available.

He nodded ominously at the receptionist. "Uh-huh. Then you tell Ben Wright that 'One-Armed Lou' said that he'd better take good care of himself."

The mobster's threat never came to fruition, but then again, I didn't write many more tirades against gambling and boxing.

It turned out that King had a record of bizarre behavior on the PGA Tour. John Lister, the New Zealand sheep-farmer-turned-professional-golfer, had once played with King but refused to attest to King's scorecard. Lister, it seems, felt that King had cheated during his round by "using the leather mashie" and kicking the ball through the rough into better positions. King, enraged by Lister's charge, grabbed Lister in the locker room and forcibly pushed him into a locker. He then slammed the door and tossed the key away before storming out.

Lister was not alone. When Gibby Gilbert once refused to sign King's card, again under suspicion of cheating, King followed Gilbert to his car in the parking lot. Catching Gilbert at his car, King threatened to beat him senseless if he didn't sign the scorecard. Gilbert knew that he was overmatched by the hulking King, who was capable of quite handily following through with his threat. Gilbert refused King's demand anyway, and instead chose to remind King that although he was small, he had "the equalizer." King was confused until Gilbert opened the glove box of his car so that King could see the revolver waiting inside. King backed off because he was, after all, a bully-coward.

Hearing these stories only made me more concerned, although I did opt to return to the Tour in the winter. Then PGA Tour Commissioner Joe Dey asked me to appear at a Tour hearing for Jim King, which was to be the Monday after the Jackie Gleason Inverrary Classic. Dey explained to me how important my testimony was, because King had apparently frightened off the other two witnesses.

"Wait a minute, Joe," I interrupted, "how did he frighten them off?"

Dey explained that a preliminary hearing was held in Boston immediately following the Pleasant Valley tournament. According to Dey, before the witnesses went in, King approached a female witness.

"Lady," he inquired, "do you have any children?"

"Three," the woman answered.

"Two, if you go in there," King told her, holding up two fingers.

The woman made for the exit, and then, according to Dey, King approached the other witness, who was a dental surgeon.

"You're a witness against me in this," said King. "Do you have an office in which you perform your dentistry?"

"Of course I do," answered the man, "with all of the most modern equipment."

"Ah," said King, "then you must have drills there."

"Yes."

"Well, I'm going to have to put one of those drills through your head if you go in there and testify."

Needing none of that, the dental surgeon was out the door.

Here I was at the Jackie Gleason Inverrary Classic at Lauderhill, Florida, having agreed to testify at the Tour tribunal after the event, and finding Jim King's name on the roster sheet. King, having not yet been judged by the Tour, was being allowed to play in the interim.

The night of the first round of the event, the CBS golf announcers went to dinner at a restaurant called "Stan's" on the Intracoastal Waterway in Ft. Lauderdale. We were just finishing our meal when I noticed that King, along with two equally big and ugly thugs, was entering the restaurant. Whitaker and Chirkinian helped to smuggle me out of the back of the restaurant along the waterway, and CBS Sports president Bill McPhail settled up the tab and followed us directly back to our hotel. McPhail contacted the authorities once again and I was given another police escort to shadow me wherever I went.

Summerall stayed in the restaurant, and approached King.

"Jim, you've got to back off of this vendetta," Summerall said. "You're going to get into real trouble here. I've been in your shoes, Jim. I was in professional sports, and you've just got to take the rough with the smooth," Summerall advised. "You have behaved very badly and you'd better just cool it and stop all of this bullshit about Ben Wright."

King listened to Summerall, but was noncommittal in his response.

When King missed the cut that week, he was once again roaming around with time on his hands.

Bang, bang, bang came the pounding on the office door to the CBS trailer. An unwitting secretary opened the door, and King entered with his two thugs, whom he then introduced to everyone around as his "legal advisors."

"I want to see Ben Wright," King insisted.

The secretary told King that I was not present, although I was in the office. Summerall chose to go to the door and confront King again, with much the same advice as he'd given the night before.

"I'm going to kill that bastard," was King's only response. "That limey's going to change his story or I'm going to kill him!"

"Jim," Summerall reasoned, "Ben can't change his story. We've all had disappointments. Just take the punishment as is required and get it over with."

King began to stare down Summerall when the secretary called the police. She then ordered King and his thugs out of the trailer and reported the incident to Tour Commissioner Dey. Armed guards were then positioned on the rooftops during the tournament, which afforded them good vantages in the "concrete canyons" of Inverrary Country Club. The "gentleman's game" had gone haywire. Was this real? Was it really happening?

I safely completed the Inverrary event, and flew up to Tampa for the Tour tribunal hearing, which was to take place the following morning. I was housed in a hotel room next to Dey, and a police officer lodged with me. The guard tipped a chair against the door and sat in it all night, guarding me while I slept.

It was a long night, and I appeared at the hearing the following morning as requested. The chairman of the tribunal was J. Paul Austin, the top man at Coca-Cola, who was the director of the Tour Policy Board. Dey was seated next to me.

"Take courage," Dey kept whispering in my ear to reassure me. "Take courage."

King did not show up at the hearing, but Pete Zaccanino, his bejeweled Connecticut lawyer, did attend. Zaccanino, in his cross-examination of me, began to insist that I didn't have my facts straight. He began to attempt to confuse me and get me all a mass of misgivings. He was screaming and shouting, but he failed singularly in his attempt to convince me to change my story.

My memory was clear. Dey was clucking beside me like a bloody old hen when it was ruled that King was to be suspended from play for one year.

I thought my ordeal had finally come to an end, but in the days to follow, King sent the word through intermediaries that he was still planning to kill me. In attendance with Chirkinian at a reception in Marco Island for the Tony Lema Memorial Tournament, Frank and I spotted King across the room.

"Ben, let's just see if we can't stop this thing once and for all," Chirkinian offered, full of bravado and bluster.

"If you want to try, Frank, I'm willing to go along." We strolled across the room and casually approached King.

"Hello, Jim, I'm Ben Wright," I said, extending my hand.

"I know who you are," King growled, ignoring my hand.

"Cool it, Jim," Chirkinian gently suggested. "Hear the man out."

Buoyed by Chirkinian's presence, I continued. "Jim, in England, we have an expression called 'let's bury the hatchet,' which means that you let bygones be bygones and patch it up."

King snarled. "The only way I'll bury a hatchet is in your head, you limey bastard!"

Chirkinian, suddenly meek, quickly turned to me and said, "I don't think it worked, Ben. Let's go!"

We beat a hasty retreat, in one of the only times I've ever seen Chirkinian on his heels.

The situation continued to be very serious when King showed up at the Doral tournament, and Summerall once again had to smuggle me out of a Miami restaurant to avoid him.

Thinking the situation was beyond hope, I approached the CBS brass. "I'm going home to England after this tournament," I told them, "and if you guys don't get this guy off of my back, I'm not sure I'm going to return."

Safely ensconced at home in England, I received the strangest telephone call from golfer Dave Marr.

"I've heard you're having this trouble with Jim King," Marr said. "You know Ben, King has a real record for violence." Marr then related stories about King physically intimidating players and otherwise behaving like a ruffian.

"Look, Ben, I'm pretty disgusted about this and you shouldn't be victimized this way," said Marr. "I have some friends in the Mafia that I got to know when I was working in the East over the years. I'm going to tell them to warn Jim off."

Frustrated to my wits' end and pleased to hear a voice that was willing and able to help, I listened to Marr, and gave tacit approval in his judgment in this matter. I was, by this point, looking for any help I could get.

Marr was convinced that King would listen to the people he would send, and he must have been correct, because that was the last I ever heard of Jim King and his threats. Gentle Dave Marr had saved me, though he was the last person I would have ever thought would have those kinds of connections. To Marr and his memory I am eternally grateful.

I thought golf was a gentleman's game, and here I was involved in police escorts, bloody armed guards, death threats, and the Mafia. I can make light of it now, but I was scared out of my wits at the time, and it made me consider the merits of lights, cameras, and show business altogether.

If that ordeal didn't prove my bravery, diligence, and maybe even stupidity to remain in "show biz," the following story does show some measure of grit and blind loyalty.

I was with CBS to broadcast the 1976 Western Open in Chicago. On Friday night, Summerall and I decided to treat ourselves to a high time, bar-hopping on Rush Street via limousine. We darkened the doors and brightened the rooms in many of Chicago's famed nightspots, finally returning to our hotel at 4:00 A.M., after, you might say, "a job well-done."

Exhausted and bleary-eyed beyond belief, I dragged myself into my darkened hotel room and tumbled face down into the percales with not even an attempt to remove my clothes.

After some fully dressed and restless sleep, I stumbled to the bathroom in my hotel room in the early hours of the morning to answer nature's call. As I sleepily stood and relieved myself, I was overcome with a violent coughing spell brought on by my summer allergies. It is no time to have a coughing fit when one is relieving oneself, because the two are utterly irreconcilable. Hacking and coughing away until my eyes filled with tears, I was also battling to manage my aim and control. I blindly reached for the lever and flushed, and finally the tickling cough ceased.

As I dried my eyes, I happened to look down into the commode and could not believe what I saw. There, caught in a despairing eddy, my upper bridge, having apparently been propelled out of my mouth by the intensity of the coughing, went 'round and 'round in the tide!

I made a splashy reflex grab to try to catch them, but they were moving too fast for my dizzy head, and evaded my desperate and clumsy grasp. Down they dove, sucked down in the whirlpool, and then disappeared into the abyss.

The total horror of the situation became painfully evident when I looked into the mirror to see only my two front teeth protruding from my mouth. The real peril was that in a few hours, I would be required to broadcast a golf tournament on national television, and could not speak without a terrible and annoying lisp and whistle.

I telephoned the hotel maintenance man immediately.

"This is Mr. Wright in room 625," I lisped at him. "I must solicit your help in retrieving my upper bridge, which I have accidentally flushed down the toilet."

"Mr. Wright," he answered with a calm, yet, incredulous tone, "are you suggesting that I dredge through 22,000 gallons of disgusting, flushed excrement in search of your dentures? And, Mr. Wright, are you further suggesting that even if I should find your teeth in that 22,000 gallons of foul mess, that you would even think of putting them back in your mouth and wearing them?"

The man had a point.

I was desperate, though, and knew that I would face the wrath of Chirkinian were I not able to broadcast that day. I had no choice but to wake Chirkinian by telephone and explain the whole tale.

"What bar are you in?" Chirkinian immediately asked after hearing me out. "Just tell me, Ben, and I'll have someone come and get you."

Sounding ridiculous, I insisted to Frank that I was very serious, very sober at that moment, and in my room just down the corridor.

"Then meet me in the lobby in half an hour," Chirkinian commanded, still wracked with disbelief and skepticism.

One look at my toothless grin, and Chirkinian was speechless. Shaking his head, Chirkinian noticed Whitaker roaming through the lobby at this early hour. Whitaker was checking in at the desk because, once again, he'd accidentally sent his rental car keys out with the hotel dry cleaning service in the pocket of his pants.

"Jack, you can be comfortable in the knowledge that this time the limey has outdone you," Chirkinian boasted. "Open your mouth and show Whitaker your plight," Chirkinian demanded with a wry insistence and a condescending tone.

Whitaker's rage about his keys vanished as he laughed out loud at my "Bugs Bunny" appearance, and the fact that I'd uttered not one word due to the shrieking whistle that was produced by my attempts to speak.

For once Chirkinian, who'd been forced on countless occasions to shepherd his announcers out of all manner of trouble and complication, was baffled. It was a Saturday morning, and finding a dentist to craft a new bridge seemed to be an impossible task.

Nonetheless, by a certain amount of grace, CBS producer Chuck Will actually happened to have a Saturday morning appointment with a dentist he was acquainted with in the Chicago area. Will, as a favor, had asked the dentist to see him on Saturday to tighten a loose cap that was bothering him.

Will agreed to give up his appointment so that instead I might pay the visit to the dentist. His name was Dr. Russell Fu.

Fu was a golf fan, and all too happy to help. He created an impression of my upper jaw, and quickly put a new bridge together just in the knick of time before I went on the air. Needless to say, that dentist never needed to wonder where his tickets to the Western Open were coming from ever again. I was eternally grateful that he'd literally rescued my career.

The rest of the CBS crew, however, was eternally grateful that I'd given them another reason to tease the limey. During rehearsal that day we viewed the hole introductions, which had been taped earlier. I waited eagerly to see how my teeth looked on camera when the "stand-up" piece of me describing the 17th hole was shown. My voice came on all right, but the dastardly scoundrels replaced the video portion with a close-up shot of wind-up mechanical teeth next to the flagstick, chattering away to the sound of my voice.

When I think about the tale of my teeth, it seems that the question left unanswered still is whether or not, just to be on television, I would really have put those choppers back in my mouth if they had been retrieved from the foul cesspool. In my attempt to answer, I am reminded of the metaphorical man who walked behind the elephants at a circus, scooping up their manure with a shovel. When the man was asked why he didn't quit such a dirty job, he answered plainly:

"What...and give up show business?"

"The Mah-stuhs"

———◆———

Player	Score	Thru
Nicklaus	−10	14
Weiskopf	−10	13
Miller	−8	13

That is how the gleaming white leaderboard read in 1975 as three of the world's greatest golfers were entering the top of the stretch at the world's greatest tournament. Henry Longhurst, legendary British announcer and my guide and mentor, was in the tower behind the 16th green, and I, in my third opportunity to broadcast the Masters for CBS, was only 100 yards away behind the 15th green. Jack Nicklaus, Tom Weiskopf, and Johnny Miller were headed right for us. While the gathered crowds had politely applauded the players perfunctorily passing through earlier, the sense of urgency heightened as the cheering and roaring wended its way from Amen Corner to our positions at the nearly adjacent 15th and 16th greens. These giants of golf, larger than life, were now to begin appearing at the top of the hill on 15.

Nicklaus stood on the par-five 15th fairway, bathed in brilliant sunshine, clothed in an appropriately green golf shirt striped horizontally with white. His longish blond hair scruffed over his ears as he shook his head and considered the options for his second shot. He ran his fingers over the tops of the clubs, as if summoning them to speak to him or feeling for the hot one. No one grew impatient with Nicklaus's painstaking deliberation because the suspense was palpably thrilling. Afraid even to look away, the gallery, the viewers, and I saw Nicklaus put his hands on his hips and stare, this time as if waiting for the scene to change. It didn't, and so now Nicklaus was tossing grass into the air, and listening to the closing arguments of the debate in his head. Finally pulling a long iron from his bag, Nicklaus then went into his standard pre-shot routine. Three times over the ball he looked up again to review his target and see an intermediary spot on the target line to the 15th green, which had still failed to move from its position behind the pond.

In fact, the 15th hadn't moved since 1931, when Bobby Jones founded the Augusta National Golf Club and he and Dr. Alister MacKenzie built it there. Although the front and back nines were reversed to their current position before the 1935 tournament, the 15th green held firm when Gene Sarazen holed his second shot there for the double eagle that time will never forget.

After Nicklaus finally let loose with his swing, he began immediately to walk toward the hole, as if chasing the ball in mid-flight, scaring it forward with his piercing, laser-blue eyes. The ball returned to earth, over the pond, a few paces in front of the flagstick, hopped softly two feet next to the hole, and gently rolled by. It seemed to willfully stop at the sight of the back fringe, coming to rest only three paces behind the hole.

Nicklaus smiled fully at the delirious ovation as he continued to walk, and even playfully patted his caddie on the head, knowing the game was on and enjoying it fully.

The buzz at 15 never subsided, but as the cheering began to quiet, it immediately cross-faded with roaring applause from the 14th green, where Tom Weiskopf had just steered in an eight-foot birdie putt to take the lead. Nicklaus continued to walk without looking back, and gracefully smiled at the gallery when the applause grew for him as he neared the green.

Player	Score	Thru
Weiskopf	−11	14
Nicklaus	−10	14
Miller	−9	14

Tom Watson, clad in then acceptable lime green, was paired with Nicklaus but was five shots behind, and virtually invisible as Nicklaus's very presence parted the Georgia pines. Jack was crouching in the shade behind his eight-foot eagle putt when, on the air, Longhurst tossed it to me at 15, where I spoke of Nicklaus:

"No man living has holed as many of these vital putts when he was most required to do so as Jack Nicklaus. Can he do it now?...The putt is fractionally uphill. The hole set on a little crown...This for the eagle that will swing Nicklaus back from a one-stroke deficit into a one-stroke lead. The waters: still, as if even they're afraid to make a ripple."

The gallery groaned as Nicklaus's putt ceased its roll and trailed to the low side less than one foot from the hole. I resumed:

"It was not to be. But with Weiskopf watching from the top of the hill, Nicklaus taps in and once again is tied for the lead at eleven under par."

Player	Score	Thru
Nicklaus	−11	15
Weiskopf	−11	14
Miller	−9	14

Weiskopf, playing in the day's final group, was preparing to hit his shot from the 15th fairway, just left of where Nicklaus had deliberated only moments before.

"Back to the top of the hill at the 15th, this 520 yard par-five, and now it's time for coolness, nerve, and courage as Weiskopf goes for the green with a long iron...

Weiskopf's shot cleared the water, but was not near the pin, and bounded clean over the green to the down-slope behind:

"That's going to be just about the most difficult shot he could think of if he was going to miss the green and stay out of the water, because he's only got about 20 feet of green with which to work."

After Weiskopf's playing partner, Johnny Miller, hit his second shot safely onto the 15th green with a chance for eagle, I "tossed it ahead" to the 190-yard par-three 16th, where it was Longhurst's turn:

"And here, on the tee looking from behind, a familiar figure now, Jack Nicklaus. Dead calm here amid all these tall Georgia Pines... Not a movement on the flag, not a movement on the water..."

The Golden Bear's shot at the watery hole was airborne. "Get up," groused Nicklaus as the ball touched down on the front of the green and nowhere near the Sunday placement. Longhurst droned:

"Ahh, a disappointing one there. Leaves him 40 feet, at least, short on the left, and a long slope to come up now. It's rather a disappointment for Jack Nicklaus."

No other voices on the CBS announcing team interrupted the dramatic back and forth happening between Longhurst and myself on the 15th and 16th holes. It was very well known that Weiskopf and Nicklaus, heralding from the same college, were fierce rivals, and loaded with enough talent left over for all of the other players on Ohio State's teams. They were now physically only a stone's throw apart, and in full view of each other with clear sight lines. After Weiskopf's poor chip from the back of the 15th green, the rivals lined up their respective long birdie putts, tied for the lead.

Nicklaus on the 16th green, Weiskopf on the 15th green.

A distant subplot, but not lost on me, was the fact that the aging Longhurst, in the golden twilight of his career, was issuing his celebrated droll British commentary in the 16th tower only a stone's throw apart from me at the 15th. While I may have been awed by the fact that I'd gone from being his student to his heir apparent, his presence most assuredly inspired me to attempt to prove my mettle to Henry and the viewers. Longhurst, of course, was not to be outdone by this young lad—not that he could ever be.

Longhurst behind the 16th green, Wright behind the 15th green.

We now pick up my commentary at 15, which admittedly was getting a bit heavy:

"This glorious scene, bathed in the pale afternoon sunlight that had been much brighter earlier in the day. A perfect day that has been one of the most intriguing and exciting finishes one could invent if one was a best-selling author."

As Weiskopf, his receding hairline revealing beads of perspiration on his forehead, lined up his 10-foot birdie putt, director Frank Chirkinian interspersed live shots of Nicklaus, who had yet to putt on the 16th green. Nicklaus, full of experience, was fearful that a roar would disturb his putt. Jack was leaning on his putter waiting, and watching Weiskopf, who likely could feel his stare on the 15th green, where I continued my call:

"Now, yet another totally vital putt. Weiskopf really has not been treated too kindly by this 15th hole this week: 4,6,5 have been his scores here. Nicklaus has had a very long wait on the 16th, and the atmosphere electric and almost totally silent on the respective greens. Weiskopf…for the birdie…"

The crowds erupted at the sight of Weiskopf's ball running straight into the hole for a scrambling birdie.

"Oh, what a tremendous putt by Tom Weiskopf, and that is going to be evil music lingering in Nicklaus's ears as Tom Weiskopf grabs the lead once again at 12 under par. Over to the 16th..."

Player	Score	Thru
Weiskopf	−12	15
Nicklaus	−11	15
Miller	−10	15

"Here's Nicklaus. He's got to putt up the hill, 35 to 40 feet, only about 100 yards from where Weiskopf hit that putt, the way his head is facing at the moment...Now, up the hill..."

With Chirkinian now cutting to shots of Weiskopf watching from the 16th tee, Nicklaus's long, curling putt broke left toward the water. Nicklaus's caddie, Willie Peterson, a local club caddie who'd been tending the pin, began to openly and visibly root, leaping into the air and urging the ball into the hole. As the ball vanished into the cup, Nicklaus lifted his putter above his head and broke into a victory gallop. Against the roar of the amazed crowd, even Longhurst showed emotion:

"Who-ho, have you ever seen one like that? Who-ho. I think that's one of the greatest putts I've ever seen in my life...Back on the tee, Weiskopf has to take it this time, having dished it out on the hole before. I never saw such a putt in my life."

Player	Score	Thru
Nicklaus	−12	16
Weiskopf	−12	15
Miller	−10	15

Weiskopf, drained from this dramatic game of "can you top this," took his turn at 16 once Nicklaus cleared the green and the ovation ceased. Weiskopf hit his ball woefully short to the front collar of the green. One wonders if the Nicklaus putt hadn't already defeated Weiskopf. As Tom looked down in dejection, Longhurst offered bold observation:

"It started well enough, but that's terribly, terribly short and disappointing for Weiskopf, and...that...might...be...it.

"If he does lose, I think that, perhaps, will be the one that did it. That was disappointing. It hasn't even reached the green."

Weiskopf was 45 yards from the hole when he putted uphill from the front of the 16th green. The ball, taking the hard slope left toward the water, trailed cruelly away from the hole, as Henry described:

"It's resisting the hole very well, but falling away at the end, and now it'll roll down farther and farther, and with it may go Weiskopf's hopes...to about 18 feet away. If he holes this one, it'll be one the bravest putts he's ever holed in his life."

Weiskopf left short the 18-foot putt to save par and maintain a share of the lead. Longhurst and I were now off the stage, our act completed, as the play moved to the final two holes.

Player	Score	Thru
Nicklaus	–12	16
Weiskopf	–11	16
Miller	–10	16

Weiskopf, clearly shaken and beginning to give in to his Nicklaus inferiority complex, then also left a 15-foot birdie effort short at 17, where Miller made birdie to pull to 11 under par.

Player	Score	Thru
Nicklaus	–12	17
Weiskopf	–11	17
Miller	–11	17

With Miller and Weiskopf waiting in the 18th fairway, tied at one shot behind Nicklaus, Jack tapped in for his par-four to finish at 12 under. Once Miller and Weiskopf hit two breathtaking approach shots to the 18th green, the day's final pairing found themselves staring at two realistic chances to force an 18-hole playoff. Weiskopf would putt last, since he very nearly holed his approach to win the Masters, and his ball settled only eight feet from the hole. How much more drama could the viewers endure?

Miller, who had shot 75 in the first round and 71 in the second, recovered by posting 65 in the third round. Now, he needed one more shot: a 15-foot, downhill, sidehill putt that would give him another 65 and a share of the lead. Miller's effort slipped past the hole on the low side, and he grimaced hard with his putter over his head. To his credit, he quickly moved away to make room for Weiskopf, who needed his eight-footer to force a playoff and avoid the ignominy of becoming a four-time Masters runner-up.

Squinting in the sun, Weiskopf stabbed at the putt and pushed it past the top edge of the hole. Weiskopf became a jilted bridesmaid for the fourth time, and Jack Nicklaus became the first player in history to slip on the green jacket on a fifth occasion.

I felt badly for Tom, who desperately needed a big win against his rival to climb out from under Nicklaus's shadow. My personal heartbreak was that there would be no playoff between these dueling masters. I wanted it never to end, as did Chirkinian, who to this day considers that 1975 Masters coverage to be his finest golf telecast ever. Tension, emotion, rivalry, heartbreak, elation, and history made before the very eyes of a worldwide television audience.

M y inaugural visit to the Augusta National Golf Club also marked my coming to America. Imagine viewing the United States for the first time as I did. Masters tournament chairman Clifford Roberts, who was Bobby Jones's administrator in the operation of the club and the tournament, once again displayed his savvy when in the late 1960s he realized the importance of creating an international appetite for the season's first major tournament. When measured against the other three "major championships," the Masters was comparatively the new kid on the block. The United States Open had already been held 39 times when Horton Smith won the first Masters in 1934. The British Open had 74 years of history before the Masters began, beginning at Prestwick, Scotland in 1860 and the PGA Championship matches, won in the first two instances by James Barnes, were first contested in 1916.

Another major distinction was that the other three championships moved from glorious venue to storied tracks each year, while the Masters remained nestled in the former azalea nursery on Washington Road in northeastern Georgia. This venue provided color and beauty that was a welcome sight the world over, and a definite rite of spring for golfers everywhere.

By the time I prepared to make my first ever trip to the Augusta National in 1966, the tournament had been won 28 out of 29 times by Americans, with South African Gary Player's win in 1961 the only international triumph. Player won the tournament twice more, maintaining that distinction until 1980, when Spaniard Seve Ballesteros became only the second foreign winner.

Therefore, Roberts was very keen on attracting foreign journalists to cover the greatest private club invitational in the world. As the first-ever golf writer for the *Financial Times* of London, I was invited, or rather, summoned, by Roberts to come across the pond and smell the flowers along with a few other British writers. Henry Longhurst, who wrote for the *Sunday Times*, Leonard Crawley of the *Daily Telegraph,* Pat Ward-Thomas of the *Manchester Guardian,* and Peter Dobereiner of the *Observer* all joined in on the junket. Jackson T. Stephens, who would one day become chairman of Augusta National, orchestrated the itinerary of our group of British journalists, who were picked up by Stephens's private plane in New York after being jetted over from Heathrow in a first-class cabin. We wanted for nothing on any leg of the journey, including refreshments in the limousines that ferried us from Augusta Airport to the golf club. Welcome to America, indeed!

When the car turned through the gate and onto the incredible Magnolia Lane, the hairs on the back of my neck stood up. Stately magnolia trees covered the entire entrance, and it was breathtakingly charming. The clubhouse was, and is, an insignificant farmhouse-type building, but dainty and pristine. The edifice was perfect in its Old South setting. In 28 years of going to the Masters, I have never been any less affected upon arriving at the National. I never found it one bit less attractive than I did on that first visit, and I find it hard to describe the rejuvenation I experienced each year when I would hop into a golf cart and have a look at the old place again. It was as if the ghosts of great glory had risen up to greet me and provide scenes of years gone by.

It seems fashionable to knock the Masters as an elitist, limited-field event, with a group of contestants that includes amateurs, but it is the finest-run tournament on earth.

Indeed, I enjoyed the maximum comfort during my first visit, including lodgings with ample domestic help in a privately owned area mansion. The accommodations were provided by an Augusta

National member, who also made sure that our needs were attended-to by white-coated domestic servants who ferried drinks to us beside the elegant pool and managed the housekeeping duties.

In contrast, I happened down the road one evening to come across a huge, nearly naked man in the road! Difficult as it was to view this creature, I did notice that he was a man I had seen earlier in the day at the club.

"What is it that you are doing?" I inquired.

"Going to bed in the Pinto," the man growled, "I don't have money for a room."

He then finished getting naked and climbed under the blankets in the car. That was my first of numerous encounters with the color-ful golf writer and sports gadfly Bob Drum...one hell of a grizzled character from Pittsburgh.

My first experience at Augusta culminated with a victorious de-fense by American hero Jack Nicklaus, who had now won two con-secutive Masters and a sum of three in a span of four years.

Two years later, in 1968, it appeared that Gary Player would be joined amongst the ranks of international players who won the op-portunity to slip on a green jacket. Everyone knows how Argentinian Roberto de Vicenzo, a sincere and likeable favorite, inadvertently returned an incorrect scorecard and cost himself a chance to win the Masters through an 18-hole playoff with Bob Goalby.

Everybody knows the story. Each player is responsible for mark-ing his playing partner's scorecard. Tommy Aaron, playing in a two-some with de Vicenzo, marked Roberto's card incorrectly, putting him down for a four when he'd actually made a three at the 17th hole. Roberto admits that his math is minimal, so he never bothered to check his card. He had little formal education. He was a caddie kid at the Railway Club in Argentina.

Upon being informed of the error, de Vicenzo called himself "el stúpido" repeatedly. It was an unceremonious end to de Vicenzo's bid to win the Masters, a bid that began on Sunday morning when he holed his second shot for a two at the par-four first hole. Roberto won the hearts of the fans, many of whom felt bitter about his fate.

There was little doubt to me that de Vicenzo would have beaten Goalby in a playoff. Goalby became the most unpopular man alive because he had "cheated"—in the opinion of the great public—the lovable Roberto out of his chance to win the Masters. My sympathies in the matter go out to Bob Goalby. I remember that for the following tournaments, Goalby was not received as warmly as he should have been. That is absolutely unconscionable. The guy who should have been admonished was Tommy Aaron, who marked the wrong score. Even when Aaron won his own green jacket in 1973, he did no justice to de Vicenzo or himself. Many people, myself included, felt that Aaron should have at least invoked de Vicenzo's name or dedicate the victory to him.

This entire scene was unsettling to all. Why wouldn't a guy be able to keep his own score and have the marker just check it? If ever there was a time when the governing bodies of golf should have taken things by the scruff of the neck, this was it. There's no way they could have changed the rules to accommodate de Vicenzo, but they could have changed the rules there and then so that this kind of incident could never happen again. It probably will reoccur, however, and in an honorable game like golf, it is quite ridiculous.

My further understanding of the poignancy and sometimes heart-break of the Masters occurred at the event in 1970. Again covering the Masters for the *Financial Times,* I requested—and was honored to be granted—a visit with Mr. Robert Tyre Jones Jr. It was Jones, the greatest amateur golfer ever, who conceived and founded the Augusta National Golf Club and the Masters. As evidence of Jones's gentle demeanor, he was reluctant initially to give in to Clifford Roberts's desire to call the event "the Masters," protesting that the title was too presumptuous.

I myself had also experienced an example of Jones's gentle nature. In 1968, I was sent a surprising but most welcome letter from Jones concerning a review I'd written of his book *Bobby Jones on Golf:*

Robert Tyre Jones, Jr.
75 Poplar Street NW
Atlanta, GA 30303

Ben Wright, Esq.
The Financial Times
London, England

May 20, 1968

Dear Mr. Wright,

A veteran golfer, who apparently came to this country from England, sent to me the piece you wrote for the Financial Times discussing my latest book. At first, he sent me only the first half of your article, so that it required some prodding by me to get the balance of it. For some reason, he had the notion that he was sparing me by holding back the second part; I suppose because of your reference to emotionalism, or maybe because you indicated that Arnold Palmer might not agree with some of my thoughts.

I have assured my correspondent that I am indeed most pleased by the entire article. My high-strung temperament has been well advertised and is also well recognized by me, and no one, I think, expects complete agreement when he begins to theorize concerning our enthralling game.

All this, of course, is beside the point. My reason for writing is to thank you for your most generous comment. I hope my book merited the treatment you gave it.

Most sincerely,

Bob Jones

Bobby Jones, however, was granting very few interviews at this time in 1970, and was not appearing in public. Jones, the Augusta National Golf Club's president in perpetuity, had even been removed from view on the Masters telecast. As I was led in to see him in his cabin, I grimly learned why. His debilitating spinal disease was winning the battle in its vicious effort to claim the hero. The manner in which Jones stirred the audience and defied his disease by walking unaided to the podium to accept the "Freedom of the City" at St. Andrews in 1958 was now an impossibility for Jones. There would now be no defying this disease.

Jones, unable now even to sit up, lay in his bed, with the room darkened. I struggled to present myself as upbeat and respectful, but I was so very saddened. Here was this great athlete, this giant man, gone to nothing. It was awful. At intervals through our conversation, a nurse entered the room and turned Jones over. He was so significantly weakened that he was unable to shift his own body into a new position.

Even with his body in this condition, Jones's spirit for the game was fully intact and plainly evident, and he gamely tried to ignore his malady and talk about golf issues like the bane of slow play and his beloved Masters.

When I emerged from the cottage and into the light of day, I breathed deep the fresh air of life and wondered whether it was some divine plan or just a random irony that had reduced this sophisticated athlete, the larger-than-life Jones, to the current indignity of merely waiting to perish.

Bobby Jones would not live to see the 1972 Masters.

It was in 1972 at the Augusta National, while I was stringing for *Time* and *Sports Illustrated,* that I nearly made my debut on the CBS Masters announcing team. I'd like to tell you that I positioned myself for the opportunity, or that I had somehow convinced CBS that they could not do without my significant knowledge and depth of insight, but "blind luck" would be a simpler and more accurate explanation.

"Does anyone know a goddamned limey who can speak halfway decent?"

The pleading question from then CBS president Bill McPhail broke the peace in the upstairs grill where golf writer Dan Jenkins and I were enjoying a remedial breakfast. It seemed that announcer Henry Longhurst, who was on loan to CBS from his usual position as the BBC's resident golf historian and commentator, had suddenly taken ill. He'd contracted pneumonia as a result of the unseasonably cold weather he'd suffered through in Palm Springs at the Dinah Shore tournament the previous week.

"Does anyone know a goddamned limey who can speak halfway decent?"

Hardly a clarion call.

Jenkins, pointing his finger over the top of my head, offered, "How about our man in London, here?"

McPhail, clearly in a bind, walked over to our table and presented himself. Jenkins introduced me, and I could sense McPhail inspecting the delivery of my speech.

"Ben," McPhail asked in a dramatic tone, "would you like an opportunity to announce the Masters?"

"Mr. McPhail," I sarcastically responded in "goddamned limeytalk," "I'm not familiar with this parlance. Was it not announced over 30 years ago?"

"Are you trying to be a wise-ass?"

"No, Mr. McPhail, I don't employ that expression. I say 'commentate.'"

"Alright, alright. Announce, commentate, whatever! Will you do it?"

"I couldn't possibly," I told McPhail, while maintaining eye-contact with him in an attempt to gage just how serious he was about using me on television.

I explained to McPhail that because I had three different editions due for my reports to the *Financial Times,* I couldn't possibly spare the time. It was a very sincere game of "hard-to-get."

"Of course you can," he insisted. "Get someone else to do it!" McPhail needed to know within two hours, so I went into the pressroom—then a glorified Quonset hut—and recruited Dai Davies to assist with my writing and filing. He was the *Birmingham Post* golf writer, and I paid him 50 pounds sterling per day to ghostwrite three daily editions under my name.

After all of this scheming and plotting, Longhurst, upon hearing the news that another "goddamned limey" was ready to step in for him, experienced a miraculous recovery, and performed the broadcast himself after all. Henry well knew who I was, as we had worked together broadcasting golf events on British television. Now the great Longhurst had risen to beat back the competition! In recompense, McPhail and CBS promised to try me out the following year.

That occasion was the 1973 Masters. After putting me through my paces on one tournament in 1972 and CBS's early season events in 1973, CBS had me fly in from England to be a part of the broadcast team on the 1973 Masters Tournament. It was a most momentous occasion for me, and my colleagues at CBS knew it, so they were very celebratory in the manner in which they welcomed me to Augusta. I arrived in the United States completely exhausted from the flights, and went directly from the Augusta airport to the home at West Lake Country Club that CBS had rented and provided for my lodgings.

I had fallen blissfully asleep when, in a dreamlike state, I realized that somebody was on top of me. I sat bolt upright. I peered down through the dark. Indeed, it was not a dream. A gorgeous woman with flaming red hair was indeed straddled over me, looking down.

"What the hell is going on?" I stammered.

"Don't worry, honey. I'm Ginger. Lay back and enjoy. It's all paid for."

The CBS crew had sent me this hooker as a welcoming present upon arrival at my first Masters as part of the broadcast team. These were my colleagues-to-be, some of whom I hadn't even met yet! It was their way of saying, "Welcome aboard!" I was fast learning about the delicate intricacies of American network television in the '70s.

My next lesson in these delicate intricacies of network television was when McPhail explained to me that I was to have my credentials reviewed and approved by Mr. Clifford Roberts, chairman of the Augusta National and the Masters. Roberts, who had been Bobby Jones's right-hand man for so many years, had the reputation of running all aspects of the club and tournament in a staid and formal manner. Roberts was considered to have an iron fist snuggled tightly in an iron glove. I was quite nervous.

Although I cannot say that I had any sort of relationship with Mr. Roberts, I did believe that I might be in reasonably good standing with Mr. Roberts. Three years earlier, I had received a letter from Roberts, which arrived on Augusta National letterhead:

May 14, 1970

Mr. Ben Wright
Financial Times
Cannon St.
London, EC4,
England

Dear Mr. Wright,

   Someone was thoughtful enough to air mail me a copy of the May 1970 issue of GolfWorld Magazine. I do not know to whom I am indebted to but at any rate, I am anxious to compliment you on the splendid story that you prepared.
   I am also writing your editor to commend him not only for the space devoted to this year's Masters Tournament, but the unique presentation of your day to day coverage of our tournament.
   You did an exceptionally fine job of reporting and I want you to know that we at this club appreciate your interest and your efforts.

With all good wishes, most sincerely yours,

Clifford Roberts

That letter, however, seemed a million miles away as McPhail tried to calm me when he walked me to the all-white, understated Roberts cottage, where he quickly abandoned me at the front door. I entered Mr. Roberts's very proper sitting room, where he greeted me. Roberts, in his age and pomposity, spoke very slowly, as if each of his words carried the weight of the world. He paused deliberately in between phrases.

"Ah, do you like tea, young Wright?"

Young Wright? I was all of 41 years old, but to Roberts I was "young Wright." My mind nervously drifting, I mumbled in what I thought was the affirmative.

"Ahh, young Wright, do you like to drink tea?" he repeated.

"Yes, Mr. Roberts. Yes, I do like to drink tea."

"Thought so. All, ahh, limeys drink tea. Pour yourself a cup."

I had never considered the prospect of ever being nervous just pouring myself a cup of tea, but I was trembling as I mixed in the milk. I tried to sip the tea, but found it boiling hot, prepared in the proper English manner.

"Ahh, take your time, boy. Take your time," Roberts slowly advised.

Eventually, I slopped the cup of tea down and Roberts continued.

"Now, ahh, ...talk to me boy, ahh...talk to me."

"What exactly would you like me to talk about, Mr. Roberts?"

"Ah...I don't care. Just talk to me, boy."

I began to list the pitifully mediocre details of my career to that date, and I had probably been rambling for a full 28 seconds when Roberts commanded that I stop.

Oh, hell, I thought to myself, *I've blown this one. Obviously, I've said something that has offended him.* There was a long and painful silence as Roberts stared at me. Finally, he spoke, as slowly and as painfully deliberately as ever.

"Young Wright, ahh, you probably want to know why you're going through this procedure."

"Yes, sir."

"Ahh, well, last year that bastard McPhail snuck one of your countrymen onto the air right under my nose. His name was, ahh, Bob Ferrier. He was a Scotsman from Glasgow, and I couldn't understand a single word he said...but...ahh, you'll do. I hope you have a lovely week."

With relief, I left the cabin with the roof of my mouth singed from the boiling tea, and my spirit lifted by the vote of approval from Roberts. He was the supreme ruler at the National, and many of those involved in the tournament had their own tales of being handled by the intimidating man.

One tale that has been told reportedly occurred in 1965, when Bob Murphy, the United States Amateur Champion, was invited to the Augusta National to compete in his first Masters. Like other amateur invitees, he stayed in the "crow's nest" at the top of the clubhouse and enjoyed all of the perks that went with being a Masters amateur invitee. Murphy arrived on the Saturday before the tournament and played his first practice round at the Augusta National on Sunday.

In those days, the use of Augusta National caddies by players was still mandatory. The club caddies, a group made up of largely African-American locals, had course knowledge by caddying for members during the months that the club was open. They, like the caddies today, were outfitted in the gleaming white jumpsuits with their player's name emblazoned on the back in green.

By the Wednesday morning of his Masters stay, Murphy had fired three of the caddies appointed to him. This action, unheard of by an invited amateur, raised a few eyebrows, and Murphy was summoned to Mr. Roberts's cabin. Murphy went, cap in hand, to face Roberts, knowing full well that Roberts had the ability to end his stay at any time, and prevent any future participation.

"Mr. Murphy," Roberts began, "it has come to my attention that you have seen fit, in, ahh, three days, on your first visit to this club, to, ahh, fire three of our Augusta National caddies. Perhaps you'd better explain to me the reason for your conduct."

Murphy cleared his throat, and began to explain, speaking into the penetrating and unflinching eyes of Roberts.

"Mr. Roberts, I made a successful practice round on Sunday with the first caddie appointed to me, but when I arrived for play on Monday morning, all of the golf balls were missing from my bag. Since I left the bag with the caddie on Sunday night, I considered him responsible for the equipment. When all of the balls turned up missing, I decided to dismiss him and look for a new Augusta National caddie."

Roberts said nothing, waiting for Murphy to continue.

"The new caddie that made the loop with me on Monday did a very suitable job, but when I arrived for play on Tuesday, he didn't show up for work. So, again, I was appointed another Augusta National caddie."

Again, no response came from Roberts; not a nod, not even a grunt. Murphy, beginning to get dry-mouthed, continued.

"The third caddie made his way with me down the first fairway, but when I asked him how many yards it was from the bunker to the center of the green, he told me, 'You're the player, you should know. I'm just carrying the bag.' I turned him around and we went right back to the clubhouse, where I fired him and asked for another Augusta National caddie."

Murphy was finished explaining, but Roberts, apparently, was not finished considering Murphy's explanation, because there was a long silence in which Murphy began to wonder what the hell would happen next. Finally Roberts, after hearing the entire story, spoke.

"Ahh, Mr. Murphy, I've listened to your reasons and your explanations. Ahh, I have to admit, your behavior is indeed justified. I hope you have good luck with your fourth one. We'll be watching. Good day, Mr. Murphy."

No doubt Murphy, though startled by Roberts's brand of interrogation, breathed a sigh of relief just to get out of Roberts's presence.

Again, with Roberts's blessing, or at least approval, I was set to make my Masters debut, hidden in the woods where all newcomers are stuck: at the 14th hole. I was very eager to excel in my broadcast efforts, and I wanted an immediate critique of my first-round performance. What better opinion to canvas, I thought, than that of my mentor and British colleague Henry Longhurst, the veteran announcer who was calling the 16th hole for CBS during the event?

Henry agreed to offer his opinion after the broadcast if I agreed to drive him out to his tower before the telecast, fetch him from his tower in my golf cart and ferry him to the clubhouse when it was over, and ply him with an unspecified amount of drinks. In hindsight, it would have been wise to specify the amount.

I agreed, and carted Longhurst out to his tower at 16, where I assisted him in climbing the ladder and getting settled into his position. As Longhurst sat down at his desk and began to get comfortable in his chair, I noticed that, as I had heard rumored, Longhurst's cameraman, George Drago, had again fulfilled his charming tradition of placing a single red rose in a slender bud vase on Longhurst's tabletop. It seemed to me to be a very civilized gesture.

"Henry," I asked, in what I'm sure was both an impressed and puzzled tone, "why does George leave you the rose?"

"Well, my boy, it is the way in which George and I always celebrate our camaraderie for every broadcast we've had together here," Longhurst explained in a serious and sentimental fashion.

"Well, Henry, I hope that maybe someday I could build that kind of sincere relationship with my cameraman."

Longhurst admired the rose and vase, and his lips broke into a tart smile as he sighed and nodded appreciatively at Drago. Longhurst then gingerly plucked the rose from the vase with his thumb and forefinger, and laid it on the edge of the booth. Then, before I could realize what was happening, Longhurst carefully lifted the vase to his lips, tilted it and swallowed up its contents!

I gasped.

"Ahh ... my man George knows my tipple," Longhurst exclaimed.

Not quite believing my eyes, I stood in my tracks, no words coming to my lips.

Longhurst broke the silence. "Nothing like the taste of gin to commence another Masters broadcast."

I shook my head and repaired to my own tower for the broadcast, which seemed to go quite well. Upon its completion, I rambled over, as promised, to pick up Longhurst and drive him in from his tower.

When we got to the clubhouse, Henry needed a drink because he'd come in from the cold and the damp after his afternoon's toil. He was very morose and uncommunicative, getting stuck into the gin. After four or five drinks, I finally broke down and asked, "Henry, when are you ever going to tell me what you thought of my performance?"

"One more drink," Henry answered. "One more drink and maybe we'll talk about it."

I got him another drink, and still another. Finally, I insisted. "Alright, Henry, that's it. No more drinks until you tell me."

"Well then, Ben, I've been dreading this. Yes, I've been really dreading this."

"What is it, Henry?"

"You were absolutely dreadful. You were totally awful. You ran off at the mouth like a dripping tap. You must have been nervous. Were you?"

Nearly speechless, I said, "Yes, Henry, of course I was."

"Well, that's when you get to talking too much. You know you've got to remember that when you get nervous, try to say as little as possible."

I grudgingly thanked Henry for the advice and asked, "Was I really that bad?"

"Yes, yes, you were really that bad."

"Oh, dear."

"Ben, I've got a piece of advice for you to try to remember at all costs. We are nothing but caption writers in a picture business. If you can't improve the quality of the pictures with your words, then keep your damned mouth shut."

Through the gin and the experience of an aging Henry Longhurst came the most valuable piece of advice I have ever learned.

The broadcast that year was plagued by rain delays, and at one point, my European compatriot, Peter Oosterhuis, was in the lead. When CBS began trying to fill though a rain delay, I was summoned to come to the studio to interview Oosterhuis because no one else on the broadcast team knew anything about him. Although Oosterhuis had appeared on the British Order of Merit in 1971 and 1972, Pat Summerall didn't even know how to pronounce his name. I had known Oosterhuis, a big English boy, since he was 15 years old.

I climbed down from the tower, and a man in a club station wagon whipped me over to the studio. I was immediately thrust in front of the cameras and television lights, still wearing the cashmere turtleneck sweater and leather coat I was using in a futile attempt to ward off the chill in the cold woods at 14. Summerall, especially generous with the microphone, threw it to me, the newcomer, and left me to fill with Oosterhuis for 17 straight minutes. I amounted to a pool of sweat by the end of that interview, but I had begun to prove my worth to my colleagues, to Longhurst, and more importantly to producer/director Frank Chirkinian. Beforehand, Chirkinian wasn't exactly keen on my participation because it was McPhail who had selected and hired me without the express approval of Chirkinian.

Tommy Aaron won the tournament, and my performance must have improved since my brief tea with Roberts because following the tournament Roberts posted a letter to McPhail. The letter insisted that I had done such a good job that I should be moved to a position of more prominence the following year. Henceforth, I was taken from the woods of 14 and repositioned at the 15th hole. On every other tournament televised by CBS, I was positioned at my regular post behind the 17th hole. Chirkinian gave me the option of maintaining that position at the Masters, but the 17th at Augusta is the dullest hole on the inward half, so I opted to remain at 15, which was and is a pivotal hole in the fate of any would-be Masters champion. From there, I also enjoyed being able to view the 16th hole.

E ach year on the day preceding the tournament, the CBS announcing team was instructed to attend a meeting conducted by a gentleman named Bill Kerr. Kerr was a stockbroker, an Augusta National member, and a member of the Augusta National television committee. The point of his meeting would be to inform the announcers of what we could and *could not* say on the air, as the Augusta National was again very protective of its tournament and the way it is presented. Attention to details is what makes the Masters the Masters.

I walked with earnest to the Butler Cabin for the meeting. When I arrived, my esteemed colleague Henry Longhurst said to me, "Well, we've got to put up once again with this dreadful little man from the floor of the San Francisco Stock Exchange telling us how to broadcast." He continued, "I would never dream of going onto the floor of the San Francisco Stock Exchange to tell Bill Kerr how to do his job, and it makes me very resentful that he would presume to do the same to me. I shall therefore see fit to take a nap through his entire meeting."

I soon learned that Longhurst wasn't kidding. He sat down in the chair next to mine, with his head nodding off as Kerr ran through his monologue. Occasionally, Longhurst would wake and inquire, "Is that pompous ass still talking?"

Kerr detailed similar guidelines each year: Announcers were forbidden to talk about money. Competitors were presumed to be playing for a green jacket, not for the prize money. Announcers were forbidden to mention any other tournament by name. If, for instance, we needed to mention the fact that Craig Stadler had won at the

Andy Williams Shearson Lehman Hutton Open, we could only mention that Stadler had won "in San Diego." If Nick Faldo had won the Heritage, we were to refer to it only as "Hilton Head."

We were keenly aware of the danger in saying something on the air that was deemed inappropriate by the Masters television committee, which would convene following each tournament and judge the performance of the broadcasters. The committee would then send its "report" to the president of CBS.

Jack Whitaker was summarily banished from broadcasting the Masters when he offhandedly and nonmaliciously referred to the enthusiastic and teeming Augusta gallery as a "mob" as they scurried up the 18th fairway.

On two occasions, I harbored grave concern for my status as an announcer at Augusta.

When Lee Elder made his debut at the Masters, he was the first black golfer to appear at the Augusta National as a competitor. On the air, I referred to Elder as "the world's leading black golfer." For this, I was castigated by the television committee in its postmortem analysis. The committee determined that I should have referred to Elder as "the leading golfer of his race." Talk about hairsplitting.

Years later, it unfortunately became fashionable for a certain level of badge-holder to shout "You da man!" after shots at PGA Tour events. During the broadcast, a gallery member shouted the annoying and disturbing utterance a fraction of a second before a player made contact with the ball. I responded on the air sharply: "Even at a place like the Augusta National, you've got the occasional idiot."

As soon as the droll comment passed my lips, I thought, *Whoa, maybe I shouldn't have said that. Damn, I'm going to get in trouble for this one.* Luckily, I never heard a peep about it from the green coats. The committee must obviously have been in agreement, and must have been surprised, as I was, that someone would introduce that trashy trend to the Masters.

The latest offender to the Masters's preferred lexicon is my one-time broadcast nemesis Gary McCord, who should not have been surprised that he offended the committee, since he knows full well that his mere presence is offensive to most. Opening his mouth only cements his secure position in the museum of mediocrity. The committee banned McCord from the Masters telecasts after his 1995 performance.

I do not think the comments that McCord made were too terribly egregious. McCord suggested that the Augusta National greens weren't mowed, but rather bikini waxed. He also warned that the area behind the 17th green was so dangerous for players who, upon venturing there to find their balls, would encounter body bags. Reportedly, the club received complaints from American Vietnam veterans who don't find the prospect of body bags humorous in any context.

Working against the silly McCord was the fact that it became plainly known that he scripted his ad-lib comments on his IBM Think Pad in preparation for tournament coverage. In other words, his disrespectful comments were premeditated, so no defense of temporary insanity could be employed. In my opinion, McCord's Think Pad approach, in which he crafted and created all of his quips, diminished the freshness of his commentary anywhere on Tour.

Chirkinian was very angry with McCord, and felt that Gary should have been more careful. If the truth be known, I warned McCord repeatedly to select his words carefully, but he cavalierly refused to pay any attention to my alerts. Past club chairman Hord Hardin had an immense dislike for McCord and had let it be known to me that if McCord put one word out of place, he would seize the opportunity to vanquish him.

We teased McCord about his outlaw status, and he boastfully claimed that he would not even bother to watch the 1996 Masters. Despite McCord's brave stiff upper lip, one could tell he was hurt by being left out of America's most colorful golf happening. He was never one to relish missing anything and never wanted to be left behind. I find some irony in the fact that the Masters is now broadcast without both McCord and me. Once celebrated partners in mirthful crime, McCord and I, at the height of our imagined powers, are absent from our high-profile roles on CBS's Masters coverage. Speaking for myself, it is literally painful for me not to broadcast the event. Words do not adequately express how much I miss the sights, the scents, the galleries bursting with anticipation, and the palpable sense of historic tradition.

Maybe McCord and I will someday enjoy a reunion on the Masters telecast. Perhaps new Augusta National chairman William W. "Hootie" Johnson will see fit to reinstate McCord. After all, an accomplished man who allows himself to be known as "Hootie" must have some semblance of a sense of humor.

McCord, however, failing to see the humor in the situation, in 1999 insisted that CBS stipulate in his new contract that he can never be commanded to work the Masters telecast, even if Augusta National lifts the ban. That's typical McCord.

"Ben, I may have lost the battle, but I'll win the war," McCord told me.

When Whitaker was reinstated after an eight-year banishment from the Masters, it was Roberts who allowed his return. Even Roberts's chosen manner of reinstating Whitaker was singularly his own. Again desperate to find an announcer when Longhurst suffered another failing of health, CBS officials approached Roberts to beg permission to use Whitaker on the telecast.

"I don't know why you wouldn't use him," was Roberts' matter-of-fact response. Puzzled and frustrated by his maddening response, CBS officials were once again left merely to shrug and accept Roberts's way of handling the situation.

Longhurst's failing health finally prevented him from broadcasting for CBS, and it came to pass that in the early 1980s, I was given the charge of announcing both the 15th and the 16th holes. Chirkinian felt that Longhurst would be impossible to replace, and that I was most suitable to fill his role at 16. I felt it was a feather in my cap to follow in the footsteps of Longhurst. I gladly accepted the challenge, and soon learned how difficult it would be to call the action from 15 and 16.

From the CBS broadcast tower behind 15, I had a bird's-eye view of both greens. However, looking at 15 meant that my back was turned to 16, and vice versa. I had to sometimes spin very quickly in my swivel chair if I heard a great roar from behind. CBS eventually provided me with eight monitors so that I could see action over every inch of those two holes, as well as the broadcast feed.

A little-known drama was one that I viewed from my tower at 15. Like the rest of the viewers, though, I had no idea of the depth of the drama I was watching.

In order to play a ball from the edge of the pond, Nicklaus had removed his right shoe and sock, and plunked his foot into the water that guards the hole. The galleries were intrigued and waited with anticipation. After sinking his bare foot into the silt and muck, Nicklaus took a fearless swipe at the ball. Mud and water flew everywhere, and the result was magnificent. I was indeed treated to the spectacle of the mighty Nicklaus making birdie from the water.

I climbed down from the tower after the broadcast and came across Joe Dey, the former PGA Tour commissioner who was serving as the rules official on the 15th hole.

"Joe, you don't look too good," I observed, only half joking since Dey indeed looked piqued. "Has the heat gotten to you?"

"No," said Dey, "but the snakes have."

"What are you talking about, Joe?"

"I have never been in such a quandary in all of my life," Dey explained. "Just before Nicklaus went into the pond, I saw just an absolute flurry of water moccasins in that spot. I just didn't know whether it was my job to warn Nicklaus about the chance he was taking."

I listened with unfettered interest, sympathizing with what I knew must have been severe inner turmoil for Dey, who was one of the foremost rules experts who ever lived.

"I decided," Dey concluded, "that I couldn't intervene because I didn't see any when he was in there, but how could I explain if something did happen?"

It was a chilling account, and I'm certain that Dey breathed a huge sigh of relief when Nicklaus pulled his foot from the peril unscathed.

My television monitors at that time did not pick up the sight of any snakes in the pond, and from my vantage, the water below the green front was not visible with the naked eye.

CBS eventually chose to provide me with an excess of monitors, due to a miserably failed attempt to move my broadcast position. A lengthy report was issued by the Masters television committee after the 1978 tournament. The report claimed that "from his position behind the 15th green, it seems that Ben Wright has difficulty determining whether shots fell into the pond in front of the 15th green." Without a camera specifically trained on the pond, it was nearly impossible for me, from the tower, to see down the bank to the water's edge.

The committee insisted that my commentary position be moved to a flanker tower just beyond the Sarazen Bridge on the left-hand side of the 15th hole at the end of the bleachers. It was a terrible ground-level position and I despised it. Dr. Gil Morgan hit a 236-yard slinging hook that nearly decapitated me. Clearly, I had enough to worry about without fearing being in the line of fire.

The position, which thankfully was an experiment that lasted through only one tournament, was also in the line of fire of contestants making their way from the 15th green to the 16th tee. This proximity helped create one of the saddest moments in the whole of my career. I had grown close to Ed Sneed, a fine player on tour. Years later, when he would visit Britain while covering the British Open for ABC, we would lodge together in stately rented homes.

While stuck at this hated flanking tower, I called the action as Sneed, playing in the final group, birdied the 15th hole to take a commanding three-stroke lead with three holes to play in the 1979 Masters. CBS cut to one of its rare commercial breaks, and Sneed, at that point, walked within steps of me, at ground level, to get to the 16th tee.

As Sneed passed, I gestured to him with a "thumbs-up" signal and said to him, "Edgar, I believe you have got it now."

"I believe so, Ben. I believe I have," was Sneed's reply.

The short commercial break ended, and to my disappointment but very slight concern, I watched as Sneed bogeyed the 16th. With my part of the broadcast completed, I jumped in a cart and quickly dodged the crowds on my way to the CBS trailers to see Sneed win his jacket. It was a long process for me to make it from 16 back to the compound, and when I finally arrived, I saw, to my horror, that Sneed had bogeyed 17 as well.

With my eyes glued to the monitor like those of a driver passing a motorway accident, I watched Sneed bogey 18 to squander what I had thought was an insurmountable lead. As Sneed could not get his putts to fall, my heart fell. Sneed now faced a sudden-death playoff with Tom Watson and Fuzzy Zoeller. I felt ill, and knew there was no way that Sneed could recover sufficiently from that kind of slide.

Zoeller was fetched from the bar inside the clubhouse, where I don't think he was having lemonade. Like everyone else, Fuzzy expected that the jacket was Sneed's to wear. That may explain why, when Zoeller won the playoff, he threw his putter high into the air. He behaved like a joyful lunatic.

The next time I came across Sneed, which was at Harbour Town the following week, I told him how shattered I was. Sneed claimed to be over it, but I knew he wasn't, and I know he will never be. Nor will I.

That 1979 sudden-death playoff served to introduce the golf world to Fuzzy, the joking, easy-going good 'ol boy who became the first Masters rookie to wear the green jacket since Gene Sarazen in 1935.

Zoeller went on to join the 1979, 1983, and 1985 Ryder Cup teams, win the 1984 United States Open, and, in 1985, receive the USGA's Bob Jones Award for "distinguished sportsmanship in golf."

Aside from being a "distinguished sportsman," Zoeller was a fan favorite everywhere. His antics and personality were a welcome relief to the beginning of the age of cookie-cutter, flat-bellied PGA Tour golf pros. Unfortunately, it was his swagger and aversion to political correctness that gave him great grief at the 1997 Masters. Having completed his round, Zoeller, again drink in hand, was approached by a camera crew in the shade of the giant tree behind the clubhouse where media types are known to lurk. When questioned about Tiger Woods and his historic and total victory, Zoeller, loved by the media for his ad-lib humor, uttered an ill-advised attempt at a quip. He used the word "boy" and made a reference to "collard greens" as a potential Woods menu choice at the following year's traditional champions dinner.

The subsequent media criticism was intense, and Fuzzy lost his sponsorship arrangement with the Kmart Corporation, which quickly attempted to distance itself from him. Zoeller, under great pressure, tearfully withdrew from playing PGA Tour events—including his beloved Greater Greensboro Open—until he could speak personally with Woods. This took longer than most expected, reportedly due to Tiger's heavy endorsement schedule. Many players on Tour resented Woods for avoiding Zoeller and letting him hang out to dry.

Zoeller's jokes were poorly chosen, but I don't believe they were meant with any harm. He's always been risky with his comments, but that has been his charm. Sometimes he is charmingly witty, and sometimes his cracks miss the mark. Zoeller is the last guy on earth I would consider to be racist, and it seems harsh that he was dropped so quickly by his business partners. Without doubt, though, corporate America will come knocking on Zoeller's door once he hits the Senior PGA Tour. My guess is that Zoeller will experience a rebirth in popularity and success on the course when he takes his jovial act to the more relaxed and colorful circuit at the end of 2001. Zoeller will shine, and his star will be irresistible.

The behavior of the CBS Golf broadcast team was certainly less than saintly during our yearly stays in Augusta. In fact, the CBS crew even created an award, dubbed the "Jerry Danford Award." The award was named after Danford, a CBS salesperson with a remarkable tolerance for alcohol, and was awarded to the person who behaved so disgracefully at the Masters that he'd distinguished himself to be more than worthy of such a dubious honor. The Jerry Danford Award was physically housed at Mike Manuche's Sports Bar in Manhattan, which was also the home of the "5:42 Club." Anywhere in the world we found ourselves, 5:42 P.M. commenced the evening's cocktails. We'd smile at each other, point to our watch, and simply remind each other: "5:42!"

One of the key figures of the 5:42 Club was Bill Brendle, a World War II vet who served as CBS director of press information. Brendle was a popular character because he was quite plainly nuts. Having been in the Battle of the Bulge, I suppose he may have been shell-shocked.

When I lived a sometimes lonely existence in Manhattan, Brendle would phone me at home at midday to convince me to come out to lunch with him. He was famous for daylong lunches that sometimes stretched until 5:42. Sportswriter Mike Lupica once wrote that when Brendle was asked how long he had been working for CBS Sports, Brendle answered, "I've been with CBS Sports for 18 years. But if you take out the lunches, it's 7 years."

Lupica also wrote of Brendle's expense account, and the way Brendle once asked a waiter to date his restaurant receipt for the next day. The waiter asked why.

"Because I used up today last night," was Brendle's explanation.

There were many extended "last nights" for Brendle, though, who was famous for his dedication to partying. At a New Orleans Super Bowl party for CBS, he once collapsed on the stage while Al Hirt was playing jazz. Brendle was left to lay there and sleep amongst the band as they played on.

One year, announcer Jack Whitaker was driving me, sportswriter Pete Axthelm, and Brendle back from a very rowdy party when he was pulled over for running a red light. The officer recognized Whitaker immediately, and was about to let him off with a warning. Brendle, drunk in the backseat, shouted, "For Christ's sake, Jack, tell that cop to get lost!"

Whitaker was immediately arrested, the car was impounded, and Whitaker was sent to spend the night in the cooler. Brendle, motivated by guilt along with the knowledge that Whitaker was needed for that day's telecast, managed to secure Whitaker's release the next morning with some fancy bantering with the local officers. For this remarkable crisis management, Brendle became a winner of the "Jerry Danford Award."

Pat Summerall had managed to drink enough to drive not one, not two, but three rental cars into ditches in the space of a week. He, therefore, was a winner of the "Jerry Danford Award."

Another winner of the "Jerry Danford Award" secured the prize virtually before he ever set foot in Augusta. Gene Peterson, a broadcast engineer, arrived at the Augusta airport and was placed under arrest as soon as he stepped off the plane. It seems that Peterson, traveling with Summerall, had drunk so much liquor during the flight that he accused a flight attendant of being a "fag" and knocked a tray of drinks out of the lad's hand. The airline phoned ahead from inflight to alert the authorities, and a policeman apprehended Peterson and began to question him until Peterson threw up all over him from head to foot. No further questions...straight to jail. No further questions..."Jerry Danford Award!"

I befriended a local woman who was the manager of a club called "the Cadaver" in Augusta. Each morning, on her way to work, she would find it in her heart to stop by my rented house for some dalliance. Very late one night, she invited me to her place, where she and I were occupied in full passion. While enjoying our spirited lovemaking, I was startled to feel something hit me on the side of the hip and knock me to the floor. In a heap on the floor, the lights went on and I looked up to find myself staring into a revolver. I quickly learned that the woman was married. Her husband, frothing at the mouth with rage and shakily pointing the revolver at me, didn't much appreciate my presence in bed with his wife. I affected my best British accent to hastily explain to the chap that I was a long way from home and had no idea the woman was married. Indeed, there is no apology like an accommodating British apology.

"I'll give you two minutes to get out of here," the man growled.

I made three quick attempts to get my trousers back on before giving up and fleeing from the home stark naked and jumping into my CBS rental car.

I pulled into the driveway of the rented home I was sharing with other members of the CBS crew, hoping that no one would yet be awake. I scurried into the home, still buck naked, only to find two lady housekeepers in white uniforms and white shoes preparing breakfast for the CBS crew, including Bob Drum, who was sitting at the table shaking vodka on his eggs.

I was caught, naked, and could only calmly nod, hold up one finger and say, "I'll be right back properly dressed for breakfast, ladies." The ladies went into shrieks, and I was named the winner of that year's "Jerry Danford Award."

Of course, television announcers weren't the only ones that should have qualified for the "Jerry Danford Award." I would like to have nominated the former Masters champion who was almost ejected from Augusta National when two women turned up with Masters access badges reserved ostensibly for that player's wife. It was further revealed that *neither* woman was indeed the player's wife, but rather, practitioners of the world's oldest profession who had been contracted by the player.

N eedless to say, gambling was another of our many indiscretions. The CBS crew would hold a Calcutta gambling event at the Masters each Wednesday night. The CBS announcers, executives, producers, director and salespeople, clients, VIPs, and invited guests would gather in one of the homes that we were billeting and get a chance to bid on Masters participants in an auction-style setting. Whoever bought the eventual winning player won the pot. The scene typically became a drunken gathering, with large amounts of money tossed around.

The irascible Bob Drum, who'd been hired to star in "the Drummer's Beat" features for CBS, served as the auctioneer. Drum presided over this scene, and called out the players' names, describing them in very raunchy terms.

Being a betting man, I participated gladly, and confess to winning the Masters Calcutta seven times. I collected a five-figure sum seven times, including a $26,000 prize. Of course, I was shrewd in my bidding. The most I ever bid for a player was $500 to claim Seve Ballesteros, who won for me in 1983. To think I once thought the $85 I paid for Tommy Aaron in 1973 was extravagant—that is, until he won. I purchased a station wagon for my wife with the $12,000 that bid won me.

My most frugal buy and biggest bargain occurred in 1979, when I shouted out a bid for a player not expected to win.

"You know," cackled Drum, the dirty auctioneer, "only a dumb limey would buy a guy like Fuzzy Zoeller playing in his first Masters. It's common knowledge with anybody that knows anything about the game that you can't win here on your first attempt."

"What can I have him for?" I shouted back.

"Fifty dollars and he's yours, you limey fool."

I'd long forgotten Drum's chiding while collecting the big prize when the rookie Zoeller won the three-man playoff mentioned earlier.

When Greg Norman came to Augusta National for the first time in 1981, I speculated to fellow announcer Pat Summerall that the heralded upstart could win the Masters.

"No way," piped Summerall. "American boys are the best golfers." Summerall, being very insular and patriotic, felt that foreigners had no chance to win a major on United States soil. Indeed, the record of internationals at the Masters was not so good then. However, I could see the fin of the so-called "Great White Shark" making its way across the ocean toward Augusta.

A wager was placed when I contacted my bookie, and I informed Pat that the odds on Norman winning the Masters were set at 20-1.

"20-1! Bah, I'll give you 40-1," Summerall croaked.

I took the bet for $100, at 40-1.

After two rounds, Greg Norman was leading the Masters.

"Still think he can't win?" I taunted Summerall.

"No chance," he replied with certain bravado.

"Care to give me double, then?"

"Deal."

Now Summerall had allowed me to put $200 on Greg Norman at 40-1 odds! Norman led into the final round until the 10th hole and I *know* Summerall was sweating all the way. The $200 I lost to him was well worth the agony Summerall endured at the thought of losing an even greater amount of money, and having to admit that a "foreigner" might beat his "American boys."

My further revenge on Summerall came six years later in 1987, when I had bought both Greg Norman and Larry Mize in the Calcutta. I paid a hell of a lot more for Norman than I did for Mize, a one-time Tour winner whom I picked because he was born and raised in Augusta. I claimed Mize at a bargain price, while Summerall, finally abandoning his prejudice against foreign-born golfers, paid big money for two-time Masters champion Seve Ballesteros.

In the final round, Mize birdied the 18th hole to wiggle into a sudden-death playoff with Norman and Ballesteros. Despite that nervy performance, I knew that Summerall liked his chances with Ballesteros in the playoff.

Has there ever been a more sorrowful sight in televised golf than the shot CBS presented to viewers of a lone man walking back up the hill away from the tenth green? Solitary in his thoughts, defeated, marching up the quiet 10th fairway, away from the buzzing crowd and the two competitors that would continue in the battle without him?

That man was Ballesteros, eliminated on the first hole of the sudden-death playoff.

As bad as I felt for the clearly heartbroken Ballesteros, my spirit was somewhat lifted by the fact that Summerall was defeated as well. On top of that, I now held all the cards, having claimed both Mize and Norman in the Calcutta.

As you know, Mize, the hometown Cinderella story, sank a 140-foot chip shot at the 11th green to begin Greg Norman's tantalizing run of major championship defeats, and continue my streak of wins.

The Calcutta, frowned upon from the start, was eventually done away with, leaving us with only side wagers.

Summerall and I, indeed, have had our moments. But we grew very close, sharing a house for many years at the Masters. The finest time I ever had at the Augusta National was in the company of Summerall. Pat and I were the invited guests of Hord Hardin, the chairman of the Augusta National Golf Club.

We lodged with Hardin in the famed Eisenhower Cabin on the Augusta National grounds just off of the 10th hole. Hardin and Summerall stayed on the ground floor, while I was lodged in Eisenhower's studio and bedroom. It was a magnificent experience for me—a child during World War II—because on the walls hung photographs of every base at which Eisenhower had been stationed throughout his long and illustrious military career. I felt immeasurably privileged.

Our itinerary each day was identical. Each morning, we would enjoy breakfast in the upstairs grill of the clubhouse and then tee off at 9:30. This being only one week before the Masters, the golf course was in a condition better than even that of tournament week, since there was not a divot or spike mark to be found, nor a rope-line in sight. Everything was as pristine as a Christmas morning package waiting to be opened.

Summerall and I played as partners against Hardin and our CBS producer/director Chirkinian, who made his residence in the Augusta area. Hardin was a class golfer in his youth, competing in many amateur championships. Age and other factors had forced his handicap to evolve to 18, which was terribly high for a player of his ability.

We had fine matches in the ultimate setting, not without a certain amount of civilized gamesmanship. As I stood over an important putt, I muttered to the group in my heavy British accent: "Well, gentlemen, it seems I am in need of this putt for a half."

Hardin broke the silence and made fun of my accent by asking, "Just what the hell is a 'haw-lf?'"

Upon completion of the round, Hardin would take us all to lunch in the men's grill just off the locker room. After lunch, Hardin would excuse himself, claiming that he had some work to complete. I suspect more often than not, though, that he went for his afternoon nap.

Summerall, Chirkinian, and I, in the absence of Hardin, would walk over to the par-3 course and play 54 intensely competitive skins holes all afternoon, eventually returning to the cottage to clean up before cocktails at 5:42.

Cocktails to Hardin meant a number of martinis. Hord, in private, was the greatest fun, nothing like his stiff and dull public persona. He loved to tell rude and filthy jokes. Chirkinian and I once hosted Hardin in Scotland, where he was attending the British Open with his wife Esther. Hardin noticed a snooker table in the game room of the stately home CBS was renting and enlisted me to teach him the game, claiming that he was an old pool shark from St. Louis. Hardin and I beat a couple of CBS engineers and Chirkinian out of more than a few quid. Hardin was brilliant and we won game after game at 50 pounds sterling apiece.

The lighter and warmer side of Hardin was never visible to viewers, who saw him each year when he read the chairman's message and represented the club during the jacket presentation in the Butler

Cabin at the conclusion of the Masters. Hardin hated being on television, and Chirkinian tried very hard to get him to relax during his reading of the chairman's message, which was taped and played at the beginning of the tournament broadcast. Chirkinian would have Hardin read take after take, sometimes nearly 50 in all, until the chairman's message was at least acceptable. Chirkinian tolerated this plodding monotony because he was a great friend of Hardin.

The jacket presentation, on the other hand, was broadcast live, so there was no means by which Chirkinian could steer Hardin through that event, in which Hardin was to interview the winner. Hardin would have such a hard time with the jacket ceremony, asking damn fool questions like the one he posed to Ballesteros. On national television, he asked Seve: "What is your weight?"

After our cocktail hour on the ground floor of the Eisenhower Cabin, the four of us would walk over and have dinner in the formal dining area of the main clubhouse. Each day, we consumed three meals in three different rooms of the clubhouse. By the end of a gourmet dinner and the fine wines that accompanied it, we would all be ready for bed. I retired each night and was left to my dreams, having lived a day that was the dream of countless golfers everywhere.

The most courageous performance in the history of the Augusta National has, to this day, remained unknown. To any man who has ever held a golf club, it must perhaps serve as the most inspiring and unbelievable accomplishment of all time. The most courageous performance in Masters history, told here for the first time, is surely the most incredibly secret subplot I have ever witnessed at the Augusta National Golf Club.

The CBS announcers, as I have stated, were lodged in rented homes at the West Lake Country Club during Masters week. On the year in question, I was paired in a home with Tom Weiskopf, who, when he wasn't in the field, served on the CBS announcing team during the Masters. That year, though it was late in his playing career, he was still an invited competitor in the tournament.

Our wives were coming in for the weekend. Weiskopf's wife Jeanne, my wife Kitty, and my daughter Margaret arrived, and we all were enjoying a dandy time. To add to the excitement, Weiskopf had played well enough through Saturday to possibly finish in the top 24, which would put him amongst the players who automatically qualify to return the following year.

Early Sunday morning, Kitty went downstairs to pour cereal for our daughter's breakfast. The next sound I heard emanating from the upper level of the house was a terrible wailing noise. Kitty came rushing up the stairs to roust me from bed.

"Ben, come quickly, come quickly," she breathlessly pleaded. "Tom needs you. He's got some kind of problem!"

I rushed down the passage, half asleep and still in my nightshirt. I charged into Weiskopf's bathroom, where the first thing I noticed is that both of us are wearing identical nightshirts. Yellow and black little cubes in a pattern. We looked like a couple of overgrown bumblebees. Upon further inspection, however, I begin to realize why I'd been hurried to the macabre scene. Weiskopf was sitting on his bathroom floor, with his legs apart, clutching his crotch...his yellow and black checked nightshirt stained with a large amount of blood. He was obviously bleeding profusely. My heart jumped with fright.

"Tom, what's going on?" I urgently asked.

"Ben, about three weeks ago I had some surgery."

"Surgery?"

"Yeah, Ben, I, uh, well I had some warts removed from an embarrassing place."

"What are you saying?"

"I was instructed by the doctor that I must not make love to my wife for at least one month. But Ben, Jeanne and I have a kind of tradition that whenever I have a chance to win a tournament, we have it off on Sunday morning before I go to play."

"Good lord, Tom!"

"The whole thing is ripped open. I'm bleeding pretty badly. You've got to help me"

I rushed to phone Chirkinian, but found that he'd already left his Augusta home bound for the golf course. I explained as much of the scenario as was decent to Chirkinian's wife, M.J., who'd answered the phone. She could tell it was an urgent matter.

"I have a doctor friend I can send over," M.J. offered. "Sherman Blaylock. He's a brain surgeon, though, Ben...but I'll send him right over."

Chagrined at the perfect irony of a brain surgeon on his way over for this particular problem, I thanked M.J. and rushed back to Weiskopf's side to calm him.

Blaylock arrived in short order and examined Weiskopf.

"Jesus, Mr. Weiskopf, what time are you scheduled to play this morning?"

"11:10," Weiskopf glumly revealed.

"Let's get you into my car. I'll run you over to the hospital and stitch you up."

In a timely manner, Blaylock escorted Weiskopf down to University Hospital, where he stitched him up and wrapped everything in gauze.

"You can play, Tom, if you like, but you're going to be in terrible pain," Blaylock warned.

Weiskopf made his 11:10 tee time, and gingerly played a gritty final round of the Masters. I told no one of the occurrence. The CBS cameras picked up Weiskopf trudging up the hill at the 18th hole, and he was in such pain that I could see that he was absolutely drained. The announcers at 18 had no idea what he was going through, and I wasn't about to tell them.

Weiskopf shot 76 that day. It was probably the greatest round of golf ever played—freshly stitched, bound, and bandaged only minutes before he went out in the heat to trudge up and down a very hilly golf course in front of a very attentive crowd.

I can't say enough about his performance, which helped him narrowly hang on to a precious spot in the top 24, allowing entrance for next year's event.

To be quite serious about courageous performances, there is no doubt that Jack Nicklaus has accomplished nearly supernatural feats at the Masters. I have never seen a player make things happen like Nicklaus has done among the dogwoods and pines. Time after time, he seemed able to will the ball into the hole just when he needed to the most. Aside from his record six wins, he finished second four times. In 1998, Nicklaus was a factor in the final round going into the back nine and shot a 68 to finish only three shots behind. What's more astounding is that the gallery believed he could win. The Nicklaus buzz was soaring through the galleries and through living rooms throughout the world! What Jack was doing was phenomenal.

Of course, in my heart, I hoped that Jack could pull out some of the magic at age 58. But in my mind I knew that, despite his enormous will, he could not. Though it may not be visible to television viewers, the back nine at Augusta is so very demanding on the legs. I never believed that Nicklaus could hold on. It is a very hard walk to get back to the clubhouse having descended so rapidly down 10.

That's the reason Raymond Floyd lost to Nick Faldo after two holes of sudden death in 1990. At age 48, he could barely bloody walk.

Nicklaus will surely be most remembered for his sixth green jacket win in 1986, when at the age of 46, he became the oldest winner in Masters history. I feel very fortunate to have witnessed his back nine charge during which he held off the youthful likes of Greg Norman, Seve Ballesteros, Tom Kite, and Corey Pavin.

Nicklaus, in the middle of a full-blown birdie barrage on 9, 10, and 11, made bogey on the par-three 12th. At 13, Ken Venturi, amazed by the supportive and respectful silence of the teeming gallery, called the action as Nicklaus birdied. Gary McCord, hidden in the woods where he belonged at 14, described Nicklaus tapping in for par there. The leaderboard was stacked in this order:

Player	Score	Thru
Ballesteros	–9	13
Kite	–7	13
Pavin	–6	15
Nicklaus	–5	14

Eleven years earlier, I viewed Nicklaus as he stood in this same fairway, in the heat of battle with Miller and Weiskopf, peering at the 15th green, just as he was now. This time, the 46-year-old in the yellow shirt and checkered pants was 214 yards from the green. With eleven years more experience, his deliberation was very much shorter. Pulling the 4-iron, Nicklaus determinedly stood over the ball, knowing full well that an eagle 3 on 15 could not only vault him near the lead but, more importantly, shake up the other competitors.

"A 3 will go a long way here," Nicklaus told his son Jackie, who was serving as his caddie.

Only seconds after addressing the ball, Nicklaus took a nicely compact swing and sent the ball skyward. As in 1975, he began to walk after the ball, shielding his steely eyes from the sun with his hand, which may as well have been saluting the shot, because the ball was like a missile that landed breathtakingly close to its target.

The screams of the crowd were delirious as the ball landed just in front of the pin and hopped to about 10 feet behind and to the left of the hole.

"He's got a chance!" I said loudly on the air, struggling to be heard over the roars. *"He has got a very, very good chance of an eagle 3 to make him seven under par. The old Bear is back!"*

Nicklaus allowed both of his fists to give a little pump, and began walking very quickly toward the green, smiling, waving, nodding, and knowing again, just as he did in 1975, that the game was on.

The CBS coverage cut back to me when Nicklaus was ready to putt:

"Jack Nicklaus and his son Jackie, his oldest son who is himself a North and South Amateur champion, have really looked at this one from every conceivable angle. Jack has backed off because there is applause from the gallery at the 16th hole nearby. He has this putt for an eagle that will slide a little to his right....He will wait for absolute silence..."

Nicklaus hit a firm putt that broke about eight inches left-to-right.

"Yes sir!" I shouted as the ball charged into the hole. *"Magnificent stuff. That information will percolate back to Seve Ballesteros as he stands on the 15th tee."*

Ballesteros's bid to hold off the Nicklaus opus ended with his own 4-iron approach to the 15th green, an ugly hook that ended in the bottom of the pond. For the longest time, Ballesteros insisted that his shot was not a poor one. Eventually, though, Ballesteros admitted to me that his swing was indeed hurried because he was fearful of the next boisterous cheer for Nicklaus. Whether he admits it or not, Ballesteros was also genuinely puzzled and bothered as to why the whole of America seemed to be pulling for Nicklaus while his own bold efforts were met with muted applause. Ballesteros had been to the Masters enough times to know that the crowd noises he was hearing were not of the usual variety. He knew there had never been a sound like it rolling through the Georgia pines. The partisan crowds clearly and unabashedly wanted Nicklaus and not the swashbuckling Spaniard. That bothered him. Thirteen years later, his countryman José-María Olazabal would suffer the same indifference.

The galleries were witnessing a miracle being staged by no mere mortal, and the atmosphere turned into a Nicklaus revival. Ballesteros was correct to fear the noise interfering with his swing because the roars were the loudest I had ever heard at the National. Were our eyes to be believed on that sunny April day? Did Nicklaus indeed go on to birdie 16 and 17? Was it not the final scene of a Hollywood script when Nicklaus came off of the 18th hole hugging his son Jackie, who'd carried his bag every step of the way?

The esteem for Nicklaus at Augusta, however, will never subside, and neither will my fondness for the best-run tournament in the world: the Masters. Each year, my wonderful memories of Augusta bloom like the cherished azaleas, and I feel renewed with the rite of spring and the fullness of three decades with the Masters.

Revolutionary Rematches

When the flags present on the golf course are no longer only attached to flagsticks stuck in greens, one can be certain that patriotism and emotion will be the two most prominent thoughts. The sight of the Union Jack and the Stars and Stripes means that Great Britain (and now Europe) and the Colonies have once again engaged in battle, this time represented by the best of their respective golfers in the biennial Ryder Cup Matches.

Samuel Ryder, born in 1858 and a remarkable gentleman by all accounts, was the donor of this prestigious trophy. As a young man, the demonstratively innovative Ryder worked with his father, who toiled as a struggling market gardener in Cheshire, England. At that time, packet seeds were sold by the mail through only two British companies, each of which offered the product at a price prohibitive to the working class. Ryder's idea, rejected by his father, was to establish a market for packet seeds amongst the working class by making the seeds affordable.

Thinking that the idea of selling packet seeds for the ridiculously low price of a penny each was preposterous, Ryder's father scorned his son's idea, forcing Ryder to strike out on his own at the age of 28. Because of the access to three railway stations, Ryder founded his mail order business in a cathedral city 20 miles north of London called St. Albans in 1886.

Through Ryder's ingenuity and innovative mentality, his new company gained over one million regular postal customers and grew to become a significant major corporation. Ryder's toil postponed his involvement in the game of golf until he was over 50 years of age, when he contracted the professional at a local nine-hole course to visit him daily, rain or shine, for rigorous instruction on the grounds of Ryder's mansion. Ryder even went to the measure of carving golf holes into his croquet lawn and through the hedges of his formal garden. Alone and with the professional, he worked arduously at his game for over a year until he was satisfied that he could make a comfortable application to Verulam, the nearby private club to which he was accepted in 1910.

Again, with determination and drive, Ryder became captain of Verulam three times and generously used his financial resources to rescue the club from financial distress. It would not be fair to say that he was more than an average golfer, but Ryder was in love with the game and amazed by the skills and talents of its best players. Like Henry Cotton and Walter Hagen, Ryder was uncomfortable with the lowly status accorded to golf professionals at that time. With meager wages and images equal to that of caddies, golf professionals were considered to be, if you'll pardon the metaphor, "beach bums of the links."

Again, Ryder generously conceived to share his financial means by creating a golf tournament to give the professionals a chance to win some of it. His 1923 "Heath and Heather Tournament," named after Ryder's herbal remedy company, was the first professional golf tournament ever played in the United Kingdom. Ryder even paid the players what amounted to an appearance fee and covered the players' expenses, which guaranteed a strong and talented field. British Open champion Arthur Havers won the first prize of 50 pounds sterling and assuredly had trouble spending it in one place, since it represented a great deal of money at that time.

Ryder supremely enjoyed the company of these wonderful players, and, with a generous salary, hired Abe Mitchell to be his personal professional golf instructor. Mitchell, considered to be the best player never to win the Open Championship, told Ryder of a friendly meeting of American and British players that sometimes took place adjacent to the Open when the Yanks would travel all the way across the sea by boat.

In 1921, for example, a friendly match between the British and American players was conducted at Gleneagles, just a drive from the Open site of St. Andrews. The British won handily, 10½ points to 4½ points. Ryder was intrigued by the concept.

At the 1926 Open, such a large field attempted to compete at Royal Lytham and St. Anne's that three qualifying courses were designated: Sunningdale, St. Anne's Old Links, and Western Gailes. It was over Sunningdale's Old Course that Bobby Jones played one of the most famous rounds of all time—a 66 that was comprised of only fours and threes: 33 out, 33 in, 33 shots, and 33 putts.

Jones went on to win that Open, and another friendly meeting of the British and American professionals was arranged at nearby Wentworth. This time, Ryder was in attendance, eager to see how his friend Abe Mitchell would fare partnered with Scotsman George Duncan against Jim Barnes and Walter Hagen in a foursome match. Mitchell and Duncan were successful in beating back the big-name Americans by a shameless 9 and 8. In his singles contest the following day, Mitchell again barely broke a sweat in finishing off Barnes by 8 and 7. British victory in the exhibition was total and complete: 13½ to 1½.

The competition, coupled with the sporting and chivalrous attitudes toward each other by the teams, impressed Ryder, who was so moved that he purchased a solid gold trophy from the Royal Jewelers in London. The small figure swinging a club atop the trophy is that of his friend Abe Mitchell, and the trophy became known as the Ryder Cup.

Mitchell was justly chosen by the selection committee of Harry Vardon, J.H. Taylor, and James Braid as captain of the first British team to travel to play for the glorious trophy in the Ryder Cup matches.

The British team sailed for New York to play in the 1927 match at Worcester Country Club in Massachusetts, but it was to be an ill-fated journey for the Brits. A rough ocean crossing by the ship *Aquitania* left many of the players seasick, the foremost being George Gadd, who never recovered his land legs and pulled out of the competition. Mitchell himself went down with appendicitis, and had to be replaced as captain by Ted Ray, who'd won the 1920 U.S. Open at Inverness Country Club in Toledo, Ohio. Ray would be the last British player to win the U.S. Open until Tony Jacklin accomplished the feat 50 years later. Herbert Jolly was called upon as a substitute player, and sailed alone to the States four days behind the team. Two consecutive days of 36-hole matches—the first-day foursomes and the second-day singles—would take their toll.

Perhaps, though, it was the stark difference between the United States and the United Kingdom that most affected the British. The boys from England had been given a posh and tumultuous welcome by their gracious hosts, and after losing the first-day foursomes 3-1, Arthur Havers summed up the British team's feelings:

"Everywhere we went, we were submerged by hospitality and kindness," Havers allowed. "Suddenly, we were in a world of luxury and plenty, so different from home. It was something we had never expected. Even the clubhouses were luxurious, with deep pile carpets, not like the rundown and shabby clubhouses at home."

It is certainly ironic that 56 years later, European captain Tony Jacklin, upon assuming captaincy in 1983, was to insist on creature comforts for his squad. Jacklin demanded travel by Concorde, tailored uniforms, and luxury hotel accommodations for his team to dispel the very feeling of inferiority that had developed as the Americans dominated the series for so long.

The 1927 singles matches were equally disastrous for the British, with only the dour Duncan winning a match by beating Joe Turnesa at the final hole. The legendary American match play expert Gene Sarazen came back from five holes down to halve his match with Charles Whitcombe.

The United States won the first official Ryder Cup 9½ to 2½ on their home soil.

After 12 years of trans-Atlantic battles, the U.S. led the series 4-2, leaving the Americans full of dominant confidence.

The 1939 match, to be played at the Ponte Vedra Club near Jacksonville, Florida in November, was cancelled due to the outbreak of World War II in September. The Americans, confident that it would be a short war, actually nominated a team for the 1941 match that included Hagen as captain, Jimmy Demaret, Vic Ghezzi, Ben Hogan, Harold "Jug" McSpaden, Lloyd Mangrum, Nelson, Sarazen, Smith, Snead, and Wood. Due to the Japanese involvement in the war, the series, in fact, was not renewed until 1947.

The state of British and Irish golf had been badly battered by the war. There was, in fact, little interest in reviving the matches so soon after such a debilitating struggle to survive. Gasoline and food rationing were still being implemented in Britain, and golf equipment manufacturers had insufficient materials to reestablish any semblance of production.

Britain was simply not prepared to send a team on a long and expensive voyage to Portland, Oregon to renew the series. Many of the best British players were still in uniform when American Sam Snead won the first postwar Open at St. Andrews in 1946, and were quite put-off when Snead compared his experience in the UK to "camping out." It was a very ungracious thing for the winner to say, but Snead has always been a very crude man.

Much more gracious was a man named Robert Hudson, a wealthy Portland businessman who was a bit of an Anglophile and a lover of the game. My late, great friend Fred Corcoran, at the time executive director of the American PGA, appealed to Hudson—who was an advisory member of the PGA—to assist in resurrecting the series. Hudson realized that Sam Ryder's dream of establishing international goodwill was then more important than ever. He agreed to personally underwrite the British effort until they were back on their feet financially. When one thinks of how significant that show of sportsmanship was, it can clearly illustrate what the game of golf can do to promote civility. Imagine bankrolling your opponent's efforts!

Hudson personally met the 1947 British and Irish team, headed by playing captain Henry Cotton, when the Queen Mary landed in late October 1947. The subsequent rail journey to Portland took a further three and a half days. Doused in rain each day, the British team was bound to struggle against an American team led by playing captain Ben Hogan.

Further complicating matters, Cotton, desperate for victory and grasping for any edge, called for an unprecedented, and apparently unjustified, inspection of the American team's clubs, implying that some of them had illegal grooves designed for excessive spin on the ball. Nothing untoward was discovered by the officials, but Hogan did not forget what appeared to have been an unseemly attempt at gamesmanship. Cotton, in desperation perhaps, also gathered his team the following morning and held up a Bible, asking his players for a period of meditation. None of Cotton's tactics proved effective, and in fact, they may have backfired.

Nelson, Snead, Mangrum, Hogan, Demaret, Lew Worsham, Ed "Porky" Oliver, and the rest of the Americans retained the Cup by humiliating the British 11-1.

The 1949 match returned to Britain for the first time in 12 years, and despite nearly losing his life in an automobile accident in February, Hogan was on hand in September as the American's nonplaying captain at Ganton, near Scarborough, Yorkshire. Hogan, forced to walk on crutches, proved that despite his physical injuries, his competitive fire was still present. It was evident that he had not forgotten Cotton's gamesmanship in the Portland incident when, on the eve of the Ganton competition, Hogan demanded an inspection of the British team's clubs.

When officials could not agree on the holes, rather than grooves, in the British clubs' faces, the clubs were hurriedly driven to Scarborough, where Bernard Darwin, the brilliant golf writer who was then chairman of the Royal & Ancient's Rules of Golf committee, was dining. The irascible Darwin, after inspecting the clubs, delivered his verdict swiftly and succinctly. "Nothing that a little filing won't put right," said Darwin before resuming his meal. The clubs were duly returned to Jock Ballantine, the Ganton professional, who duly filed the night away.

The Americans further inspired hard feelings among the British team when it was revealed that the Yanks arrived with 600 steaks, 12 sides of beef ribs, 12 hams, and 12 boxes of bacon. Since food rationing was still in effect in Great Britain, this was probably an unwise move in a diplomatic sense. In retrospect, however, I am sure there was no malice on behalf of the visitors.

The British seemed to have an advantage in the match. Though seven of the Brits were part of the team humiliated in Portland, they were now on home soil, and amongst the Americans only Snead and Demaret and Mangrum had ever played in Great Britain. The loss of Hogan as a player was also bound to hamper the American efforts.

A large partisan crowd watched the British win the opening day foursomes 3 to 1, with only Demaret and Clayton Heafner preventing a whitewash. Great Britain and Ireland needed only 3½ singles points for their first postwar victory.

The Americans, however, possibly stung by harsh words from Hogan the evening before, staged a brilliant comeback. The Yanks won six of the eight singles matches, and Mangrum—as one might have expected of a gentleman who had been decorated for his bravery in combat on the Normandy beaches on D-Day—sealed the comeback with a late win over Fred Daly.

The 1951 match at Pinehurst was forgettable for the British because the American nucleus of Snead, Mangrum, Demaret, and

Hogan was at full strength. Alas, a 9½ to 2½ drubbing by the Americans had this young Brit wondering if we'd ever win again, and how long we'd be forced to maintain our stiff upper lips.

In recent years, the much closer matches have come down to the last putt. It is then that the greatest pressure lies squarely on the shoulders of those at the bottom of the singles matches. So it was on Wentworth's west course in October 1953. There was a feeling that once again the British and Irish would have a very good chance of victory. Hogan—whom I had gone AWOL as a young Army cadet to watch win the British Open earlier that year—had also won the Masters and the U.S. Open, but was not to play in the Ryder Cup. Lloyd Mangrum assumed the role of playing captain, and the American team included newcomers Walter Burkemo, who'd won the PGA Championship; Canadian Open winner Dave Douglas; Ted Kroll; and former U.S. Open champion Cary Middlecoff.

The British team presented the debuts of the fiery Scot Eric Brown, young Englishmen Peter Alliss and Bernard Hunt, and the first Irishman ever to play, Harry Bradshaw. The semiretired Cotton captained without playing.

After spirited play, the fate of the matches lay on the young shoulders of Alliss and Hunt, who were to play last in the singles.

Both were ahead as they came down the stretch, Alliss 1-up with three to play against Jim Turnesa. Turnesa hit a terrible drive far to the right at the 16th, but the ball bounced back into play off a spectator. Turnesa got up and down from a greenside bunker for a winning par when Alliss made a sorry bogey from the fairway. Worse was when Alliss drove out of bounds to lose the 17th, or 35th. Turnesa then hit his drive so far to the right of the 18th hole that although he was able to chip out he would plainly do no better than make six. Off a perfect drive, Alliss was just to the left of the green with a well-played 2-iron shot. He then completely fluffed his chip, and then ran the ball three feet past the hole with his second attempt. Turnesa missed his putt for five, but alas, so did Alliss—to lose his match. To say Alliss has been haunted by this incident ever since would be an understatement, and further indignity and aspersions are possibly cast upon Alliss every time a golfer anywhere mutters the cliché phrase, "Nice putt, Alliss," upon misfiring on the putting surface. Though there is no proof that this is where the phrase came from, there is no doubt that it still must sting. Homophones can be cruel.

Everything now depended on Hunt, 1-up with the final hole to play against Douglas. Hunt was short of the green and to the right in two shots, and allowed himself the luxury of thinking that he had only to run the ball somewhere close to the hole for his par five to win. Instead, he pitched the ball to the back of the green and took three putts to only halve his match. The U.S.A. had won again, 6½ to 5½.

The near victory, instead of stimulating the British and Irish to great efforts in Palm Springs two years later, must have left the British dispirited, because they fell to the Americans 8 to 4 at Thunderbird Golf and Country Club. My former television commentating colleague and world renowned golf teacher John Jacobs won both his foursomes and singles matches, but there was little else to view as positive.

The drama that unfolded before, during, and after the 1957 match at Lindrick Golf Club, Nottinghamshire, England, could well have been scripted by a Hollywood screenwriter, although it would admittedly be considered a "B" movie.

The British and Irish had not won the biennial fixture since their mostly long-forgotten victory at Southport and Ainsdale in 1933. Only a few months before the 1957 match, the British PGA was still seeking both a sponsor and a venue for a series that had become ridiculously one-sided, and therefore hardly worthy of public interest. The situation cried out for a sort of fairy godfather like Robert Hudson, and in the nick of time, the British PGA found one in the unlikely shape of Sir Stuart Goodwin, a Sheffield steel magnate with no previous experience of, or interest in, golf. In fact, as he tramped about the Lindrick course in black bowler hat, crumpled raincoat, and trousers above his ankles, he cut an anything but imposing figure.

In 1956, Goodwin had been lured onto the Lindrick course for the first time because he had nothing better to do one afternoon when his lunch appointment was cancelled. It so happened that Welshman Dai Rees—who was to become the central figure in our drama as the British and Irish team's heroic playing captain—was the same, fateful day playing an exhibition match at Lindrick for charity. Also participating were Ulsterman Fred Daly, the 1947 British Open champion; Jack Jacobs, the professional at Lindrick and older brother of John; and the unfortunately named Sheffield club professional Jack Shanks of the Hillsborough Club.

Despite match-long rains, Goodwin apparently enjoyed himself so much that he invited the four golfers and retired Naval Commander Charles Roe, secretary of the British PGA, to dinner that evening.

When Goodwin said that he would like to see more top class golf in the area, Rees, always the opportunist, was quick to point out that the city of Sheffield had a population quite large enough to accommodate a major tournament. Goodwin asked how much money such an event would cost, and the then princely sum of 5,000 pounds was mentioned. Goodwin immediately wrote a check to the PGA for 15,000 pounds to guarantee a professional foursomes event in his name to be played in the area for the next three years.

In his desperation in early 1957, Roe went back to the well and Goodwin promptly and generously saved the Ryder Cup from almost certain extinction, as had Hudson before him on the other side of the Atlantic. Goodwin advanced a sum of 10,000 pounds, and told the PGA secretary that he could also keep all the gate receipts.

Controversy was to surround the match long before it began, and lasted long after the dust had settled. Firstly, an American team that did not include the magical names of Ben Hogan, Sam Snead, Jimmy Demaret, and Cary Middlecoff was dismissed by some golf wags as "not fully representative," while there were those quick to reply that the best players cannot retain their reputations without earning them.

Nevertheless, most of us in Britain believed that American captain Jack Burke had enough talent on his team to once again sweep aside the underdog home side.

Max Faulkner and Harry Weetman, who had lost by 4 and 3 to Burke and Ted Kroll, were quick to admit that they had both played poorly, and did not deserve to play in the approaching singles matches. Rees, who had read their figures hole by hole on the main scoreboard, readily accepted their "resignation" and nominated Peter Mills and Bradshaw as their substitutes in the singles. The meeting was both quickly finished and entirely amicable. So one can imagine Rees's amazement when, after he had exchanged singles lineups with Burke, he was stopped by a reporter and asked for a statement as he made his way out of the club. Apparently Weetman had just announced to the press that he would never again play on a team captained by Rees. Rees, who had been a long-time friend of Weetman, was quick to suspect that the villain of the piece was Mrs. Freda Weetman, who had let it be known from the outset that she felt her husband—not Rees—should have been British captain.

Mrs. Weetman was quoted widely the following day that it was quite ridiculous that the players' wives had been forced to stay in a different hotel from their husbands. Peter Alliss described the break-up each evening as "like leaving a hospital after visiting hour."

I well remember talking with some of my fellow scribes over a few drinks that evening that this was about the last straw. If we couldn't play together as a team without this kind of nonsensical situation arising, we all agreed, then let's forget the bloody Ryder Cup matches.

The sequel to this disgraceful incident—every petty detail of which was splashed across every newspaper with huge headlines the following morning—was that Weetman was immediately called before the PGA's disciplinary committee and suspended from all British PGA tournaments for a year. The harsh sentence was commuted some months later at the insistence of Rees. Rees himself refused to make any statement to any reporter, saying that he would give his version of the incident in his official report to the PGA after the match.

For some strange reason quite beyond my ability to fathom, this "phantom" row seemed completely to unite the home team on a cold and blustery day, rather than the expected reverse. A wind change during the night, which produced greens of appreciably faster pace for the singles, caused the Americans to opt for the British ball, which penetrates the wind much more readily, and flies further, but is now generally recognized as being less easy to control around the greens. In hindsight, this controversial American decision was probably a tactical blunder. In fact, five of the visitors took three putts apiece on the first green, including captain Burke. The American captain had been allowed by Rees to substitute himself for Kroll, who had taken ill overnight, one of the few friendly gestures displayed during this most furiously exciting of days.

Rees had purposely put the flinty Eric Brown at the top of his singles list in the hope of having him play the irascible Tommy Bolt. Bolt had been all sweetness and light the previous day, when he and Dick Mayer, the reigning U.S. Open champion, had crushed Brown and Ireland's Christy O'Connor by 7 and 5. There was no love lost between Brown and Bolt.

"You're beat, sucker," were the words uttered by Bolt after he walked across the first tee and approached Brown.

Soon, though, the cocky Bolt was muttering darkly that the crowd was acting very much in favor of the former Scottish railway fireman. What, indeed, did he expect? Bolt's irascible reputation had preceded him, and the crowd became more and more enthusiastic for Brown.

When Brown finally closed out Bolt by 4 and 3, the angry American swiped Brown's ball clean off the green as his way of conceding the hole and the match. Bolt admitted that the Scot had beaten him but that he had not enjoyed a single minute of the round because the crowd had behaved so badly toward him.

Brown told me later that he had heard U.S. teammates Ed Furgol and Doug Ford chewing out Bolt for his behavior. In addition, Bolt smashed a club, which was really not unusual behavior for him, but then he refused to attend the closing ceremonies and presentation of the cup.

No doubt Brown's success against Bolt served as inspiration to the rest of the British team. The crowd on hand also helped by scampering all over the course to catch glimpses of the tight matches between Mills and Burke, Bousfield and Lionel Hebert, Rees and Furgol, Hunt and Ford, O'Connor and Dow Finsterwald, Alliss and Hawkins, and Bradshaw and Mayer.

I can see and hear the scene as if it happened yesterday. Just as Seve Ballesteros was unnerved by the charge to victory of Jack Nicklaus in the 1986 Masters, so the remaining Americans became unhinged as a succession of ear-splitting roars came drifting over the course like clouds of poison gas. The Americans folded like a house of cards.

Rees was determined to put his man away as quickly as possible after lunch so that he could get out into the field and cheer on his team. He disposed of Furgol by 7 and 6, by which time Brown had crushed Bolt and Mills had overcome Burke by 5 and 3. Although Alliss lost to Hawkins by 2 and 1, Hunt polished off Ford by 6 and 5 and O'Connor won six of the first eight afternoon holes to see off Finsterwald by 7 and 6.

Only one point was now needed for the momentous British and Irish victory they craved so fervently after so many years of suffering, food rationing, and failures on the golf course.

While 7-up on Hebert, British hope Bousfield lost three holes consecutively, and a collapse appeared imminent when momentum swung back to the Americans. Rees and Faulkner came charging through the undergrowth as Bousfield halved the 15th hole to win by 4 and 3. Rees and Falkner told their bemused teammate that he had won the vital point. By then, it mattered not at all that Bradshaw had only halved with Mayer. The home team had finally accomplished the impossible—taking the singles by 6½ points to 1½ and winning back the Ryder Cup 7½ to 4½. As a British subject, a golfer, and a journalist, I enjoyed my first-ever Ryder Cup victory.

What struck me as so pathetic about the Ryder Cup at that time was that when the matches were played in Britain, the Americans were only interested in coming over here with their wives so they could buy up all the cashmere. I hope they had good shopping that year, because there was plenty of room for packages on the plane with no Ryder Cup to take up valuable space.

If anyone remotely close to the game thought for a minute that Great Britain and Ireland's momentous victory at Lindrick would prove a lasting inspiration to the perennial underdogs, they were quickly disillusioned at the 1959 contest at Eldorado Country Club. The first bad omen for the British reared its ugly head when, on the short hop from Los Angeles to Palm Springs, the visiting party was tossed all over the sky in its charter plane as it flew into a violent storm over the San Jacinto mountains.

My late colleague and good friend Ron Heager of the *Daily Express,* London, longtime golf writer for that paper, was to make the front page with his story of that terrifying flight—the first time ever the Ryder Cup had achieved this distinction. The plane eventually landed safely back in Los Angeles, which prompted John Letters, the golf club manufacturer from Scotland who was one of the party, to form the "Long Drop Club." The club included the 29-strong party that had survived. It was thus named because at one stage the plane had dropped like a stone from 13,000 feet to 9,000 feet in a matter of seconds. The club had an annual reunion for many years to celebrate the members' good fortune. Dai Rees, the British and Irish captain, insisted that the party would then make the trip by Greyhound bus, and no one argued with that decision.

The Americans, captained by Sam Snead, were thirsting for revenge. Julius Boros returned, having missed the 1957 match with a broken leg. But U.S. Open champion Billy Casper, Arnold Palmer, Ken Venturi, and Gene Littler all missed the match because they were still serving their probationary period before becoming full members of the PGA.

Peter Alliss, alongside Christy O'Connor, recorded the only U.K. foursome victory by 3 and 2 over Art Wall and Doug Ford. The United States team, employing the likes of Jay Hebert, Lionel's brother, Snead, and Middlecoff, won back the Ryder Cup by an 8½ to 3½ margin. It was the last time the British and Irish arrived in America by sea.

The 1961 match, played at Royal Lytham and St. Anne's, called for eight 18-hole foursome matches on the first day, and eight 18-hole singles on the second. A shocking development involved the disqualification of Sam Snead because he had played in an unsanctioned pro-am in Cincinnati that clashed with the Portland Open. Although Snead's six-month suspension for this PGA rules breach was commuted on appeal to 45 days, Snead was never again to play in the series. In seven singles matches, he had been beaten only once: by Weetman in 1953. Doug Ford, Snead's last-minute replacement, was exactly the same size and thus able to wear Snead's uniform issue.

The British, playing at home, virtually lost the match on the first day when the Americans took the foursomes by 6-2. The singles matches offered no heroics by the British, and the Americans won handily 14½ to 9½.

A third day of play involving eight fourball matches was introduced into the matches at East Lake Country Club in Atlanta in 1963. Rees was replaced as British playing captain by John Fallon, who actually captained from the sidelines. It had become abundantly clear when the series had reverted to 18-hole play that the days of a playing captain were numbered.

Although Neil Coles traveled to the States by sea because of his aversion to flying, the rest of the challengers flew across the pond in coach. Playing captain Arnold Palmer had at his command too strong a team to be denied, although there were four newcomers on board: Tony Lema, Billy Maxwell, Johnny Pott, and Dave Ragan. Brian Huggett, George Will, and Geoffrey Hunt, the younger Hunt brother, all made their debuts for the visitors.

Great Britain and Ireland surprised themselves by sharing the morning foursomes 2-2, but were whitewashed in the afternoon. Although the visitors took the morning singles by 4½ to 3½, they had already lost the fourballs by 6-2, and it was never remotely possible to make up a 12-4 deficit on the final day.

As it turned out, only Alliss halved with Lema in the afternoon singles, with the Americans winning the remaining seven for a resounding 23-9 victory.

The golf result in Atlanta had led me to fear that the series was once again fast becoming a farce. It had been a most ridiculous decision by the British PGA to agree to play two series of fourballs, a game at which the Americans have always excelled. But such pathetic underdogs could hardly argue, even if the move to a third day merely increased the margin of defeat. The Ryder Cup match in this, its present form, appeared to be living on borrowed time unless we either recruited the rest of the Commonwealth, the world, or, God forbid, the rest of Europe!

The 1965 match, played at Royal Birkdale, ended in a bitterly frustrating defeat for the British and Irish by 19½ to 12½. In those days, Birkdale was famous for its finish of *four* par-fives in the last six holes, most often out of range in two shots. Consequently, the magnificently skilled wedge play of the Americans came very much into focus in the closing stages of every match that reached this point, and British players Dave Thomas, George Will, Peter Butler, and Lionel Platts all saw leads slip away there.

The United States, which then dominated the singles, completed their 13th victory by 19½ to 12½.

The 1967 match was played at Champions Club in Houston, with Ben Hogan selected to captain a team that contained Arnold Palmer, Hogan's undisputed successor as the king of American golf.

Hogan quickly made it clear who the boss was when the two met in the locker room before the first practice round. Shortly before, Hogan had surprisingly declared that the Americans would use the British 1.62-inch diameter ball instead of the more familiar American 1.68-inch variety. According to someone who was there, the exchange between Palmer and Hogan went like this:

Palmer: "Say, Ben, is that right, we're going to play the small ball?"

Hogan: "That's what I said."

Palmer: "Well, supposing I haven't got any small balls?"

Hogan: "Who said you will be playing, anyway, Palmer? And by the way, are you sure you've brought your clubs, or would you like to borrow those as well?"

Palmer may have been "The King," but Hogan still reigned supreme over all he surveyed. Even off the golf course.

Reportedly, at the dinner for the teams before the match, British and Irish captain Dai Rees stood and introduced each of his players, detailing their accomplishments. When Hogan took his turn, he asked the attendees to hold their applause until the end and introduced each of his players by name only. He then stated, "Ladies and gentlemen, the United States Ryder Cup team. The finest golfers in the world."

If the Americans didn't have a psychological advantage already, Hogan, by undercutting Rees, gave them one at that moment.

Thomas and newcomer Tony Jacklin were the challengers' only winners in foursomes, beating Doug Sanders and Gay Brewer by 4 and 3 in the morning, and Gene Littler and Al Geiberger by 3 and 2 after lunch.

In the following day's fourballs, the same duo won the visitors' only ½ point, again against Littler and Geiberger. The Americans took the other 7½.

The singles were a mere formality. No wonder the three major television networks refused to touch the match with a barge pole. If it achieved one thing, it forced the underdogs to give the American ball a three-year trial, despite all the squealing of the British ball manufacturers, who enjoyed a worldwide monopoly turning out millions of the smaller pellet, which is hardly seen anymore.

The historic match at Royal Birkdale in 1969 was remarkable for many more reasons than the well-documented generous gesture by Jack Nicklaus.

I was present during the overheated match between Americans Dave Hill and Ken Still and opponents Brian Huggett and Bernard Gallacher—four volatile characters—on the second afternoon when the two sides almost literally came to blows. Certainly, the shouted insults and fists shaken at each other across the eighth fairway were as close to fighting as I have ever seen on a golf course. It was a disgusting business that incensed the partisan crowd. The uneasy intensity boiled and bubbled, replete with dirty looks, glares, and cold stares from each of the opponents. In retrospect, I believe that Still was mostly to blame.

On the first green, Hill was asked to stand still while Huggett was trying to putt. Then Still was asked to move because he was basically breathing down Huggett's neck.

Never one to back off, the little Welshman told Still, "I want you behind me from now on."

At the second hole, Gallacher had completed his preparation and was about to putt when Still told his caddie not to hold the flagstick because it was "Bernard's caddie's job to be doing that."

I continued to shadow this group with great intrigue. These were the most volatile players in the game and more fireworks were sure to occur.

At the par-three 7th, Gallacher putted up three feet from the hole. Still followed slightly closer to the hole on the same line, and then holed out. The British pair protested and demanded that Still's ball be remarked until after Gallacher had putted. David Melville, a British professional refereeing the match, was still delving in his rule book when Still snatched up Gallacher's marker from the green and yelled, "You can have the hole and the goddamned Cup!"

The unseemly argument raged down the eighth hole until captains Eric Brown and Sam Snead arrived with Lord Derby and demanded a cooling-off all around. Still promptly fell to pieces, but Hill became inspired, and carried his partner to victory by 2 and 1.

The foursomes and fourballs were closely contested, and with 16 singles left to play, the teams were tied at 8-8. When the home side took the morning singles by 5-3, the excitement became even more intense.

In the afternoon, Gallacher beat Lee Trevino by 4 and 3 and Butler closed out Dale Douglass by 3 and 2. The Americans were really up against it. Hill, however, beat Brian Barnes by 4 and 2, Miller Barber demolished Maurice Bembridge by 7 and 6, Dan Sikes beat Neil Coles by 4 and 3, and Littler squeezed through by 2 and 1 over O'Connor. The four points for the Cup-holders squared the match, with two pairs still fighting it out on the course.

I vividly remember that when Huggett came to the last hole all square against Billy Casper, he was of the opinion—albeit mistaken— that behind him Jacklin was 1-up on Nicklaus. In actual fact, Nicklaus had taken a one-hole lead on our new hero—the newly crowned British Open champion—by taking the 16th.

Huggett was over a three-foot putt for a half with Casper when a huge roar rent the heavens above the 17th green. Jacklin had squared his match with an eagle three. Huggett, however, wrongly imagined that Jacklin had won his match and that his putt for a half would now ensure victory for his team. When the putt went in Huggett broke down completely, weeping openly in the arms of captain Brown.

By the time Huggett found out the true situation, Nicklaus and Jacklin were marching down the 18th fairway, knowing that the fate of the match lay in their trembling hands as they tried to control the emotion that swelled with the responsibility of representing their countries.

From the back of the green, Jacklin putted up to about 2½ feet. Nicklaus, going for the win, characteristically putted three feet past the cup. Having the honor, Nicklaus then holed his return.

A 30-inch putt was now all that stood between Jacklin and a half with the Americans. He was a man alone under incredible pressure. However, before Jacklin could get over a putt that I was convinced he was going to miss, Nicklaus calmly picked up the Englishman's marker and warmly shook his hand.

"I am sure you would have made your putt," Nicklaus told Jacklin, "but I was not prepared to see you miss."

The world seemed to stand still as the suspense turned to confusion, and then, finally, to a warm realization of what had just happened.

The gesture, granting Jacklin the half and ensuring that, for once, Great Britain and Ireland would escape defeat, was incredible. Nicklaus did not think that such an epic three-day struggle should have to depend on a single putt of that tantalizing length. The Americans retained the cup and Nicklaus spared Jacklin from any chance of suffering what surely would have been a shattering and unbearable miss. The exciting clash ended in a 16-16 tie, and Nicklaus's concession of that putt to Jacklin was the single most sporting gesture of my experience. That is what the Ryder Cup should be all about, and the spirit that attracted Samuel Ryder in the first place.

Alas, the Americans won by five points in 1971 at Old Warson, St. Louis; by six at Muirfield, Scotland in 1973; by ten at Laurel Valley, Pennsylvania in 1975; and by five at Royal Lytham in 1977. It was the 1973 match in which I had seen the other side of Nicklaus's gamesmanship ability. Drawn against England's Clive Clark and Ulsterman Eddie Polland in the second afternoon fourball, Nicklaus and playing partner Tom Weiskopf were heavy favorites to beat Clark and Polland.

Barbara Nicklaus, eight months pregnant, had followed Jack for 18 holes in the morning, and was in doubt as to whether she could make it all the way in the afternoon.

"Don't worry, Barbara," Jack said loudly, and easily in earshot of the Brits, "it won't be a long walk."

I watched both British players drop their heads.

On the first hole, Nicklaus and playing partner Weiskopf both hit the green in two shots. Weiskopf's ball was only ten feet from the hole, while Nicklaus' shot finished twice as far away. As Nicklaus examined the putts, he walked past his partner.

"Pick up your ball, Tom," he said matter-of-factly.

"What the hell are you talking about?" asked Weiskopf.

"I said, 'pick up your ball, Tom.'"

A puzzled Weiskopf picked up his ball, whereupon Nicklaus rammed in his putt to make birdie and win the hole. Talk about supernatural powers! Nicklaus not only psyched out his opponents, but also bewildered and intimidated his own teammate and partner, who was already in the midst of a career in Nicklaus's shadow that would keep him forever behind the "Golden Bear."

American bravado was apparently in full bloom in 1973. Lee Trevino, feeling like a world-beater at Muirfield—where he'd won the Open Championship in 1972—made a bold and randy pronouncement:

"If I cannot beat Oosterhuis in the morning singles, I will..." Trevino began, pledging to orally please each of his American teammates.

Much to Trevino's surprise and horror, he could manage only a halve with Oosterhuis, and his American teammates were all too ready to make the "Super Mex" "put his money where his mouth was." At a gleeful American team victory reception that evening, Palmer, Tommy Aaron, Dave Hill, Billy Casper, Lou Graham, J.C. Snead, and Nicklaus playfully needled Trevino by dropping their trousers in mock expectation of the spoils of victory and the humbling of Trevino. I have a photograph as proof, though Jack told me he'd kill me if it ever got out—and quite frankly I believe him.

Two years later, in the 1975 match at Laurel Valley Golf Club in Ligonier, Pennsylvania, Nicklaus suffered an embarrassing experience ... actually, two in one day! As the Americans were on their way to a 21-11 victory over Britain and Ireland, I walked along and watched the mighty Jack Nicklaus lose both of his final-day singles matches to Brian Barnes. I'm a very close friend of Barnes, so I followed him the whole time. It was damned exciting, I must say, for a team that was so starved for success to have "Barnesie" make two of the teams 11 points by beating the greatest golfer in the world—not once, but twice! Barnes somehow managed to handle the pressure and stare down "the Bear."

During the afternoon round, I suddenly realized that Barnes had been smoking a pipe since the beginning of the day. Oddly, though, I also realized that I hadn't seen any smoke come out of it. "What's wrong with your pipe?" I finally asked him as we walked down a fairway. "Are you having trouble keeping it lit?"

Barnes took the pipe out of his mouth and showed me that there wasn't even any tobacco in it. "This pipe, Ben," he explained, "is just to keep my bloody teeth from chattering!"

Nicklaus's gesture to Jacklin in 1969 was heroic, and the way he handled the double defeat in 1975 was admirable. Both examples of his sportsmanship paled into insignificance, however, alongside his approach to Lord Derby, president of the British PGA, after Great Britain and Ireland's defeat at Royal Lytham in 1977. Nicklaus bluntly told Lord Derby that the matches could not continue in their present form or they would surely die an obscure death. Without international television coverage and the genuine interest of other media, golf fans would consider the event—if they bothered to take notice at all—as an insignificant exhibition. After all, when the old Hughes Network attempted to air a live two-hour broadcast of the final day's singles matches at Old Warson in 1971, the competition was so one-sided that the Ryder Cup result had already been determined before the American network had even gone on the air! The U.S. eventually won 18½ to 13½. There was still golf to show as the matches were played out, but they were meaningless. It was a long period for the

Hughes Network to try to keep interesting, and I was summoned to their broadcast booth to assist with an interview.

Nicklaus's point was well-illustrated by the Hughes Network, which was left with egg on its face. The media—and the general public for that matter—could not possibly be interested in rout after rout. The years of tradition and heritage of the event were beginning to fade from awareness, and interest waned.

Later, Nicklaus backed up his frank, realistic words with a letter to Lord Derby in which he emphasized that the selection procedures would have to be widened to include players from continental Europe if the Ryder Cup were to continue to enjoy its past prestige.

Ken Schofield, executive director of the PGA European Tour, was promptly summoned to Knowsley Hall, Lord Derby's estate in Lancashire. He was told that Brian Huggett, the 1977 captain, and Peter Butler, a member of the Ryder Cup committee, were to help him complete the negotiations to bring about this radical change of format. Sure enough, only weeks later, Don Padgett, then president of the American PGA, announced that at the 1979 match venue— The Greenbrier in West Virginia—the challenging team would subsequently be known as just plain old "Europe."

In a sense, it was Nicklaus's words of wisdom that again saved the matches and made them the major sporting event they have become today.

The debut of the first European team in Ryder Cup history at The Greenbrier resort was anything but a happy one. The two Spaniards brought in to bolster the British and Irish—Antonio Garrido and the swashbuckling savior Seve Ballesteros—had the misfortune thrice to meet arguably as good a combination as America had ever fielded: the fiery, self-confident Lanny Wadkins and the modest, self-effacing Larry Nelson, who proved unbeatable. In fourballs they beat Ballesteros and Garrido by 2 and 1, and by 5 and 4, and in foursomes by 3 and 2. For good measure, they took out a tried and tested Scottish combination in Bernard Gallacher and big Brian Barnes in their other foursome by 4 and 3. Gallacher gained a measure of revenge by beating Wadkins by 3 and 2 in the top singles match, but Nelson ground down poor Seve by 3 and 2 to complete his extraordinarily triumphant debut and subject the Spaniard to an utterly humiliating one.

Incidentally, Nelson was one of no less than eight newcomers to the American team. The others were Andy Bean, Lee Elder (the first black golfer ever to play in the series), Tom Kite, John Mahaffey, Dr. Gil Morgan, Fuzzy Zoeller, and Mark Hayes, who was a last minute substitute for Tom Watson, who left for home and the imminent birth to wife Linda of their first child, Meg.

Because John Jacobs, my co-commentator on British commercial television, had been so instrumental in establishing the European Tour, he was awarded the honor of captaining the first European team. Some honor, as the young British pair Ken Brown and Mark James behaved so badly throughout the trip that, two months after returning home, Brown was fined 1,000 pounds sterling and suspended from international team golf for a year. James was not suspended, but he was fined 1,500 pounds.

As a professional observer of the event, I am convinced to this day that this pair cost Europe a real chance of victory and, despite their subsequently much improved behavior, should have been banned from this series forever—an opinion shared by several of the American players I consulted.

James, who withdrew with a quite genuine chest injury after he and Brown had lost their first morning fourball, did not play again. Brown, who had the temerity publicly to declare that he wished only to partner his friend James, treated his afternoon partner, Irish Cup debutant Des Smyth, with complete contempt and disdain—not once even talking to Smyth. Brown then won his only other match, beating Zoeller by one hole in the singles, adding further insult to injury.

Captain Jacobs first smelled a rat when James arrived at London's Heathrow Airport looking like an unmade bed instead of being dressed in the obligatory uniform designated by the PGA rules. Both he and Brown failed to show up at mandatory team meetings, and at the opening ceremony and flag raising the ridiculous pair wore their uniforms with garish socks, repeatedly crossing and uncrossing their legs.

But it was Brown's senseless treatment of Smyth that incensed members of both teams. Hale Irwin, who partnered Kite to the easiest of victories by 7 and 6 over the recalcitrant Brown and the bewildered Smyth, told me at the time, "I was sorry for poor Des, but Tom and I were quite determined his partner wouldn't get away with such sickening behavior."

Poor Jacobs had to make apologies all around, to Smyth, to Irwin and Kite, and to the American captain Billy Casper.

There was yet another format change at the 1979 match. Instead of the 1977 pattern of five foursomes the first day, five fourballs the second, and 10 singles the third, at The Greenbrier, four foursomes and four fourballs were played morning and afternoon the first two days, and then 12 singles on the third day—six in the morning and six after lunch—involving every member of both teams. Because of this, there had to be some clause inserted in the rules to allow a match not to be played in the event of illness or injury to a member of either team.

It was agreed at a press conference that the team captains would exchange sealed envelopes at the end of the second day including the name of the player each would drop if the opposing team was reduced to 11 men. Jacobs obviously nominated the injured James. But to the European captain's astonishment he was approached by the American PGA official later that evening asking that Casper be allowed to change his nomination because he had misunderstood the procedure. Instead of nominating his weakest player, Morgan, whose ailing shoulder was later to require serious rotator cuff surgery, Casper had named his strongest: Lee Trevino.

To his great credit, Jacobs told his team he did not want to risk winning the match in such a manner, so the Morgan versus James match was never played and declared halved. Trevino eventually beat Sandy Lyle, another Cup rookie, by 2 and 1. Although only one point had separated the teams going into the singles, the Americans leading by 8½ to 7½, the home side won 8 of 11 for a convincing victory by 17 points to 11. It was an inauspicious start for the new Europe, but the worst was to come in two years.

The Greenbrier was a terribly expensive resort. When I went to the desk to check out, I came across ABC announcer Jim McKay and his wife having trouble with his checkout. It seemed that McKay was contesting a charge on his bill. Although McKay had generously waived his usual fee to emcee the "Meet the Players" dinner, he was charged for two dinners for him and his wife when he checked out. He was having a row with the desk attendant when I arrived with my leg in a plaster cast, broken in a moped spill in Bermuda. That was when I learned that the hotel had applied a charge for $150 on my bill for "sporting activities."

"Wait a minute," I protested. "How the hell do you expect that I engaged in sporting activities when I've got my leg in a cast?"

I refused to pay my bill, and phoned the *Financial Times* to alert them of the bogus and unreasonable charge since I was at the Greenbrier under their aegis. It was not for two years that the dispute was finally resolved and the hotel removed the charge. I hope McKay was spared that kind of wrangling.

At Walton Heath in September 1981, in miserably wet and cold weather, I watched the strongest team America had ever fielded, captained by Dave Marr, inflict on the challengers the most devastating defeat ever on British soil: 18½ points to 9½. Masters champion Tom Watson, British Open winner Bill Rogers and PGA Champion Larry Nelson, who bumped Howard Twitty off the team with his PGA victory a month before the team flew to England, had a supporting cast that had between them won 36 major titles. Only Ben Crenshaw, Kite, and Bruce Lietzke had yet to win a major.

By stark contrast the European team took the field without Ballesteros and Tony Jacklin, arguably Europe's preeminent players of the era. Ballesteros was dropped because he was still feuding with the European PGA over the vexing subject of appearance money, and had even refused to pay his dues to the association. The three selectors—captain Jacobs, chairman Neil Coles, and Cup newcomer Bernard Langer, leader of the Order of Merit—chose to omit Ballesteros, preferring Canadian Open champion Peter Oosterhuis for the first of two special places. This left the 12th place between James, 11th on the money list, and Jacklin, who had played indifferently all season. When James was chosen unanimously, Jacklin was both hurt and insulted, particularly in view of James's behavior at the 1979 match.

So, in addition to West Germany's Langer, the European team contained three more newcomers: Spain's José-María Canizares and rock-solid Manuel Piñero, and Scotland's Sam Torrance.

When the Europeans took the honors at the end of the first day by 4½ points to 3½ points, James, Lyle, and Smyth were the heroes. James and Lyle won their two matches as a team. Smyth won both his matches, partnered with Gallacher in the morning and Canizares after lunch.

But, as ever, the Americans were most dangerous when threatened. Of the 20 points at stake over the next two days, they took no less than 14. Not surprisingly, it was the extraordinary Nelson who almost single-handedly ripped the hearts out of the Europeans. The Americans took the second morning fourballs by 3 points to 1, but it was Nelson's finish in the second match that did all of the psychological damage.

Lyle and James appeared to have their match under control when the former put his tee shot stone dead at the par-three 17th hole, making it all square against Nelson and Kite. But Nelson made a huge putt for a two to halve the hole, and another monster on the 18th green for a winning birdie three.

In the dreadful weather of the afternoon, the Americans were so brilliant in making a clean sweep of the foursomes that only Trevino and Jerry Pate were taken as far as the 17th hole—yet not one European pair was over par. The day's end tally of 10½ to 5½ gave Europe scant hope in the 12 singles, when Trevino scampered around the following morning in two hours and ten minutes, trampling all over Torrance by 5 and 3. Jack Nicklaus and Eamonn Darcy had not even teed off in the final match.

It was wholly appropriate that Nelson should gain the vital point for the Americans with a victory over James by two holes. Nicklaus ended his Cup playing career with a victory over Darcy by 5 and 3.

In 1983, Europe served notice that the balance of power between the two continents was about to change. The all-exempt U.S. Tour and ever-escalating purses were to breed a fatal complacency among the traditionally dominant Americans.

At the PGA National Golf Club in Palm Beach Gardens, Florida, the two teams contrived a finish almost as thrilling as it had been 14 years earlier when Nicklaus and Jacklin had come down the 18th fairway all square in the final singles match. This time the same pair was scampering all over the place as respective nonplaying captains, with a splendid sense of irony.

Eventually, everything depended on the last two singles matches. With the score tied at 13-13, Canizares came to the 578-yard 18th hole—water lurking insidiously down the right—one up on Lanny Wadkins. At the same time, Gallacher approached the tee at the par-three 17th, now only one down to Tom Watson and with the honor. The approach of lightning, flashing in the sky like camera bulbs, made the scene all the more dramatic. If today's modern lightning detection equipment had been employed at that time, I'm certain that play would have been halted to ensure the safety of the participants and the gallery.

Oblivious to the danger from above, both Canizares and Wadkins went about their business of laying up on their second shots, each leaving themselves with a third of around 100 yards over a guardian bunker in front of the green. With Ballesteros urging on his countryman, poor Canizares came up inches short under the lip of the bunker. Characteristically, Wadkins pounced swiftly and decisively, almost pitching it in for the win and a half point, making it 13½ to 13½. Wadkins's shot, which stopped stone-cold next to the hole, was akin to the plunging of a sword into the stone heart of the Europeans. Later, members of Wadkins's American team would present him with a wheelbarrow that held two big balls, symbolic of his fortitude and courage.

Gallacher had not been at his best all week, gaining only one game on the first morning. He and Lyle had quickly lost their foursome to Watson and Crenshaw by 5 and 4, and he had asked to be dropped. But Gallacher had always been a formidable competitor. Here in the singles, at the 17th, he now thought he had hit a perfect 191-yard 3-iron. But with the adrenaline rushing through his system, he was betrayed into hitting the ball over the green into a poor lie. Watson missed the green to the right. Although the pressures on both were tremendous, there followed the most sorry anticlimax: Gallacher's delicate chip did not even reach the green, whereupon Watson promptly flubbed his, too. But he at least then got his next close enough to be certain of a bogey, while Gallacher left himself an awkward four-footer for a half—and missed. Watson won by 2 and 1, and America won by 14½ to 13½.

Jacklin's disappointment was monumental, as was that of his team members. Even Nicklaus admitted, "It should have been another tie." But what was naturally overlooked in the awful agony of the moment was that, in Jacklin, the Europeans had found the best captain to have ever led either side in the entire series.

Having watched matches only since 1953, I realize that I have no right to express such a sweeping opinion. But hindsight is definitely 20/20. Jacobs was almost shy, unless it came to golf instruction, of which he was a master. John never stamped his authority as a captain. He was a tough guy, as he proved as a player in the 1955 matches by winning both foursome and singles points. Jacobs was also the first Tournament Director-General of the European Tour, from 1971 to 1974. As a team leader, though, he had little presence. He was, after all, a quiet-spoken Yorkshireman.

Tony Jacklin was asked to succeed Jacobs as captain by Ken Schofield, who was Jacobs's successor as executive director of the European Tour. The proposal to Jacklin occurred the previous May on the practice putting green at Sandmoor Golf Club, Leeds, Yorkshire, England. Jacklin, who was playing in the Car Care Tournament, demanded but one condition—that his team should travel to America in the front—in first class—instead of in the back of the plane. Better than that, he and his men actually flew on the Concorde, and for the first time were accompanied by their own caddies, all expenses paid.

"Too many times in the past the Cup had been run, it seemed, more for the officials than for the players," said Jacklin. "Priorities had been in the wrong place, and if I was to be captain, it would be run and organized with the players in mind." Jacklin was determined to do away with the built-in inferiority complex that he felt hampered Europe's chances to win against the Americans.

Jacklin did everything right from the outset. Firstly and very importantly, he persuaded Ballesteros to play in the match, a task made only fractionally easier because both had been summarily rejected in 1983. Jacklin came to Florida with his pairings already mostly settled. He paired Ballesteros with Paul Way, a Cup rookie at the tender age of 20. Ballesteros was apparently far from happy after the pair lost their morning foursome by 2 and 1 to Kite and Calvin Peete, the latter one of the newcomers to the American team, which incredibly did not contain Nelson, the U.S. Open champion, because he had not accumulated sufficient points. Seve told Jacklin that he felt "like a father to Way and was holding his hand." Jacklin insisted that this was the very idea of the pairing in the first place. Ballesteros immediately accepted his captain's evaluation of the situation, and he and Way promptly won twice and halved one match thereafter.

Team spirit reached an all-time high because Jacklin and his late wife Vivienne entertained his players and their wives and girlfriends in his own hugely impressive suite at the hotel right on the edge of the golf course. The suite was always open to them and was the venue for team dinners. In addition, Jacklin ordered specially made absorbent shirts to battle the awful humidity and extra shoes to combat much casual water. The die had been cast for the momentous victories that were to come under Jacklin's inspired captaincy. Easily the most important aspect of Jacklin's leadership was to persuade the British, Irish, and Europeans to meld as one unit, truly submerging their nationalistic instincts, which had appeared to be so divisive in the debacles of 1979 and 1981.

The finest moment of Jacklin's dreams became reality with the Europeans' victory at The Belfry, Sutton Coldfield, England in 1985. After 27 years of futility, the Ryder Cup was finally out of the hands of the Americans.

I must comment that The Belfry is simply an awful golf course, and it was only money that brought this historic series to such an unsuitably undignified venue. When Dave Hill compared Hazeltine National to a "cow pasture" at the 1970 U.S. Open, it was only because he had yet to lay eyes on The Belfry.

Nonetheless, it was an emotional victory. Coming down the stretch, Scotsman Sam Torrance was three down after 10 holes in his singles match to Andy North. Andy, however, was plainly unnerved by the occasion and the hooting and cheering of the admittedly overly partisan crowd. Torrance, therefore, was able to level the match after the 17th.

On the 18th, Torrance hit a huge drive and North's collapse became complete when he popped up his tee shot into the lake. Torrance's birdie was superfluous, since North took four shots to reach the green. But the Scotsman, tears pouring down his face into his fulsome black moustache, raised his arms in triumph as he was engulfed by Jacklin and several of his teammates under a thunderous ovation. Sam had just clinched Europe's fourth win in 58 years. The Concorde was soon to sweep noisily over the course twice, dipping its wings in salute. There was scarcely a dry eye at The Belfry, and few dry or empty glasses there for many hours into the night.

The final score was 16½ to 11½. Jacklin's personal victory over his opposing captain Lee Trevino did much to assuage the numbing wound he had suffered when Trevino had "stolen" the British Open from him 13 years earlier at Muirfield, Scotland.

Perhaps Jacklin's smartest ploy in his entire four-match captaincy— he bequeathed the position to Gallacher after the 1989 match—

was perpetrated after the moving flag-raising ceremony at Muirfield Village in 1987. Jacklin invited Schofield, executive director of the European PGA Tour, and three of his chief tournament administrators—Tony Gray, George O'Grady, and John Paramor—for drinks at the team's headquarters alongside the 18th fairway. What purported to be a pleasant cocktail hour was anything but, as one by one the players stridently voiced their complaints about their inferior working conditions on the European Tour.

Since Muirfield Village was in the kind of condition more easily associated with Augusta National, with facilities for the players to match, Jacklin's ploy was obviously perfectly timed. It took his players' minds off the Herculean task ahead, but at the same time got them fired up to face it.

The Europeans needed but four singles matches on Sunday to retain the trophy and record their first victory on American soil. It sounded simple, but it was no easy trick.

At the top of the order, Woosnam was beaten at the final hole by Bean, who had three 2s on his card. Howard Clark beat Pohl by the same margin in the second match, and then Torrance halved with Mize. At this stage, with all of the remaining matches having turned for home, the Americans led in six.

Ballesteros appeared to be in control of his match with Strange, and Ireland's Eammonn Darcy was 3-up at the turn against Crenshaw, who had broken his putter in anger after leaving the sixth green and was putting with his one iron or sand wedge—an embarrassing predicament. "Gentle" Ben somehow fought his way back, however, and even took the lead with a par three at the 16th. Suddenly, the hopes of Europe were centered on the gangling Irishman with his eccentric swing, who was still in search of his first Ryder Cup point after 10 attempts.

Faldo had lost to Calcavecchia, Olazabal lost to Stewart, José Rivero to Scott Simpson, and Langer had only halved with Neslon, who still had the fire in his belly for competition. To his everlasting credit, Darcy struck a wonderful 6-iron for a winning birdie at the 17th to square the match. Crenshaw hooked his tee shot into the creek at the 18th, and was bunkered in three, but somehow scrambled to a five. Darcy was also in the sand in two shots, and his recovery came to rest almost five feet above the hole.

The Irishman's putt for victory was difficult enough to be almost unwatchable for the 3,000 European supporters present. He somehow made it, and although Ballesteros actually made the match-winning point, it was almost anticlimactic since the unlikely hero Darcy had ensured that the precious trophy would return to the Belfry until 1989. Certainly it was a sweet victory again for Jacklin, who led his team to a win over a team captained by Nicklaus and literally at Nicklaus's home club—which he designed and created—in Dublin, Ohio.

America was finally beginning to pay attention, though, and it showed in some of the naïveté of the U.S. fans when it came to the nature of match play. I arrived at the 18th green in late morning on the first day's play, and to my bewilderment, found a large number of spectators assembling there to view the golf.

"What are you waiting around here for?" I asked one of the gallery members.

"For the first match to arrive any time now," he told me.

I tried to explain that in a match play format, there was no real guarantee that any of the four matches would even reach the 18th hole. The crowd gathered anyway, and only one of the matches that day reached Muirfield Village's 18th green. The golf along the way, however, was excellent.

The 1987 match had finally attracted the attention of one of the three major American television networks. ABC covered the event live, albeit sketchily.

Although the rest of the world found the 1989 match fascinating in prospect—again at the former potato field, The Belfry—it was left to the USA Network to broadcast it live to the United States for the first time. Alas, my fellow announcers and the viewers at home were condemned to take the BBC's pictures, which were almost laughably inadequate. But the event attracted 380 writers (over 50 from America), 170 photographers, and more than 500 television technicians and broadcasters. The worldwide television audience on the final day was estimated at 200 million people.

I lost count of the telephone calls and letters I received after the broadcasts that Gary McCord and I and our USA Network team sent back live, for the first time ever, from rural England. Nary a one of them was negative in any way—rather gushingly the reverse. This appreciation came as a complete surprise, so distraught were McCord and I about the abysmal pictorial coverage of the play supplied to us by the BBC. Having worked for that state-owned corporation in the 1960s, when I served part of my apprenticeship alongside the late, great Henry Longhurst, it almost made me weep to witness the depths to which the BBC camera coverage had plunged. In addition to failing to follow the ball in a very favorable sky, the BBC hardly ever managed to relate it—when they did find it—to either tee or green. There it was, just a lonely golf ball sitting forlornly on a screen full of grass.

On this occasion, because Payne Stewart, the PGA Champion, had already qualified on points, captain Raymond Floyd chose Tom Watson and Wadkins to make up the team he would take to The Belfry, needing their experience because his team included five newcomers: Paul Azinger, Chip Beck, Fred Couples, Ken Green, and Mark McCumber.

Because Sandy Lyle had completely lost form, he had asked Jacklin to omit him from consideration, let alone selection—a brave but incredibly sad decision for a man who had won the British Open in 1985 and the Masters in 1988. Subsequently, the European captain nominated Langer, again apparently cured of "the yips," Howard Clark, and Christy O'Connor Jr. The only newcomer was Ulsterman Ronan Rafferty, leader of the European Order of Merit.

With Europe leading 9-7 after the first two days of engagement, the singles war would tell the story.

What a battle it was! Kite drew first blood for the challengers when he went out in 31 and recorded a record victory over Clark by 8 and 7.

Azinger came to the 18th 1-up on Ballesteros in a spirited match and drove into the lake, but he got up and down from a greenside bunker for the bravest of fives. Ballesteros, who had hit his second shot into the water, couldn't beat bogey and lost. Beck played superbly to beat Langer by 3 and 1.

Suddenly the Europeans had their backs to the wall, leading in only one match: Mark James against Mark O'Meara.

The first European point arrived when Olazabal squared his match at the 17th with a birdie. Stewart then drove his tee shot at the 18th into the lake to lose it.

Calcavecchia quickly followed suit against Rafferty, compounding the felony by hitting his third into the lake for bad measure.

James then took out O'Meara on the 16th green by 3 and 2, and surprisingly it was the journeyman O'Connor who was the next hero.

All square against the far longer hitting Couples, O'Connor struck the stroke of his life, a glorious 2-iron second shot that pulled up four feet from the 18th hole. Couples was so unnerved that he missed the green with his 9 iron, and took a woeful bogey five to lose.

Canizares—at 42 the old man of the European squad—made sure the cup was retained with a superb lag putt from the back of the 18th green for his par. Ken Green three-putted from the front of the green to lose a great match, both men 'round in 68.

Thankfully, golf was the only winner of this quite magnificent contest. McCumber, Watson, Wadkins, and finally Strange—who birdied the 18th to win his match and secure the tie—all won their matches to level the scores at Europe 14, United States 14.

The tie was, in my mind, the perfect sporting occasion. I showed up at The Belfry the following morning after staying out at various parties that lasted through the night, so euphoric was the atmosphere. I had come to drink in one last heady draught of the atmosphere that had surrounded the place fully for a week and, far from incidentally, in hope of picking up some cut-price souvenirs.

The first person I met in the lobby of the splendid Belfry Hotel, which is very far superior in quality to the dreadful course that bears its name, was the renowned American writer Dan Jenkins, a long-time friend. He asked me if I had ever been present at a more perfect golfing occasion, and I had no hesitation in agreeing with him that this had been the greatest sporting event I had ever witnessed.

As we breakfasted in the lobby, several of the European team members came through, and they agreed they had seldom felt so genuinely moved because the result had been absolutely right. The Americans should have won, but they agreed it was entirely fitting that Curtis Strange had salvaged national and personal pride by at least ensuring that his team was not defeated.

The Europeans now held the Cup uninterrupted on British soil for six years by going through three consecutive contests without a loss to the previously dominating Americans. The prestige and importance of the Ryder Cup, in peril on so many occasions over so many years, was fully intact—and in fact, somewhat reborn.

Some say the enthusiasm took a bitter turn and that the competition has become too fierce, and perhaps a case can be made that that is not at all what Samuel Ryder had in mind when he conceived the event.

When the Americans won back the Cup by one point in 1991 at Kiawah Island live on NBC-TV on a course built specifically for the match, the Ryder Cup had entered a new era of intensity and awareness. This "War on the Shore" on the Ocean Course at Kiawah Island, South Carolina was highly spirited, and I suppose dubbing it a "war" didn't help to temper the charge of partisanship. Neither, though, did new European captain Bernard Gallacher, as I was to learn the hard way.

Gallacher's team lost the Cup by one point at Kiawah in his first attempt as captain. Because the clubhouse is very small, there was a very carefully policed admission to the elegant reception following the matches. Because I had done television commentary of the matches for the USA Network, I was one of the very few people from the media who had been admitted to the party.

I was standing and enjoying a cocktail with Vice President Dan Quayle and his wife Marilyn, and tension filled the room when the losing captain Gallacher entered the party. Eventually, Gallacher took notice of my attendance at the soiree.

From about 15 feet away, I sensed Gallacher trying to get my attention.

"Wright," he barked, "just what the hell are you doin' in here? You're a damn traitor!"

Gallacher, stinging from his loss, apparently chose me to vent his anger on since I was a Brit who had left Britain and moved to the United States. I was embarrassed, though, for the Vice President and Mrs. Quayle to have to listen to a Ryder Cup captain speak so crassly in a social setting. The Quayles were wide-eyed, but graciously pretended not to hear Gallacher's tactless tirade. Suffice it to say, there would be no love lost between Gallacher and me.

In 1995, I was a guest on a live transatlantic radio piece hosted by Michael Parkinson. Gallacher was the phone guest from Great Britain, and I joined the show on the telephone from my home in North Carolina. Parkinson had to cut short the interview because Gallacher began screaming insults at me on the air from his side of the pond. In Gallacher's opinion, because I lived in the United States, I was in the enemy camp. That's how infantile Gallacher was.

Of course, I was not only critical of his "war-like" mentality, but also of the way he totally mishandled his European teams during his three turns at the helm. The 1993 match at The Belfry was obviously going to be a close contest. I sat down with former captain Jacklin for lunch on the Saturday of the event. Jacklin, who'd surrendered his captaincy to Gallacher for the 1991 matches, was in a dither.

"Ben, I can't believe what I'm seeing," Jacklin said as he sat down at the table. He was disturbed and disheartened by the poor strategies that Gallacher was employing. This time, Gallacher had informed Joakim Haeggman of Sweden, only 40 minutes before the afternoon's play, that Haeggman would be making his Ryder Cup debut. Haeggman was left with precious little time to prepare for the all-important afternoon fourball, and was sent out in the last match alongside Olazabal against Ray Floyd and Payne Stewart.

"How can Gallacher throw this young guy to the lions?" Jacklin queried. "He hasn't even had time for a proper warm-up!"

Jacklin was right, and Olazabal and Haeggman were defeated by Floyd and Stewart in that last match. The good news about Haeggman was that after he'd had a chance to steady himself, he was one of only three European winners in the singles on that final day, winning his match against John Cook 1-up.

Before Gallacher was shown the door as captain, he managed to finally add a victory to his record at Oak Hill in 1995. I honestly believe that Gallacher won because the Americans threw away the singles.

Take, for instance, the example of Europe's Nick Faldo and Colin Montgomerie. On the morning of the second day, that duo beat Jay Haas and Curtis Strange 4 and 2 in the foursomes. So what did Gallacher choose to do? He broke them up! Consequently, in the afternoon fourballs, Faldo and new partner Langer lost to Corey Pavin and Loren Roberts, and Montgomerie and his new partner Sam Torrance lost 4 and 2 to Fred Couples and Brad Faxon. Therefore, the Americans won the afternoon fourballs 3 and 1, which could have proved to be the U.S. springboard to victory.

Normally, then, in singles, a captain will position some really strong players at the end if he thinks it will be a close decision. The United States was leading the matches 9 and 7 heading into Sunday. The last singles match is usually thought of as a very important position. Who did Gallacher have bringing up the rear? Per-Ulrik Johansson, who had only played two matches on the first day. Phil Mickelson beat Johansson 2 and 1.

I think Gallacher got that victory despite his captaincy. He was fortunate that the Americans gave it away. Couples only halved his match with Woosnam. Peter Jacobsen, Jeff Maggert, Faxon, Crenshaw, Roberts, Haas, and especially Strange all collapsed. Strange's match with Faldo—capturing the beauty and nerve of engaging in match play for one's country—enabled the Europeans to win by one. Gallacher's win though, was by default, and the disappointed American fans henceforth referred to the installment as "Choke Hill," an unkind sobriquet, to say the least.

Perhaps the unkind criticism that Curtis Strange and 1997's defeated captain Tom Kite have suffered is overly severe, and maybe at times the intensity and importance placed on the match is undue. No one, however, can deny the fact that the Ryder Cup now has the attention of the public, and that the excitement and pride is unparalleled by even the Olympics, which have been sullied by political statements and dirtied by charges of bribery and graft.

As the series ages, it evolves. The match has been played at Valderrama Golf Club in Costa del Sol, Spain, and a future site, the K Club, has been selected in Ireland. Even the American PGA Tour has attempted to replicate the series, with a copycat event called "The President's Cup" in which the United States competes against the world.

It is safe to assume that the Ryder Cup will no longer need saviors, benefactors, and investors. But what it will always need, and will invariably deliver, are heroes.

Making Mediocrity an
Art Form

———————

G ary McCord was born in San Gabriel, California in May of 1948.
Somehow he managed to make it through high school and into
college, whereupon he studied economics at the University of California–Riverside. He also played on the golf team, and was twice
named All-America. In 1970, no doubt amidst a field that must have
been remarkably weak, he won the NCAA Division II golf championship. In 1971—the school having seen enough of him by then—he
turned professional, which proves he retained *nothing* from his education in economics.

McCord joined the PGA Tour in 1973. In 26 years playing on the
regular PGA Tour, he never won more than $60,000 in a single sea-
son and never finished higher than 59th on the Tour money list. In
fact, his career earnings, over 26 regular Tour seasons at this writing,
have yet to top the million-dollar mark.

McCord's only notable finishes were runner-up positions at the
Greater Milwaukee Open in 1975 and 1977. Milwaukee must be
McCord's kind of place.

McCord served as a Player Director on the Tour Policy Board from
1983 to 1986, and was instrumental in developing the "all exempt
Tour," a policy that would eliminate qualifying for the previous
season's top 125 money winners. This seems ironic since McCord
finished out of the top 125 in 18 of his 26 seasons on Tour.

In fairness, McCord did dip down in class to win the 1981 Gateway
Open on the Hogan Tour. His unlikely win was so horrifying to that
tour's organizing sponsor that they eventually surrendered their involvement to Nike, and the Gateway Open was never again contested.

On the senior circuit, Gary has very nearly ruined his act and
confused his image by winning the 1999 Toshiba Senior Classic.

McCord's lifelong friend and wild fellow-Californian John Jacobs battled him down the stretch. Jacobs surely must have defaulted after five playoff holes, either weary of McCord's chatter or just bored with his presence. I don't know what gyrations the PGA Tour is going through right now to convince Toshiba not to drop its sponsorship of the tournament, but I'm certain that the Tour's assurance that McCord will not be back to defend his title is playing a major role in its effort.

McCord is a man who has seemingly gone out of his way to make his appearance look ridiculous. He sports a silly-looking handlebar mustache, which I suppose is present to compensate for his balding head.

Despite his laughable appearance and golf record, he was obviously a much better player than he ever exhibited in tournament play because his mind is so lively that he finds it difficult to concentrate for long periods of time. Eighteen holes of golf were too many for him. If golf had been played over six holes, he might have had a chance of keeping his mind on the job for that length of time. I wouldn't give him more than six, though.

He's definitely an underachiever with the talent he has. In truth, McCord possesses a great swing, and huge short-game abilities. He's tall, his swing has a wide arc, and he's sneaky-long with his drives. He should have been much better than he was.

By now, McCord has spent more time *announcing* golf than he has playing it. Down and out on the Tour, he literally begged for his job at CBS. He was definitely on his uppers and needed to find a way to earn some real money, because he certainly couldn't live off of his Tour earnings, or lack thereof. Gary hung around producer/director Frank Chirkinian and some of the other CBS guys, pleading with Chirkinian to relent and give him a chance on the air.

Fate stepped in when McCord found himself boarding a commercial flight to Columbus. As McCord made his way back to the steerage compartment, he noticed Chirkinian seated comfortably in the first-class cabin.

"Frank, you've got to help me," McCord pleaded, after pausing at Chirkinian's seat and blocking the aisle. "I may be down and out, but I know the players better than anyone and I can stir up your group."

Chirkinian stared out the window of the jetliner and tapped his fingers, having heard the huckster's pitch before. McCord gave Frank no rest. Finally, Chirkinian, concerned that McCord might drop to his knees and disrupt the rest of the boarding passengers, relented.

"Come by the tower this week," Chirkinian barked in an effort to dismiss McCord. "We'll see what happens."

The Memorial Tournament in Columbus, Ohio, is an "invitation only" tournament, and McCord's woeful winless Tour status certainly garnered him no invitation. He was heading to Columbus only for policy board meetings and had plenty of time on his hands to take Chirkinian up on his offer.

At first, Chirkinian positioned McCord with conservative veteran announcer Verne Lundquist in the tower at the 16th hole. Chirkinian made McCord serve as part of that duo because Chirkinian knew better than to allow McCord to start on his own. Gary couldn't be trusted to behave himself, and he was so wild that, without Lundquist's tutelage, anything could have happened on the air.

I remember very clearly my initial opinion of McCord's on-air performance: "What the hell do we need this yahoo from California on the air for?" I asked. "He's got no intellectual ability. He's just a smarmy, ignorant, California loudmouth."

McCord and I were natural opposites, occupying each end of the spectrum. He was a freewheeling, young, irreverent smart aleck, and I was perceived to be the pompous, elitist, stuffy British traditionalist. The perception that the British are pompous is easy for someone like McCord to embrace because, as I've said, he's an empty-headed Californian.

Unbeknownst to me, Chirkinian began a clandestine operation to play McCord and me against each other. While we were on the air, Chirkinian could communicate with his announcers through our earphones. The technology was such that Chirkinian, as he pleased, could also speak privately to each announcer.

I would offer an insightful, loquacious comment on the air, and just as I'd finish, Chirkinian would goad McCord privately on his isolate key:

"That was a weird word that pompous limey used, Gary. Why don't you ask Wright what the hell he was talking about?"

McCord would take the direction from Chirkinian and use the opportunity to make fun of my language or presentation on the air. Of course, as soon as McCord would finish his rude comment, Chirkinian's voice would enter my earphones. He would push my isolate key and privately say:

"Are you going to take that shit from McCord? Get after his ass!"

I must say that the first few times McCord took a shot at me, I was extremely pissed. On the air, McCord would facetiously say things to me like, "Ben, that word you just used, I've never heard such a funny word as 'escarpment.'"

I'd think to myself, *What the hell is this ignorant scumbag on television for, when he doesn't know a word in common parlance? What are we doing here? We're lowering the tone of the broadcast to the lowest common denominator—McCord!*

So I would then answer him on the air in an irritated manner. To viewers, it sounded as if I was scolding McCord the way one might treat a child. Of course, he *was* childlike in many ways. He loves to provoke people. He's a little boy always bent on discovering just how far he is able to go.

So this "back and forth" Chirkinian secretly created between McCord and me was entertaining to the viewers, but I mean it quite seriously when I say that I was not amused when it started. The whole relationship between McCord and me started with genuine acrimony.

Of course, once we realized how popular the sniping became, and that Chirkinian had served as the instigator, I'm afraid that it became what one might call "an act."

McCord and I held a summit meeting in a pub while on the road. We forged a gentleman's agreement that each was fair game for the other. Our attitude was "no holds barred." Go for your life, we agreed. There were no hard feelings; it was just "the act." Viewers would stop me in the street and ask me, "Do you really hate that Gary McCord? Is he really a bad guy?"

Of course, McCord was having people ask him the same. Gary would be playing in a PGA Tour event, and gallery spectators would shout to him from behind the ropes, "Hey Gary, where's your buddy Wright?"

I'd play in celebrity golf events and people would say, "I bet you'd like to have your pal McCord along with you today!"

"No," I'd respond. "I'm here because I'm trying to avoid the son of a bitch!"

"Hey, Wright," someone would yell, "get after that som-bitch from California!"

To McCord, fans would shout, "Don't let that pompous British swine get the best of you. Get after his ass!" It took on a bit of an East Coast vs. West Coast connotation.

Old Felstedians, who reached the semifinal in the Halford-Hewitt. Ben is fourth from the left, standing.

Ben, on the right, looking over a group of his father's race horses.

Ben interviewing Tony Jacklin at Augusta for the BBC.

National Airlines Pro-Am at the Country Club of Miami, with Steve Clark, Mayor of Miami, Tom Weiskopf, and Ben joined by two flight attendants.

Ben and Jack Whitaker at Augusta.

Gary Player being consoled by his wife, Vivienne, at the scorer's hut after a final hole double bogey at the 1959 British Open at Muirfield.

Ben and Jack Lemmon at Pebble Beach.

Michael MacDonnell of *The Daily Mail*, Jack Nicklaus,
Ben Wright, and Renton Laidlaw of *The Evening Standard*
in the 1970s.

Ben, Mayor Clark, and Weiskopf at the National Airlines
Pro-Am.

Ben at the burned out cross and high altar at St. Michael Cathedral in Coventry, where he was christened. It was destroyed during WWII.

Jim Nantz, Ben, Frank Chirkinian, Gary McCord, and
Vern Lundquist at President Ford's Pro-Am in Vail.

Ben and the irascible Bob Drum.

Ben, Dai Rees, George Bird, Peter Dobereiner, and Dai
Davies at the Pro-Am at Castle Harbor, Bermuda.

The CBS broadcast team at the Butler Cabin at Augusta.
Back row: Bobby Clampett, Vern Lundquist, Jim Nelford,
Ben Wright, Bill McAtee, and Peter Kostis. Front row: Jim
Nantz, Ken Venturi, and Tom Weiskopf.

Gary McCord and his infamous license plate.

Sammy Davis with Ben.

Sir Henry Cotton, Sam Snead, and Ben at the Ryder Cup
at Royal Birkdale.

Ben, Dan Quayle, Jim Nantz, and Jerry Pate at the
Admiralty House in Washington D.C.

Ben listening to Jack Lemmon describing a shot where the ball stuck to the clubface—and he swore it was true!

Charles Brakefield, Gary McCord, Ben, and Pat Summerall
at the Memphis Pro-Am.

Ben ad-libbing a column at the Alcan Championship at
St. Andrews, Scotland.

Pat Summerall and Ben in front of the clubhouse at the
Augusta National.

Ben covering one of the many sports he wrote about
during his 45-year career.

Ben at the 15th tower at Augusta with spotter and scorer
Lou Serafin.

RAYMOND FLOYD

May 3, 1996

Dear Ben

I know that it has been a tough year for you. I wanted to drop you this note of encouragement for your courageous decision to undergo rehabilitation out in Palm Springs -- along with your family, there is nothing more important in life than your health and well-being.

Maria and I want you to know that our thoughts are with you. A little education and some physical conditioning never hurts, and we are confident that you'll emerge from your treatment with a healthier outlook on life and a new enthusiasm for your business endeavors.

Ben, you have always had our admiration. We miss you and we wish you all the best.

Sincerely,

Raymond

Raymond

Even in public, we would keep the feud alive. Gary and I were urged on by a public that was plainly charged by our rivalry. Therefore, we escalated it. Were we a bit rough on each other? Sure. He had every right to ridicule me about my weight because I was pretty gross during that period. In turn, I had every right to denigrate his lack of ability as a player since he'd never proven otherwise. If Chirkinian felt we were going too far during the broadcast, he would push the all-key and cut us back by saying something like, *"Hey, hey, hey, boys...the game. We'd better concentrate now on the game. We are here to televise a golf event."* Frank was good in that respect. If McCord and I got out of hand, he'd put a stamp on it.

McCord's and my antics spread through the telecast as well, as we developed creative and amusing ways to shoot the hole introductions. Hole introductions normally were straightforward, even dull little features where the announcer would be shown on camera describing the hole he was covering, with the hole itself serving as his background. For instance: "I'm Ben Wright, and I'll be calling the action here at the 17th hole, a long par-three from an elevated tee with a giant pond lurking in front of the green..." McCord and I participated in shooting variations on the hole introductions, which were largely developed by McCord's bizarre little mind.

At the Greater Hartford Open, at the TPC at River Highlands, McCord's hole introduction was to focus on the 100-foot drop from the tee to the green. To illustrate the 100-foot drop, Gary read his introduction perched 100 feet above the earth in a bucket on a fire truck lift. He talked about the hole, and offered to demonstrate just how high 100 feet was by jumping from the bucket. Before he jumped, the camera cut to me on the ground, holding a round cloth reflective disk, ostensibly to catch McCord in when he fell.

The drama built as McCord climbed out onto the outside edge of the bucket, and I scurried back and forth with this disk, trying to line up properly with McCord's impact position. McCord then jumped, and at the last second, I snatched the disk away, allowing him to smack face first into the ground! The camera then cut to McCord, groaning, moaning, broken on the earth, asking, "Ben, Ben, tell me you didn't do that on purpose. You wouldn't have done something like that would you?"

The camera then cut to me, shaking my head "No," but giggling into the camera with a mischievous look on my face.

Of course, it was a dummy made up to look like Gary, CBS blazer and all, that had been launched off of the bucket truck. But the way the piece was craftily edited, it appeared to viewers that I had sold-out a diving McCord.

We found ourselves in Washington D.C. to broadcast the Kemper Open while Soviet Premier Mikhail Gorbachev was also in the area to participate with President Ronald Reagan in a summit meeting between the USSR and the United States. Calling on my old skill as a Russian linguist, McCord, on camera, had me translate his entire hole introduction, line by line, into Russian. When he completed the introduction, he kissed me wildly on both cheeks.

At the TPC at Southwind in Memphis, McCord seemingly did a standard stand-up hole introduction in front of the green at the 16th:

"Hi, this is Gary McCord, and I'll be calling the action here at the 16th, a very long, uphill par-five. If a player drives his ball over the top of the hill, he'll face a sea of bunkers. Basically, it's a very long shot into the green from there, and if a player misses the green to the left, there's no telling what he'll see down there..."

The camera then panned over McCord's right shoulder and zoomed in on the left of the green. There I was, dressed as Elvis in a full-body white jumpsuit, sporting sideburns and big sunglasses, with a guitar slung around my prominent belly, licking a chocolate ice cream bar. I looked preposterous! "Hound Dog" swelled up in the background, and McCord wondered aloud if former NFL coach Jerry Glanville was present at the tournament. For all the trouble we went to and as funny as the bit was, Chirkinian would not let it air. "In this town," he said, "you imitating Elvis may cause you to be put away. They may very well not appreciate you demeaning Elvis's legacy here."

McCord came up with many hare-brained ideas, only to have Chirkinian snap, "Gary, you ass, we're here to do a serious golf broadcast!"

The occasion when I realized just how popular the act was, was at the 1992 United States Open at Pebble Beach. I attended the event with CBS colleague Jim Nantz. Since it was ABC that was broadcasting the tournament, Nantz and I were present only as golf fans. Nantz stayed in a suite at Spanish Bay and I lodged in downtown Monterey at a lovely pub. We had a wonderful week, playing a bit of the game and wandering around watching golf. I enjoyed every bloody minute of it.

After the final round, Nantz and I were invited to the winner's party, in this case Tom Kite, held at the Beach Club following play. A USGA Committeeman approached me as I walked into the reception. It was Tom Chisholm, an elegant gray-haired gentleman dressed in his official USGA regalia.

"Is there any chance I can have a word in your ear?" Chisholm asked as he grabbed my arm.

"Surely," I answered. "We can do it now."

We walked together into a little anteroom, and I assumed I was about to hear a diatribe about how much of a disgrace McCord's and my antics were to the game of golf, and maybe that we were lowering it to the level of the meanest streets.

Chisholm put his arm around me and began. "What I brought you in here to tell you is that I think you and McCord are the best thing ever to happen to televised golf."

I was genuinely amazed that this was coming from the mouth of a committeeman of the normally staid United States Golf Association.

"Why, Mr. Chisholm? Why on earth are you saying this?"

"I'm saying it because you two guys embody the spirit of the two-dollar nassau," Chisholm explained. "Whether it is played at Cypress Point or on your humblest public course, you two guys have got into the spirit of golf at the grassroots level...the backbone of the game. I can't tell you how much enjoyment you two have brought to me and my family literally on days in which the golf has been anything else but stellar. You guys make the broadcast," Chisholm continued. "I really wanted you to hear this, and I really wanted to make this known to you, because we may not ever meet again. I'm not sure all of my fellow committeemen would go along with my views, but they're my views."

I thanked Chisholm for his comments, but he had one more thing to say to me.

"I've got one request of you, Ben, before we go into the party to have a glass of whatever it is we fancy. I really think it would be great if neither you nor McCord ever allowed it to get vicious. I think if it got vicious, it would destroy the whole beauty of the thing."

"You know, Mr. Chisholm, you're absolutely right," I agreed, "it must never be allowed to get vicious."

Rightly or wrongly, I felt Chisholm had given me the seal of approval that I wanted to hear. I wanted to hear someone in a very upright organization like the USGA say they thought my act with McCord was a good idea, because I expected golf's governing bodies to be very suspect in that regard.

As an aside, Chisholm went on to tell me how much he and his entire family enjoyed hearing me on a local radio show that aired in his hometown of Detroit. With some regularity, I was a guest on the "J.P. McCarthy Show," which Chisholm and nearly a million others listened to each morning.

McCarthy was a friend of Chisholm's, and for over thirty years one of the top radio broadcasters in America. The now late McCarthy was also a great friend to the game of golf, and well known among the golf community because he so thoroughly covered and promoted the sport on his radio show.

"Mr. Chisholm, I was just awakened by J.P. on Friday," I explained. "He interviewed me by telephone very early on his Friday morning show."

Chisholm grinned because, as a regular listener, he knew that the three-hour time difference between Detroit and Pebble Beach meant that his crafty Irish friend must have called me at 4:30 A.M. Pacific time. Chisholm was right.

"J.P. introduced me formally and greeted me on the air," I continued, "and then he asked me what the Friday morning conditions at usually windy Pebble Beach were.

"Well, J.P.," I answered in my best and most droll British accent, "at the moment it is particularly dark…" leaving McCarthy laughing and mildly embarrassed.

Chisholm and I shared a good laugh too, and returned to the reception for a glass of wine, and a toast to McCarthy and McCord.

A few weeks after the U.S. Open encounter with Chisholm, I attended the British Open at Muirfield in Scotland. British golfer Barry Lane approached me.

"You don't know what you've done for us, mate!"

"What?" I asked him. "What is it that I've done for you?"

"Well, Ben, the boys and I, we go to the pub after playing. Because of the five-hour time difference, we get the CBS golf coverage live here at about 9 P.M. After having a few at the pub, we all make it back to the television in time to see you and McCord go at each other. We just watch and laugh our arses off!"

Despite our apparent popularity on both sides of the Atlantic, McCord and I did have our detractors. At Doral, Tom Watson got ahold of me behind the cart barn.

"I am absolutely disgusted with you," Watson told me in no uncertain terms. "I have always regarded you as a historian of the game and I have had great respect for your love of tradition. The fact that you even talk to McCord is a source of annoyance to me. He is beneath you, Ben. He's not worth bothering with. He's just an ignorant fool who can't play."

I listened to Watson carry on, and finally answered by saying, "Tom, that may be your opinion, and you're entitled to it, but if you want Gary removed from the broadcasts, you're wasting your breath talking to me. You'd better petition Frank Chirkinian, because I don't agree with anything you say."

Watson then wrote a letter to Chirkinian demanding McCord's removal. There was a feeling amongst many people that Watson held a grudge against McCord because it had appeared that when Gary joined CBS he'd taken the job of Bob Murphy, who was one of Watson's friends on Tour in those days. That's rubbish. Murphy opted to work with ESPN and play the Senior Tour. Watson can be obstinate and just isn't a very warm man; in fact, he's a cold fish. I was surprised when Watson was selected as a Ryder Cup captain for the 1993 matches at The Belfry because he'd never won the PGA Championship, though it is perplexing that Kite and Crenshaw have also been selected, so maybe it is a changing of the guard of sorts. Most Ryder Cup captains have won that championship. I was also surprised he was selected because, no question about it, Watson is doubtful in the field of diplomacy.

I was very offended, for instance, as was British Ryder Cup player Sam Torrance, when Watson refused to autograph menus for the opposing team that year. I'm offended by many things Watson does, but I do admire him for his stubborn character. He obviously is not afraid of anybody and will do exactly as he sees fit. I agree with him on that, but I rarely agree with his point of view. A man who can win five British Opens in those conditions has got to be one helluva player, so I'm not disparaging him. But he definitely marches to a different drummer. Watson and McCord are like oil and water, and it is *no* act.

Since so many viewers were curious as to whether Gary and I really held such contempt for each other, we had to work out a proper response. Therefore, we agreed that whenever either of us would be asked a question about if we really disliked the other or was it all an act, our standard response would always be to tell the person, "It's your call." That was our reply: "It's your call," then we'd walk away, leaving the person totally mystified. At that point, people would find themselves even more confused. The response, "It's your call," was McCord's idea. I must give him credit for that because it is the only idea he's ever had.

With my very public rivalry against McCord near its natural pinnacle, it demanded a natural resolution. Resolution came in the form of a most surreal confrontation for the ages, which I shall detail here.

The move toward a showdown was made when we were broadcasting at the Memorial Tournament in Dublin, Ohio. Off the air, McCord challenged that he could beat me in an 18-hole match, giving me one stroke per hole, provided I teed from the same tees as him.

"You have a bet," I told him.

Now Gary was a professional golfer who still played on Tour, and I was roughly a 10-handicap. Over the course of the weekend, news of the bet was bandied about on the air during the telecast. We had received permission to stage the showdown on Monday in nearby New Albany, Ohio, at a course called The Golf Club. The event would be held behind closed doors, because the ultra-exclusive Golf Club, though they were excited to host our match, insisted that no galleries or cameras be allowed in.

Try, if you can, to imagine the scene that unfolded:

McCord brought as his caddie eccentric two-time Tour winner Mac O'Grady, who toted McCord's bag tuxedo-clad—in tails, no less— and with a fedora covering his head. O'Grady, who was already well known for his bizarre concepts and space-age philosophies, changed his name in 1978, abandoning his real name: Phil McGleno. In truth, O'Grady was probably too intellectual for most golfers to relate to. While I wouldn't classify McCord as an intellectual, the two could be considered kindred spirits in a kind of unconventional and disobedient lunacy that is largely and purposely absent from the structured and civilized world of golf.

A catering cart followed the group, handing out fruit and cheese with glasses of chilled Dom Perignon champagne. McCord himself showed up wearing a camouflage beret over a ninja headband, camouflage fatigue pants rolled up to the knees, white socks, and a brown T-shirt bearing a military insignia, as if he were going to war for America. McCord wore eye-black on his cheekbones like a professional football player.

I arrived for play, dressed smartly in a British Union Jack golf shirt, with former United States Open champion and fellow broadcaster Ken Venturi as my personal manager and on-course advisor.

I got off to an inauspicious start when McCord & Company intentionally popped a champagne cork during my backswing. After that ignominious beginning, this comical and unruly group made its way around the links, and, despite frequent hijinks by my opponent, which included the blasting of rock and roll music through a portable "boom box" stereo, McCord and I battled fiercely through each hole. The course was playing very wet due to overnight and morning thunderstorms. As hard as I hit it, with no roll I was having trouble reaching the fairway from the championship tees. That made it very tough on me, but I maintained my stiff upper lip, since we were playing for honor and country.

We played the nines in reverse. After the 15th, I found myself two down with three to play. With my back to the wall, I captured the 16th.

As I approached the 17th tee, I was unnerved by the sudden sight of an ugly snake near my feet. Startled, I jumped into orbit! "The whole world shall hear of this," I uttered in disgust at McCord and O'Grady upon realizing that it was a rubber fake planted by the less-than-dynamic duo. But I collected myself and won the 17th hole, giving myself a dramatic chance to win the match. We were all square going to 18.

The ninth hole at the Golf Club, which we played as our 18th, is a par-four dogleg to the left around woods and trees. I had just won two straight holes, and now McCord was chirping like a cricket.

It was my honor, so I hit a three-wood very conservatively down the middle of the fairway, just far enough to see the green. Along comes yahoo, who flashes his drive into the trees on the left, quick-hooking the ball terribly. To McCord's eternal discredit, the damned ball banged around in the branches and somehow threaded its way through the trees and out into the fairway!

Since he was giving me a stroke on the hole, I tried not to let this undeserved quirk of good luck bother me. I hit my approach shot with a 4-iron, but the ball landed in a greenside bunker. McCord needed only a short iron to reach the green. He left the ball 35 feet from the hole. My bunker shot landed and stopped 10 feet from the hole.

McCord then miraculously *holed* his 35-foot putt, giving him birdie on the last. With the wind knocked out of me and in total angst at the way fate had gifted McCord twice on the hole, I missed my 10-footer. McCord won the match 1-up, and as you may have surmised, McCord was not a very good winner. He's no good at anything, in fact.

I enjoyed revenge at McCord's expense on more than one occasion. From time to time, I would have the CBS announcers and production staff at my North Carolina home for a few days of highly competitive golf and drinks. Each player would put up $100 per day, so good golf was important unless one planned to go home significantly poorer.

Now believe it or not, McCord is a very quiet guy at night. His wife Diane is much more lively after dark. Gary, after all these decades of failure and ineptitude, is still serious about his golf. Deep down, he actually still believes he can play, and while a glimmer of his ability came through during his Senior Tour victory, I have to believe that there was some measure of untold default by the competition that week. Either way, McCord is not much of a party person, and sometimes takes his medicine too lightly.

One evening at my home, the CBS fellows and I were so disappointed at the sight of McCord asleep in a chair that we dressed him in an old grandmother's shawl and cap, complete with an afghan over his legs and a bottle of Metamucil in his lap. We all left him like that and went out to party—including his wife Diane!

Last, but certainly not least, was my favorite and most satisfying moment with McCord. Ben Hogan, who had a close relationship with Venturi and had always been very gracious to me, was admittedly a viewer of CBS golf coverage. Hogan claimed that it was only CBS's golf coverage that he found worthy to watch, eschewing the other networks' telecasts unless Dave Marr was on—Hogan loved

Marr. Hogan had taken a shine to Venturi because Venturi dressed like him and very much tried to emulate the Hogan style of golf. Hogan believed that he and Venturi shared the same belief in the principles of the game.

Venturi, though, told us how intimidated he was the first time he played a round of golf with Hogan. Venturi was a young man, and the two were paired for a practice round at the Masters. Hogan, who spoke so little, eventually peered into Venturi's golf bag, examining his clubs. Venturi, grateful for what appeared to be a chance for a breaking of the ice, was excited about Hogan's interest until Hogan began shaking his head.

"Why is it that every young player out here carries a bag full of damned 2-irons?" Hogan scoffed at Venturi, referring to the fact that touring players had taken to using irons with jacked-up loft.

Such the loner was Hogan, that he built a giant, stately home in Ft. Worth with only one bedroom; the implication was that he never wanted to entertain company in his house. However, Hogan warmed to Venturi and their acquaintance was maintained throughout Venturi's playing and television career, and included a commercial deal with the Hogan Company. In fact, in the late 1980s, the elusive and mysterious Hogan displayed his affection for Venturi and CBS Golf by granting Venturi a rare television interview, which they taped at Shady Oaks, Hogan's country club.

Chirkinian had goaded Venturi into asking Hogan for the interview. Hogan was very much a businessman, and would typically demand financial remuneration to participate in such an exercise. For Venturi, though, Hogan waived the fee but *did* insist on one condition: Hogan wanted complete and total editorial control over the interview, and demanded that he be able to approve the final edit of the taped interview before it went on the air.

There was one story told in the interview that Hogan wanted removed. It concerned the 1955 U.S. Open, when after finishing his final round, Hogan was virtually named champion. The celebration over Hogan's historic fifth U.S. Open Championship had basically begun...when young Jack Fleck birdied two of the last four holes to force an 18-hole playoff to be played the next day.

On the first tee the following morning, as Hogan and Fleck prepared to begin the playoff, Hogan uncharacteristically broke his normal silence and approached Fleck.

"I see you're playing my clubs, Fleck," he commented.

Fleck nodded proudly and confirmed that he was, indeed, using Hogan-manufactured clubs.

Hogan told Venturi in the interview, "I never should have done that," referring to his casual comment to Fleck three decades earlier. "It allowed Fleck to win."

Apparently, Hogan was aware of his power of intimidation. When Fleck stepped onto the tee to go head-to-head with the mighty Hogan, he might as well have started the round 2-down. After all, the Hogan mystique, coupled with Hogan's normal icy manner of total ambivalence in ignoring his competitors, surely would have unnerved Fleck.

Hogan's meaning to Venturi was that his acknowledgment of Fleck's mere existence on the tee broke the ice, calmed Fleck's nerves, and settled him down sufficiently to allow him to overcome Hogan's presence.

"It's the worst mistake I ever made," Hogan admitted to Venturi. He then insisted that the revelation be removed from the interview.

It was a rare peek into an even rarer lapse in Hogan's concentration. To illustrate Hogan's focus, CBS Associate Producer Chuck Will told me of an occasion upon which Will happened to be in the player's locker room after caddying at the Hershey Open in Pennsylvania. Will witnessed a brooding Hogan come off the course after his round and make his way through the locker room. Clearly deep in thought, Hogan was concentrating so intently and was so totally focused on mentally recounting his round that he eventually walked into the shower, stood under the spigot and turned on the water—while still fully clothed in his cashmere sweater and trousers!

A personal "Hogan" occurrence at Shady Oaks that I will never forget was the time I was hitting practice balls on the range in solitude. Whacking away at the ball, I suddenly noticed this dark shadow creep up behind me. Without looking back, I came to the frightening realization that Hogan had walked out to the range and was watching me hit shots. I was thrown into a total tizzy. My hands were shaking as the most inferior feeling I had ever experienced settled in my swing. My mind raced, and I thought that the best way to defuse this situation was to stop hitting the ball as pathetically as I was, acknowledge his presence, and ask him a question.

"Mr. Hogan," I began respectfully, "may I ask you a question?"

"Ask away," was his reply.

"I am right-handed, and it seems to me that I overpower my left hand with the right," I explained. "How can I stop doing that?"

"I'm a left-handed person," Hogan said. "That was probably one of the luckiest things that ever happened to me because my left hand was very strong, although I played right-handed. It's a good question that you ask," he said to my relief.

"When I find that my left hand gets sloppy or lazy," Hogan continued, "I leave the 'pinky finger' off the end of the club and hit the ball with three fingers and my thumb. It truly strengthens the left hand."

"Ahh," I nodded as I turned back to the tee, happy that I now had a valid excuse to miss a few more shots in front of the great Hogan. It was a great relief.

I was very careful of what I said around Hogan because I was cognizant of his volatility and I did not wish to destroy the acquaintance I had with the hero of my youth. On another occasion, I did have the opportunity to glean some of his golf expertise.

"Mr. Hogan," I said, "on some mornings when I prepare to play golf, I notice that my fingers feel fat and swelled. To be honest, this seems to occur after I have had a substantial night out, if you know what I mean. Have you ever heard of this condition?"

Hogan gave me a knowing look.

"Ah, yes," he said, nodding slyly. "I have some knowledge of the malady you are referring to. Before morning rounds, I drink ginger-ale to remedy the swelling." He gave no further explanation. I don't know if or why it actually works, but I have done it to this day.

My fascination with Hogan was furthered when, to my total surprise and delight, he personally invited me to tour his golf club production facility in Ft. Worth. I gladly accepted, and arrangements were made for me to fly to Ft. Worth and tour the facility in advance of my involvement in broadcasting the Colonial National Invitational nearby with CBS.

I landed at the Ft. Worth Airport, and excitedly looked for the driver Mr. Hogan said would meet me and escort me to the Hogan Company headquarters. After a thorough search, I came to the disappointing conclusion that Hogan had apparently forgotten his offer to spend time with me and provide me with a tour. Certainly he was busy, and I had no choice but to be graceful, avoid being a pest, and not embarrass Mr. Hogan by pointing out his slip of mind. Instead, I simply taxied to my lodgings at the hotel appointed by CBS.

The next morning, I answered the ringing phone in my room. It was Hogan calling.

"Where were you?" was his only greeting.

I was taken aback. Where was *I?*

"Mr. Hogan, I assure you, I was all too ready to make our appointment, but when you didn't send the driver to the airport, I assumed you had a change of plans or perhaps a conflict in your schedule."

Hogan was surprised and outraged to learn that the driver had left me stranded at the airport, apparently forgetting to fetch me. Hogan began to apologize, which I assured him was not necessary.

"May I send a new driver to get you later this afternoon?" Hogan asked, and I readily accepted. At the same time, I feared for the fate of the original driver, figuring that he would not much longer be in the employ of the Hogan Company.

The tour of the Hogan facility was marvelous, and the manner in which the employees seemed to revere Hogan was inspiring. They looked upon him as a demigod, and he moved around the facility like the royalty that he was.

Hogan was also a careful perfectionist, and brandished his own version of quality control. His frequent close scrutiny of equipment coming off the line often resulted in the abandonment of large quantities of golf clubs that he deemed imperfect following his inspection. I witnessed Hogan's insistence on very high production standards and his willingness to scrap large quantities of product, even to the point of financially damaging his company.

These stories illustrate the kind of perfection, dedication, and respect with which Gary McCord was wholly unfamiliar.

Sometime in the early 1980s, Hogan very kindly began hosting a yearly lunch for a few of the CBS announcers when we would go to Hogan's hometown to broadcast the Colonial. Chirkinian, Venturi, Summerall, and I would go and meet him at his regular table at Shady Oaks Country Club. Hogan would have numerous martinis, and then his brother, Royal Hogan, would drive him home.

Eventually, McCord joined the CBS team. The first year he went with us to Ft. Worth, Chirkinian, Venturi, Summerall, and I went off to our lunch with Hogan. Later McCord, having heard about where we went, approached me.

"Ben, I really would like to have been a part of that."

"Gary," I said quite seriously, "Hogan doesn't suffer fools gladly. He despises mediocrity, and you've made incompetence your badge of honor. You have made mediocrity an art form. You are just worthless, and Hogan would just eat you up and spit you out."

Despite my admonition, McCord, each year, would pester me to take him along to the Hogan lunch. Each year I demurred, until eventually I could no longer stand the sight of the man groveling and begging. I phoned Mr. Hogan in his office.

"Mr. Hogan, can I bring a mystery guest to the luncheon this year?"

"You can bring anyone you like, Ben."

I took the news to McCord.

"Okay, Gary, I've got you permission to go to this lunch, but you'd better keep your mouth shut. Don't get cheeky, because you are not to meddle with one of the great men of our time." It was like talking to a child, which it always was when talking to McCord.

By the time we got to Shady Oaks, McCord was getting a little on the twitchy side because I think he realized that he'd perhaps bitten off more than he could chew. We all were to sit at Mr. Hogan's round table, which was his table every day of his life in Texas.

The big moment came, and I finally introduced McCord to Hogan. They shook hands as I cautiously observed.

"Nice to meet you, Mr. McCord," said Hogan as he greeted Gary. "What do you do for a living, son?"

"Well, Mr. Hogan, I play the PGA Tour," McCord politely replied, his voice cracking in nervousness.

Hogan struggled in thought. "Goddammit!" he said finally. "When you get old, sometimes the mind plays tricks on you. I don't remember that name, Mr. McCord. How long have you been out there on Tour?"

"Seventeen years, Mr. Hogan."

"Seventeen years! Damn, my mind is playing tricks with me. I just don't remember your name, Mr. McCord. How many tournaments have you won, son?"

"None," Gary admitted, as he began to twitch and squirm, backed into an uncomfortable corner of humiliation in having to admit to his woeful record.

McCord gulped through a long pause, broken finally when Hogan asked McCord pointedly, "Seventeen years and no wins. What the hell are you even out there for?"

With that, Hogan turned his back on McCord and never spoke another word to him. McCord sat silent through the entire lunch with a queasy look on his face, while the rest of us went on merrily without him. Finally, in desperation, Gary turned to me, and I could barely contain my joy at getting the chance to utter my next four hushed words:

"I told you so."

"Out of Bounds"

A ny poor soul who possesses the unmitigated audacity to position oneself in front of an open microphone on live television is destined to suffer from the occasional "foot in mouth" malady. At any moment, without fair warning, one's keen and insightful commentary can flee in favor of a mistaken fact, poor attempt at humor, flubbed name, or inappropriate comment that offends the sensibilities of half of the free world. At CBS Sports Golf, we were not immune to these dreadful occurrences, and when they happened, we typically adopted a "there but by the grace of God go I," attitude—just before we accosted the offender mercilessly. Usually our producer/director Frank Chirkinian, nicknamed "the Ayatollah," beat us to the punch.

Frank Glieber, a CBS announcer in the 1970s, for instance, actually believed, and stated, thankfully in rehearsal, that there was a British player named "Slazenger" in the field because he saw the word emblazoned on the side of a player's golf bag.

Another all-purpose CBS sportscaster, Gary Bender, was broadcasting the 14th hole as Seve Ballesteros was on his way to winning the Masters. Ballesteros unleashed a mighty drive, drawing the ball around the corner, and left himself only a short iron—clearly a 9-iron or wedge—to the green. A very short shot indeed. The Spaniard was about to get over his ball when he heard some rowdy people, who'd obviously enjoyed their Sunday afternoon beers, making noise in the trees next to the fairway. Ballesteros backed off, took a few steps toward the offenders, and barked, "Fore, please. Fore...please!" to quiet the crowd. Whereupon, Bender, on the air, observed: "It appears Ballesteros has backed off and is now calling for his 4-iron."

Ken Squier, who specialized in automobile racing, also had his turn in the CBS Golf broadcast booth. He hovered over his microphone and described the action by saying: "Now driving from the green, in the general direction of the tee, is Johnny Miller." He was adequately roasted later that evening when the broadcast was adjourned.

Jerry West, one of the great names in basketball and now the general manager of the Los Angeles Lakers, took his turn in the golf broadcast booth at the Phoenix Open (in the early 1980s). West actually had some golf credentials. I had seen him shoot a 65 at Bel Air so I knew the guy had some knowledge of the game. Once in the tower, though, in front of the live microphone, when it came time for West to speak, Chirkinian cued West through his earphones by saying: "Alright you long streak of miserable basketball player, it's your turn now. You're on!" West, who somehow never learned the fundamental fact that you never ever reply to a cue from the director on the air, hastily blurted out: "Okay, Frank..." for all of the viewers to hear, then proceeded to begin his commentary. Well, Frank absolutely excoriated West in the next commercial break, speaking again through West's earphones: "Don't reply to me on the air, you dumb son of a bitch. I'm the director! Have you pissed away your brains jumping up and down on the damned basketball court?"

Well, damn me, after hearing that tongue lashing, the very next time West was cued through his earphones by Chirkinian, he began again by saying "Okay, Frank" again on the air, almost as if it were an involuntary reaction. That, needless to say, was West's debut and final golf broadcast.

Hale Irwin had similar problems with the headphone cue system. Hale got his debut on television at the American Golf Classic at Firestone Country Club the week immediately following his United States Open victory at Winged Foot. We went to air, Irwin with his headset on, and blow me down—about two minutes into the show he went cross-eyed and turned purple in the face. At the first break, he whipped off the earphones and cried "How the hell can you talk while someone's talking to you? I can't stand it!"

I sympathized, and offered, "I'll tell you what, just take them off. Don't wear them, and I'll just tap you on the knee when it's time to talk. I'll tap your knee twice when it's time to stop." Our hastily conceived "knee tap" system, in all of its rudimentary glory, seemed to work adequately and Irwin proved to be quite good and very insightful.

Rick Barry, on the other hand—the former basketball star—was another would-be golf commentator who had a dubious performance during the Westchester Classic. Barry had chosen to skip rehearsal, thereby violating the one Chirkinian rule that was unbreakable. Then, to add insult to injury, when it was time for the broadcast, Barry showed up with his wife in tow, wearing matching tennis outfits. Once Barry was in front of the monitors in his tower, with his earphones on, ready to begin the broadcast, Chirkinian flashed up a shot he'd taped of Barry and his companion climbing up the steps into the tower. Then Chirkinian, pressing his "all key"—which meant that he could be heard through the earphones of every announcer and production person on the course—sneered, "Oh, look at these two. Aren't they lovely in their matching tennis dresses?" Chirkinian then launched into an incredible tirade: "In addition to the fact that you chose it not necessary to show up for rehearsal, which is, on my team, totally unacceptable, you show up here after your game of tennis in your pretty, darling tennis dress. Get the hell out of the tower...now!" Frank fired him on the spot, and Barry and his consort climbed down from their lovenest of a tower, matching tennis outfits and all.

The late Jim Thacker knew to be attired in golf apparel, but probably should have worn army fatigues the day he tried out for Chirkinian and CBS Golf. Thacker was a local affiliate guy from Charlotte who Chirkinian had been pressured to try out. He was one of those all-around announcers—not really what you'd call a pure golf man. Jim, poor devil, was very, very nervous during his on-air tryout. He got to chattering, and the more he said, the more he got himself mixed up. It was sad, really, but this is a nerve-wracking business, especially for an affiliate guy trying to make it in the big time. As Thacker fumbled and stuttered, Chirkinian spoke loudly and clearly through the headphone system: "Stop....I can't stand anymore of this driveling rubbish. Jim Wacker, or Bob Thatcher, or whatever your name is because you've never made an impression on me as a person. You just waffle away from error to error and never have come to grips with this situation. I just can't take any more of it. Good-bye, you're out of there!" Frank dismissed him right in the middle of rehearsal, and down he climbed, undoubtedly stunned and scarred by a battle he wasn't prepared for.

Chirkinian once excoriated network sports announcer Don Criqui for asking one question: "How do I look, Frank?"

"'How do I look?'" mocked Chirkinian. "What do I care how you look? It's how you sound, and I think you sound awful!" Criqui was one of those pretty boy announcers like Roger Twibell, who wouldn't have lasted five minutes with Chirkinian.

Frank's rules were seemingly simple: never talk over a stroke, because nothing you could utter would ever be more important than the stroke itself; and never say anything obtuse. If an announcer said "…He's made the putt…," Chirkinian would sneer into his headphones by charging "Oh, really? We couldn't see that for ourselves, eh?" Frank wanted his product, the broadcast, unsullied, so he was always coaching, always searching for and expecting perfection.

The great Chirkinian met his match when ordered by CBS to try to make a golf announcer out of the overly sensational golf neophyte Brent Musburger. When Jack Nicklaus pulled out of the 1983 Masters due to back spasms, Musburger interviewed him for CBS: "Jack, you say your back spasms have caused you to withdraw from the Masters," Musburger said. "Why didn't you just ask for a later starting time?"

Nicklaus just roared with laughter, "Uh, you just don't do that, Brent. " He patiently explained to Musburger that the tee times were preset and unchangeable. Mercifully, it was a taped interview, so Musburger was spared the further embarrassment of having all of the golf world see that telling gaffe.

Musburger was ill suited to golf broadcasting. You'd have thought that a man who was a skilled announcer at other sports would realize that there had to be a change of pace to broadcast golf. He was incapable of realizing that golf is a game that doesn't need hyping. Musburger seemed to think it was a crime to show any reverence. Chirkinian tried very hard, indeed, to get Brent to understand what golf was about, but Musburger had only one way of broadcasting, and it was completely unsuited to the game of golf. There's a language to golf that only those who are steeped in the game seem to understand is mandatory.

Of course, Musburger was a nongolfer who only made the concession to play the game, and typically came off the last hole having made his one-footer to break 100—though he did abide by the most important Scottish tradition—he played very, very fast. The fact that the royal and ancient game is no longer burdened with the commentary of Musburger anywhere on the planet leads me to believe there is, indeed, a glimmer of hope for golf.

Jack Newton, who achieved runner-up status to Tom Watson in the 1975 British Open, made his television debut as my co-commentator on Australian television. On the air, I threw it to Newton by passing a comment about the strong play of Graham Marsh. Newton's reply to me went like this: "Shit, man, Marsh is definitely hot today..." I began to shake my head and gesture wildly. Newton just charged ahead, describing Marsh as he lined up a short putt by saying, "Marsh has a real knee-trembler here, though."

With that, I began to stutter and stammer and try to contain myself because in British parlance—understood in Australia—a "knee trembler" refers to having sex against a wall. As buttoned-up and professional as I was trying to be, Newton was letting it all hang out. Exasperated and shaking my head, I figured Newton had destroyed himself. Apparently, the casual manner of most Australians won out because no complaints were lodged, and Newton became the top golf broadcaster in Australia.

I withstood a similar experience while broadcasting the Palm Meadows Cup in Queensland, Australia on Channel 10. My co-commentator in this case was an Australian sportswriter named Jeff Roach.

Peter Senior, in the midst of an outstanding year, had dominated the tournament, and had done so with an elongated, broom handle-type mallet putter. As Senior lined up a putt, I said to Roach, "Isn't it amazing, Jeff, that Senior has had such success on the greens by switching to the long putter? He's absolutely copied the style of Sam Torrance by anchoring the grip-end of the putter on his chin. It may be unusual, but the long putter and that technique has been successful for Senior, hasn't it?"

"Yeah, mate," Roach answered. "It's especially amazing because as Senior stands there ready to putt, it looks as if he doesn't know whether to suck it or blow it!"

I was flabbergasted at his witty but bold remark, and was surprised to learn that again, not one call of complaint rang in from Australian viewers. Calls of complaint did come in, interestingly, when the Prime Network replayed the event and commentary on American cable television.

I must admit that Newton and Roach are, at least, original, authentic, and bold: 100% Aussie.

At the other extreme, Vin Scully, considered one of America's finest sports broadcasters, was a master of the cliché. His days at CBS golf were absolutely, unbelievably cliché-ridden. I recall the Buick Open at Warwick Hills, where we once decided to broadcast the hole introductions in a different manner than usual. The individual hole announcers basically stood in a line, shoulder to shoulder, and Scully was to ask us questions about the hole we were covering. Scully got to me, and damn me if he didn't ask a long, elaborate question and then answer it himself! He didn't even let me answer! Of course, Chirkinian just went after him though his earpiece. "You red-headed idiot! You've got such a damned ego that you can't even let the limey speak? You've got to give the question and the answer? You're damned Carnac, you are!"

I think Scully is a consummate baseball announcer. I have a huge respect for his encyclopedic knowledge of baseball and its history. But when it came to golf, he was out of his field of true expertise. He tried to get by with a pompous delivery, which was not backed up by enough knowledge.

Jim Nantz had a somewhat similar problem early in his career in that I don't think he's ever been able to give the impression that he's really in tune with golf history. It's hard to convince the public, when you're young, that you know what went on. That has changed for him, though, with the passage of time. Chirkinian was hard on him in the beginning, but Nantz, a tremendous guy, rarely cracked. We did, however, ride him a little on his talking about his Fred Couples/Blaine McCallister connection. He'd gone to college with them and was close to them, so he had a tendency to work that into the broadcasts—until we jumped on him with viciously ribald comments. Nantz didn't take it very well, but it worked. We even once put poor Nantz through his paces in Flint, Michigan, where we punished him by feeding him dastardly alcoholic concoctions called "Alabama Slammas." Since he was the youngest member of our group, we were just toying with him and trying to corrupt him. He was quite innocent until we got ahold of him.

It was no different than when we'd broadcast from Pebble Beach and have to hear Ken Venturi, CBS's main analyst, talk about how nice it was for him to come home. He waxed on endlessly about the

San Francisco area and Cypress Point. Every time we got anywhere near Congressional Country Club, we'd then have to hear about Venturi's U.S. Open win there. It got boring, and our man Kenny has a considerable ego. If he was in the midst of one of his mood swings, he was capable of walking right past you without even saying "hello." When Venturi was on, however, he was hilarious. He could be absolutely the funniest guy you would ever want to be in the presence of, although he was hell to play golf with. Venturi, tee-to-green still a fine player, brushes away all of his short putts because he has the yips. And if there is any slow play in front of him at all, he jumps back into his cart and skips holes, rushing around to avoid the backup.

Some of the younger players harbored some resentment toward Venturi because they got the idea that he was against the modern-day golf pro. Some thought Venturi was bitter about all of the money they were now making. They'd hear him speak of the great players of his day, and bemoan the lost art of shotmaking. Sometimes I might be convinced to agree with Kenny's alleged bias. Do we have an equal of Hogan, Nelson, and Snead today? I greatly admire Venturi for his courage in overcoming a stuttering problem that would have kept mere mortals off the air. Venturi's longevity as a lead sports analyst—over 30 years with CBS—is unparalleled and an incredible feat. Venturi somehow manages to effectively make his points compelling without conventional punctuation and syntax, and a somewhat limited vocabulary.

Bobby Clampett, who I suppose was a little naïve, to say the least, took his lumps from us for committing an all-time on-the-air gaffe. Clampett was broadcasting at the Kemper Open when a shot was hit into his green, where it landed, stuck, and drew back some 20 to 30 feet almost off the front of the green.

"Wow, that ball really had some jism on it!" Clampett remarked.

At the first available opportunity, Chirkinian jumped all over Clampett through his earphones. "You silly ass, Clampett! What are you talking about 'had a lot of jism on it?' Don't you know what jism is?"

"No, Frank," admitted Clampett, "I guess I don't."

"It's semen, you idiot!" Frank shouted back to Clampett, who was aghast upon learning the definition because he considered himself a very religious man and a born-again Christian.

The Kemper Open is contested at the TPC at Avenel, near Washington D.C. The evening of Clampett's gaffe, the CBS golf broadcast team was invited to a reception at the Admiralty House at the Naval Observatory, hosted by Vice President Dan Quayle and his wife Marilyn, who resided there. It was commonly known that Dan Quayle was a golf enthusiast and a jolly good player. During the cocktail hour, Summerall, Nantz, Venturi, I , and a few other members of the CBS Golf team were chatting away in the corner, laughing about the day's events, and I said "We ought to rename Clampett. From now on he shall be known as 'the Reverend Jism.'" That comment caused even more laughter, and then Jim Nantz added, "Yeah, we'll call him 'R.J.' for a code to use in front of other people!"

We were really carrying on, engaging in good-natured fun at Clampett's expense, when Vice President Quayle drifted over to ask what all of the laughter was about. Everyone looked at me and suddenly this poor Brit was left to explain the intense giggling that ensued. Slightly embarrassed and certainly cornered, I bravely began by explaining, "Well, Mr. Vice President, Bobby Clampett, at the golf tournament today, talked on the air about a shot hit into a green with backspin as 'having a lot of jism on it.'" After running through the entire story, I got a total blank stare from the Vice President, who, to my total amazement, didn't see the humor in the tale because he, too, apparently, didn't know what "jism" is. It was a most awkward of moments, and none of my cowardly colleagues came to my aid. Again, left to the unenviable task of explaining, I calmly put my arm around Vice President Quayle and punned: "Now, Mr. Vice President, come, come..." His eyes lit up as "the penny dropped," and thankfully, the laughter began to flow again.

The laughter was never in short supply when Jack Whitaker was committing another of his Clouseau-type blunders. While broadcasting a tournament with Whitaker in Australia, a tremendous rainstorm descended upon the golf course. It was forecast to be a short, albeit mighty shower, so we tried to maintain the broadcast through the rain delay. As host, I was "tap dancing" to fill the time, and in the process I tossed a question to Whitaker, who was positioned in the tower at the 12th hole. Whitaker did not take his cue to reply. I called for him again on the air, and when I got no response from Whitaker, the director trained one of our cameras on his tower. The camera shot revealed Whitaker, miserably bundled up in his trench coat with his hat pulled down over his head, climbing down from his now abandoned perch. We let the viewers see this piece of tape, but not before manipulating the tape to give the effect of Whitaker in his overcoat, dancing madly to the song "Blue Skies." Everyone, subject excepted, laughed at Whitaker's embarrassingly premature run for cover, and the creative genius of director Mac Hemion scored a direct hit on ol' Jack.

When it came to on-the-air mistakes, some announcers have thicker skins than others. Tom Weiskopf has done some golf broadcasting for CBS, and he once had a tremendous row with Pat Summerall when he corrected a Summerall mistake on the air. Summerall was annoyed that this happened, because he felt Weiskopf should have taken him to the side after the broadcast and told him the error of his ways rather than correcting him on the air. A serious animosity developed between the two.

At a crew dinner in Augusta at West Lake Country Club, I decided to try to end the hostilities. During the cocktail hour, I summoned Summerall and Weiskopf together. They are both tall, so I put my hands on the backs of their necks and said, "You know, you two guys are so dumb and so obstinate that I should bang your heads together." With that, I pulled their heads together, expecting them to resist, and boom—I accidentally smashed their heads together!

I ran swiftly for my life, all the way back from the West Lake Country Club to the house that Summerall and I were sharing, and promptly locked the door. Pat came rushing after me, and, since the door was locked, kicked in not only the door, but the door frame as well! Fortunately for me, he was laughing too hard at the sight of the fallen door to be angry.

There have been occasions where I, too, have angered people with my on-air commentary. On one occasion, my tower was positioned pitifully close to the green at Harbor Town. Tom Kite, lining up a putt, claimed he could hear me talking. It destroyed his concentration, and he got mad. So he stepped away from the ball, huffed and puffed, put his hands on his hips, and made gestures toward me in the tower. By now, the crowd had started to get on me as well, shushing me angrily.

I blew my stack, got up out of my seat in the tower and said, "Tom, why don't you stop bitching and moaning and do your job, and I'll do mine, because all we're trying to do is make you look good!" The gallery was stunned into silence by this imperious Brit.

When I got off the air that evening, Tom approached me in the clubhouse. I thought *Uh-oh, we're going to have some nastiness here.* But to his eternal credit, Kite said to me, "You were absolutely right, Ben. I was out of line. I know you're not doing it on purpose, and I apologize." I always thought a great deal more of Kite after that, and I was very upset that I had unnerved him.

That wasn't the first, nor was it the last time a player would complain about audible on-course television commentary. Nicklaus and Lanny Wadkins seemed to have especially sensitive ears.

When Nicklaus was associated with CBS as a part-time broadcaster, the network held a dinner for him at the "21" club in Manhattan. I was to roast Nicklaus, which I did with some aplomb, needling him for his slow play and for the fact that we never really knew if he was actually going to show up for his broadcast duties at the time he'd been richly contracted to do so.

Following my roast of him, Nicklaus rose to the podium, and began his own defense. "Ben has talked about how slowly I play," Nicklaus began. "But you folks don't realize how tough it is for me to get over a short iron and be able to hear Ben in the tower behind the green saying '...*Well, this is not the strongest part of Jack Nicklaus's game.'*"

Amidst the laughter, I realized that Nicklaus was right. I had, indeed, said that he was one of the poorer chippers in the game because he so rarely had to do so. Nicklaus had used this example as a joke, but he'd made the point clearly that he was able to pick up my voice during the heat of competition. Often truth is told in jest, and the truth is, when yours is the only voice talking on a golf course, it can easily be heard.

I recently ran into Tour player Brad Faxon's father, Brad Sr., at the "Lobster Pot Tournament" at the Mid-Ocean Club in Bermuda. Faxon told me that his son had from time to time commented that he could hear me describing his putt when I broadcast from my tower. "Brad did tell me that he could hear you," said Faxon Sr., "but he said he never minded because it was always such a joy for him to hear your delivery style and manner of speaking."

Some of the less complimentary Tour players would report being able to hear me to the Tour staff, which would accept their complaints, relay them to me with a wink, and then conveniently forget to do anything about them.

Easily, though, the most egregious and valid example took place during a 1975 CBS broadcast of the Jackie Gleason Classic at Inverrary Golf Club in Lauderhill, Florida.

Announcer Ray Scott was calling the action from a CBS tower perched very near a green. Lee Trevino had marked his 10-inch putt, and was waiting his turn to tap it in. Scott, in earshot of "Super Mex," suggested to Trevino that he stall his putt until the commercial break was over and the live CBS coverage was back on the air. The request certainly caught Trevino off guard, but the timing worked out. CBS came back from the commercial, and Scott got to call the play as Trevino, in the thick of the race, put his ball in position, picked up his coin, lined up the 10-inch putt—*and missed it!*

Now, Trevino may have a reputation for being jovial when you see him laughing and joking on television, but when he's riled, one should not aspire to be on his bad side. He is intense and demanding, as many of his caddies have learned the hard way. Even Chirkinian knew Trevino's wrath when he once caught Lee at a bad moment. While playing poorly on the course, Trevino grabbed a nearby CBS camera lens and banged on the microphone, asking the technician if it worked. When assured the microphone was indeed active, Trevino glared into the lens with a message for Chirkinian, who was watching on monitors in the control truck.

"Frank, are you in there, you rug merchant? Leave me alone, dammit!"

In fact, the media-savvy Trevino also knew how to spot a microphone that was set up to gather sound effects, usually placed inconspicuously next to a tee marker.

Bang, bang, bang, Trevino would knock on the sensitive microphone with his driver, causing the technicians in the control truck to clutch their ears. "Are you in there, Frank?" Trevino would playfully ask.

It was at the 1971 U.S. Open at Merion that one of these ambient microphones picked up the voice of Trevino, who had gone to the

18th tee in the final round with a chance to win the tournament out-right. Standing next to the microphone, Trevino called for his driver. His caddie, Neal Harvey, nervously fumbled with the club and had trouble getting the head cover off. "I'm doing the playing, and my caddie's doing the choking!" Trevino chirped.

Trevino wasn't joking, and Ray Scott must have been choking when Lee ended up losing the Inverrary Classic to Bob Murphy after Scott had asked him to pause over that putt. Trevino was convinced that the announcer had cost him a chance to win the event. After-ward, there was no lack of very vocal and visceral complaining by Trevino in the press room.

Scott was appropriately then forced to appear before the media and apologize to Trevino. Scott also admitted that it was wrong of him to attempt to influence play in that manner. Scott was a nice man, but again, not versed in golf. He was really a CBS football an-nouncer who had no idea Trevino might miss that little putt and then blame him for the loss.

I must admit here for the first time that I once cost a player a chance to win a tournament. I was covering the Waterloo Cup, played in Belgium near the scene of the infamous defeat of Napoleon by the Duke of Wellington. The event was being played in memory of Donald Swaelens, a Belgian professional who was stricken down by cancer at the age of 34.

Well, Hale Irwin was one of the big-name players imported to compete in this event, and we were all put up at a beautiful hotel in downtown Brussels. The night of our arrival I ran into Sally Irwin in the lobby, and my big mouth got to talking in great depth about Brus-sels. Hale eventually came downstairs and approached us.

"Hale, you won't believe it," Sally said to her husband. "Since tomorrow is a day off for you, Ben has offered to escort us on a walking tour of Brussels. He's going to show us all of the great build-ings and wonderful cathedrals of this city! Isn't that great?"

"Uh, gee, hon, yeah," Irwin mumbled, "that's terrific."

The next morning, we set out on foot to view all of the great medieval marvels and intricate architectural wonders of Brussels. To put it mildly, I walked their asses off. Eleven miles of streets, side-walks, and steps. Sally had a ball, and Hale ended up enjoying himself once he got used to the idea. The very next day, Irwin tried to play, but was forced to forfeit any chance to win the tournament due to a bad back.

Being the good sport that he is, Hale never blamed me publicly.

Another good sport was the lighthearted quipster Frank Urban Zoeller. Fuzzy had a maddening habit of toying with me at any chance he got. As you would expect, Zoeller was quite proficient at it. In Akron at the World Series of Golf, Zoeller breezed by my broadcast tower after he'd putted out. I was then suddenly startled by a loud "thwack!" I jerked my head and looked down to find a Maxfli bouncing off my desktop. Zoller had playfully lobbed a golf ball over the plexiglass shield in front of my booth.

It was only the beginning of an annoying, yet amusing, habit that Zoeller continued to haunt me with all over the Tour.

Greg Norman was not quite as genial, and not playful at all when my mouth caused me to run afoul of him on one occasion. It also occurred at the Kemper Open, where there were about seven players in contention coming to the last four holes. I was covering the 17th hole, which is a par-three featuring water on the right and in front. The pin was very near the water—a "sucker pin"—and generally speaking, those players in contention made every effort to keep their shots well away from the water, even if it meant missing the green to the left. Davis Love III, for instance, missed it way to the left. Norman, though, being the macho fellow that he is, took the brave line and his ball came up short and fell into the pond. "Alas," I said on the air, "Greg Norman has found yet another way to lose." It seemed like the truth, and there was no denying that Norman was becoming known for snatching defeat from the jaws of victory, as he had at various tournaments, major and otherwise.

The following week I was sitting on an outdoor stage at Shinnecock Hills, about ready to host a U.S. Open preview for Intersport Television. It was a panel show that I hosted with John Walls, and Fred Couples had joined us on the stage. We were just about to start when Greg Norman came by, having just finished being interviewed for ESPN's preview show on the next set. "Hey, big Ben Wright, you bastard!" Norman shouted. "That thing you said about me was the cruelest damned thing you've ever said. I've always backed you up and that was just unforgivable, you ass." He raged into a very blue streak right in front of everyone assembled to produce the television show. "I hit a damned courageous shot and I was just unlucky."

I said to Norman, "Can't you see I'm just about to do a show? Just bugger off!" Norman stormed away, while Walls and Couples sat there with their jaws open, as if they'd been hit by lightning. As far as I was concerned, I said the truth. He may have thought it was a great shot, but I don't reckon too many great golf shots finish in the water.

Norman and I didn't speak for weeks and then months, and finally Frank Chirkinian got us together on the telephone. It made no sense for me to quarrel with someone with whom I would cross paths so often, and one of Chirkinian's closest friends to boot. Norman had named Chirkinian chairman of the board at his vaunted Medallist Club in Palm Beach, Florida. Chirkinian, in fact, was present at Norman's home when President Bill Clinton's visit with Norman was shortened by a knee-injuring fall on Norman's porch steps. (For the curious and suspicious, Chirkinian insists that neither alcohol nor women were involved.)

So anyway, Chirkinian arranged a peacemaking phone call between Norman and me.

"Alright, Greg, I suppose I was severe with you," I told him.

Apparently, this pleased the Shark and the feud ended. It was a relief to me because Greg and I, before and after that incident, have shared an enjoyable relationship. Norman's new favorite foil is CBS announcer and golf teacher Peter Kostis, but only because Norman does not appreciate being criticized on the air by a teaching pro who has never himself been in contention or in the heat of battle.

Peter Jacobsen suffered a spell in which he was insecure about his short game. This insecurity, according to a miffed Jacobsen, was compounded by me criticizing his putting on the air. I later learned that in an effort to mentally exorcise his putting demons, Jacobsen conjured up a detailed mental image of me being hoisted from the television tower by a helicopter and carried off into outer space. He even had a Ben Wright look-alike participate in the literal staging of the helicopter scene in a photo-shoot for a magazine article on visualization techniques.

It sounded like an overly paranoid case of positive imagery to me, but Jacobsen is one of my favorite players on Tour, and if this voodoo actually helped him, I'm pleased.

To be critical of the play of a star golfer like Norman, I can assure you, is not a task I relish. But it is the duty of all broadcasters to describe the action as one sees it. We must provide truthful and insightful commentary and perspective whenever we can—good or bad. Here again, we learn the lesson that, in a "politically correct" environment, sometimes the truth hurts. The PGA Tour's network television deals are now structured in such a way so that the PGA Tour has more influence than ever over what the networks show and say. A PGA Tour representative is present in the network's broadcast truck at each telecast to ensure that PGA Tour content and direction is followed to the letter. If the networks should lose control of the content of their programs, and they start to be a shill for the PGA Tour, then no one will watch these bloody telecasts because they will just be an attempt at a public relations exercise on behalf of the Tour. If announcers can't criticize a shot for being a bad shot when it *is* a bad shot, the commentary will be ridiculous. If a Tour pro hits a sand wedge to 40 feet from the hole, it's a bad shot. There are no two ways about it. If you're going to try to hide those facts, then there'll be no honesty left. It's quite possible that the Tour is attempting to gain control of all television programming. Eventually, the Tour might opt to produce and control all of the golf broadcasts. In that scenario, a PGA Tour Productions broadcast unit will provide programming to the networks. The integrity of the broadcasts might then be open to suspicion, since the commentary would seem bound to be PGA Tour slanted. I suppose some of the players might enjoy that kind of protection, but in the long run it would seem that the Tour risks losing viewers.

Frank Chirkinian was fiercely protective of the integrity of his CBS broadcasts. In fact, his stubbornness on the issue of creative control may have cost CBS the chance to gain broadcast rights to the British Open. Chirkinian had asked me to assist in setting up caucuses with now Sir Michael Bonallack, Secretary of the Royal & Ancient Golf Club of St. Andrews, in an attempt to gain broadcast rights. I had known Bonallack, a five-time British Amateur and six-time English Amateur champion, for years, having played golf against him as a youth and having covered him during my golf writing career. In fact, Bonallack has jokingly never forgiven me for writing that he had "a swing that only a mother could love," comparing it to "that of a coal-heaver." Bonallack won by sheer force of will, dominating in match play but struggling in stroke play.

Even if a deal with Bonallack for the British Open rights equated to a break-even financial proposition for the network, CBS was interested. I believe we would have secured the rights, had it not been for IMG superagent Mark McCormack, who was handling the negotiation for the R&A. McCormack insisted that he be given an on-air position as part of the proposed BBC/CBS commentary team covering the Open. Chirkinian felt this was a clear conflict of interest and would have none of it. Could there really be honest criticism and commentary of players with a man representing the R&A and the European PGA Tour as part of the broadcast team? Could an agent who represented a good number of players in the field really be expected to put himself in a position of criticizing his very clients? The all-powerful McCormack ended up serving as an announcer on the BBC feed, while CBS and Chirkinian were left without the British Open as a consequence of maintaining editorial dignity.

I remember very nearly being put in a difficult position by a PGA Tour player on the occasion of my very first live greenside award presentation in 1974. Following play, Summerall was to "throw" the telecast to me, where I was standing with the tournament director, the tournament sponsor, the player, and his wife. On-the-air, I would then introduce everyone, ask the player a few questions, and then the tournament director would congratulate the player and the sponsor would present the beaming player with his crystal trophy and oversized check.

As we were all waiting for the commercial break to end so that we can go on the air live, the player leans over and whispers in my ear. "Ben, I know she has a name badge on...but this woman is *not* my wife. Help me out here."

I played cool in front of the crowd and the officials, but my mind was racing. How was I going to diplomatically pull this off in front of the television viewers and gathered officials?

Fate stepped in, because just after Summerall introduced me live, my microphone went dead, and Summerall had to reclaim the broadcast from the booth, apologize for the technical difficulties, and sign off. The technicians later revealed that an overserved patron had stumbled over the cables and inadvertently yanked out my audio cord.

In my television career though, I quickly and literally painfully learned that consequences can frequently be experienced as a result of legitimate editorial criticism and opinionated commentary. Christy O'Connor Sr. and I, for one instance, had a love/hate relationship due to my frank television commentary about him. It began when I was broadcasting for ITV in Europe in the late 1960s. Christy O'Connor, an Irishman, was playing exceptionally poorly in a tournament in England called the Agfa-Gevaert at Stoke Poges, west of London, where the classic James Bond golf scene in "Goldfinger" was filmed. O'Connor had played early in the day, and Harry Weetman played late in the day. Weetman was a very strong lad who was a Ryder Cup player for years and was a very good player. While Weetman was playing, O'Connor got to drinking in the clubhouse, as Christy was wont to do, particularly when he was playing very poorly. Harry, though, played well. But when Weetman walked into the bar, O'Connor made disparaging remarks to him.

Weetman was strong, and built like a brick outhouse. He growled at Christy, "I don't need to take any of this shit. You come outside." O'Connor went outside with Weetman, but it was a pathetic fight. O'Connor attempted a few ill-judged and ill-aimed blows, but Weetman just whacked him twice straight in the face, knocked him back over a hedge, and left him unconscious. Weetman left and O'Connor eventually crawled away to his lodgings.

Christy appeared for play the following day wearing a pair of very large, dark sunglasses. Thunderstorms that day had delayed play, so that when play resumed and we went on the air, we had no choice but to show the stragglers who were then on the course, including O'Connor, instead of the leaders who had yet to come into camera range. I was commentating, and it's dark as night out because even though the storms had left, it was still very overcast. O'Connor appeared on the screen, wearing these big dark glasses on this very cloudy day, and I said on the air, somewhat jokingly, "...Well, here comes Christy O'Connor Sr., not having a very happy tournament this week. You might query at home, why he's wearing a large pair of dark glasses when it is almost as black as night out here, the storm having just blown though for it to be fit enough to play, but only just. Well, the truth of the matter is that Christy met with a slight accident last evening."

The ink-stained wretches were listening to the feed in the press room, and none of those jokers knew anything about the fight, so they jumped all over O'Connor when he got in, asking what the accident was about. The next day, one of the Sunday newspapers in Britain, called *The People,* published a story by their golf writer, Jack Wood, that said that I had blown O'Connor's cover by revealing on the air the story of the Weetman-O'Connor fight. Of course, I had not done that at all. I simply had said that O'Connor had met with a slight accident, but Wood's story charged that I revealed the gossip on purpose to stir the pot. Stir the pot it did, because this newspaper story was read in Ireland, and when O'Connor got back to Ireland after the tournament, he was called before the board of the Royal Dublin Golf Club at four o'clock the following afternoon.

The board slammed the clipping down and commanded O'Connor to explain his behavior. The board gave him a serious warning because it was always away from home that Christy behaved in this wild manner. At home in Ireland, he behaved in a different manner altogether. O'Connor was one of the most talented golfers I ever saw, and moreso because it was at times when he was horribly hung over that he compiled scores in the very low 60s. It defied reason.

O'Connor got the idea that I was trying to make trouble for him, and whenever he got into a fighting drunk mood, he'd come after me. I told him repeatedly that what had happened was not my intention, and I think he believed me, but when he was drinking his feelings would again surface. At the Dunlop Masters Tournament in Gosforth Park, Newcastle on Tyne, Dunlop held a cocktail party on the evening of the event. After the cocktail party, Dunlop Managing Director Findlay Picken and I were walking across from the clubhouse to the adjacent hotel to have dinner when suddenly I heard the footsteps of cloven hooves coming up from behind. I spun around and put my hand out as Christy O'Connor grabbed onto one finger and bent it back so far he broke it. Blood actually spurted from the palm of my hand! It wasn't until the next day that he apologized, because he had been so drunk he didn't even know what he had done.

At the Italian Open, just out of the blue, O'Connor rambled at me as I was sitting on the sofa in the hotel. "You filthy rotten swine," he growled at me, "you got me into trouble!" With that, O'Connor aimed a big but swift kick at my crotch. Brian Barnes, another player sitting nearby, caught O'Connor's foot in midair, yanked it up, and dumped O'Connor with a crashing fall! Barnes, who had the more than six-foot-tall body of a hulking barroom bouncer, stood over O'Connor with his sleeves rolled up, and warned him with a growl to "Get the hell out of here." O'Connor was immediately obedient.

This love/hate relationship with O'Connor was truly that, because eventually we learned to laugh about the incident. Further, he came to understand that my commentary was not designed to hurt him.

In fact, at Royal Birkdale early one morning, I entered the clubhouse and came across O'Connor all alone, shaving in the locker room.

"What are you doing here at this time of the morning shaving?" I asked.

O'Connor said, "You know what I'm like. I had a terrible skinfull last night, and I couldn't find my hotel, so I picked a nice, friendly bunker here, and I laid down in the bunker. Perfect lovely sleep I've had."

He'd walked from whichever bunker it was he'd slept in, shaved, and still tied for second in that event. I never mentioned O'Connor's bunker incident on the air or in print that week. O'Connor must then have understood that I loved the game, and didn't want to do anything to hurt it or its participants, including him.

Unfortunately, due to my continental background, sometimes I have been accused of favoring the European players in my commentary.

Ed Fiori came at me one time in Dallas. I was passing the table where he and Fred Couples were having lunch, and Fiori, mimicking my accent, challenged me with "Ben, I'm so sick of listening to you going on and on about the 'magical shotmaking of Seve Ballesteros.' Why do you favor Seve, Ben? Are you his damned agent?"

Maintaining my composure, I mustered up my best aloof British accent and said, "Yes, Ed, I am. I would represent you as well except I don't waste time on inferior performers."

Couples recognized the touché and grinned slyly, trying not to break into a chuckle in front of a fuming Fiori.

Fiori never much liked the CBS crew. He seemed to hold a grudge against us since the time Venturi mockingly referred to him as "the Grip." Venturi gave him this witty sobriquet because of the way Fiori kept his left hand strongly turned on the club. All four of Fiori's knuckles were visible upon address.

I always tried to be impartial on the air. If there were any truth to Fiori's complaint, I would have been rooting for Ballesteros when he was trying to hold off Nicklaus's historic march to victory at the 1986 Masters. Even though I was from Seve's side of "the pond," I didn't want Seve to beat Nicklaus. Not on your life. My most infamous call, in fact, was of Seve's second shot at the par-five 15th hole.

Ballesteros himself has said that he had the tournament under control. He was in the lead, and his form appeared strong. Were the resounding gallery cheers for Nicklaus starting to rattle chains in Seve's subconscious? Did he get overconfident? Somehow the shot, which by all accounts cost him the tournament, got away from him. Ballesteros's swing was clearly out of whack. Immediately after impact I uttered, "This ball is destined for the water." Sure enough, Seve's 4-iron shot sent the ball into the pond, and his hopes for a third green jacket sunk with it. If anyone had a right to be angry with me, it was Ballesteros. Many people also remember my call at that same tournament in which my exuberance over the Nicklaus charge prompted me to shout, "Yessir!" when Jack holed a brilliant putt at 15 for an eagle just moments before Seve's fate would be sealed there.

Both calls may have sounded partisan, but they were indeed reflective of the emotion of what was happening on the golf course. Ballesteros might very well have—and probably with a measure of merit—taken offense to the tone of those calls. But they were nothing personal.

It was a thinly veiled reference to Ballesteros that put me on the wrong side of PGA Tour commissioner Deane Beman at the World Series of Golf in Akron, Ohio in the early '80s. I served each year as emcee of the event, which I suppose aided the Tour in its effort to establish the World Series as an event with international flavor. During this period, though, Ballesteros was involved in a well-publicized feud with Beman over the PGA Tour restrictions on the participation and requirements of international players. Ballesteros, even though he was the top-ranked player in the world at the time, was not in Akron to play at Firestone, which was a cause of some embarrassment to the Tour and the tournament organizers, who were repeatedly questioned about this by the media.

Serving as emcee of the opening ceremonies and presentation of honorees, I was surrounded by Beman and other golf officials, along with a suitable number of the international sports and golf press. The ceremonies went without incident, and at the culmination, I quipped, "Good luck to all of the players, and may the best man win...if he's here."

I was henceforth removed as emcee of the World Series of Golf Opening Ceremonies and told by the tournament organizers that Beman, enraged by my Eurocentric quip, ordered the change. Beman, of course, denied any involvement.

I am keenly aware that I have an enemy in Perth at the Lake Karrinyup Golf Club. In the late 1970s, I went there to broadcast an event on Australian television. Upon my arrival, I was informed that a tumultuous event had occurred during Lake Karrinyup's recent club championship. It seemed that a fine golfer who was expected to win the tournament came to the 17th hole with victory at hand. Unfortunately, his perfunctory 2-iron shot didn't make the carry to the 17th green and landed in the water. Stunned and enraged, the player violently helicoptered his 2-iron into the pond then teed up another ball, which also didn't make the carry. The club he used for the second shot quickly followed into the lake, and now, short on long irons, the player hit yet another ball into the watery grave, whereupon he threw his whole bag of clubs into the drink. The spectacle continued when the player noticed his caddie laughing. He proceeded to take furious hold of the boy and forcefully usher him into the lake. The player's embarrassing tirade resulted in the committee demanding his resignation from the club, and it left Karrinyup to search for a new leader, since the player was the club captain!

As you might expect, I just had to tell that story on the air during the broadcast. It is without reservation that we can be certain the former captain will not be asking me to autograph this book.

Of course, I have felt my own shame by misspeaking in front of a crowd while introducing Raymond Floyd at the start of the final round of a British Commercial Television mixed foursomes series in 1977. It was to be Raymond Floyd and Jane Blaylock against Gary Player and Sally Little—America versus South Africa—at the famed Waterville Golf Links on the green and scenic southwest tip of County Kerry, Ireland. General Manager Noel Cronin still keeps the scorecard from that event, with my signature, displayed in the warm and elegant clubhouse, but not due to the inauspicious beginning of the event, which was filmed for a later showing on television. I stood before the crowd, and on the cue of the director, began... "Good afternoon, ladies and gentlemen from me, Ben Wright, at the Waterville Golf Links, this magnificent track designed by Eddie Hackett, an Irish architect of genuine merit. It's my pleasure to introduce, first of all, on the team representing the United States, Raymond Floyd, *who is no stranger to mixed foursomes...*" alluding to his reputation for partying and womanizing.

"Cut!" came a voice from the crowd. We were working on film, so the cameraman stopped the camera, thinking it was the director who yelled "cut," but it was Maria Floyd who stepped out of the gallery. She walked right up to me and said "Ben, you may be a very good friend of Raymond's, and I've never met you before, but I just want you to know that I am his new wife, and we want to try and put that garbage behind us. From now on, Raymond is going to concentrate on his golf."

What courage it took for her to step out! I was embarrassed to no end, but I became great friends with Maria, and somehow managed to keep a relationship with Raymond despite my mistaken attempt at humor. Raymond and I, after years of partying and seeing each other at golf tournaments, also had a great working relationship.

Floyd and I shared a particularly hard night of drinking in London in his early days. When it came time to leave the pub in which we had done our damage, I had enough sense to realize that I should not even attempt to pilot my prized Aston Martin DB-4 and its powerful V-8 Vantage engine through the streets of London. I left it parked safely in a cul-de-sac, or mews, between some nearby houses, and Floyd and I took London cabs to our respective beds.

The next day, after eventually awakening and drying out, I came to the panicked realization that I had no idea where my car was! I walked the neighborhood near the pub, but had apparently so successfully and safely hidden it that I myself could not find it. For three subsequent days, I searched high and low for that car. Desperate for clues to jog my memory, I returned to the pub, where by now the same Irish barkeep on the night in question was back on duty for his shift.

I explained my plight to the bartender and asked if he could help me in any way.

"Well, it's like this," he began in his whimsical brogue, "I'm not knowing at all where you might have hidden your car. My only suggestion would be that you sit down here, drink as much as you did that night, and you'll probably find yourself walking straight to it."

He may have been kidding, he may not have been. Either way, I easily accepted his advice, and indulged myself with the appropriate amount of drink. I walked directly to the car, and joyously found my DB-4.

Once Floyd got serious about his game and life, I remember him ranting and raving to me about how announcer Steve Melnyk would hang around him all of the time while Floyd was hitting balls and trying to prepare himself to play. "You know," said Floyd, "it's the equivalent of me coming into your office while you are trying to concentrate or write an article when you are on deadline, and bugging you with a load of questions."

I always asked players if they minded chatting with me before a round. Most of them were happy to do it because as they started to get a nervous edge, it became a little outlet that was beneficial to their temperament. If a guy was taciturn with you, you'd just walk on if you had any brains. Only a truly insensitive reporter would pester a player until eventually the player would have to say, "Do you mind? I'm trying to do some serious practice here!" You can always tell when a player has had enough of talking to you because he'll walk away and start hitting balls again, or just quit talking, focusing on the task at hand. I move on at that point, figuring he's been kind enough to give me a few minutes. To ask for more would be selfish.

In 1981, CBS experimented with having me attempt to conduct on-course interviews with players in the middle of the round. On the second hole of a sudden-death playoff between Tom Watson and the relatively unknown Tommy Valentine at the Atlanta Classic, I did a short interview with Valentine. The hometown favorite lost the playoff on the third hole, and I was bitterly accused of distracting Valentine and costing him the tournament. In fact, as we walked down the second hole, Valentine said to me, "Stick around, Ben, I'd like someone to talk to." I only tried my best to politely comply with his request without interrupting him or affecting the outcome in either way.

At the 1982 Los Angeles Open, Tom Weiskopf played poorly down the stretch, missing a chance to compete in a playoff. Weiskopf, who is plagued with a reputation as being difficult to deal with, noticed that I was urgently in need of an interview before the playoff started. To my surprise, Weiskopf approached me.

"Ben, you can interview me if you want to talk to a loser," he offered. It was indeed a gracious thing for him to do, and at what I'm certain was a difficult moment.

Having said that, it is true that some players were more sensitive than others to the needs of the media. On one occasion on a Saturday at Doral, the day's play went very quickly so we had to fill time near the end of the broadcast. Jack Nicklaus and Curtis Strange had just come off the last hole as the final pairing. Nicklaus had shot 65, and Strange finished with an unimpressive round of 75. Pat Summerall and I were dispatched by Chirkinian to get both of them at all costs and do at-length interviews with both of them.

Pat, being the gracious and utterly unselfish person that he was, asked me which of the two I wanted to interview. "Nicklaus, of course," I answered. Pat agreed that he would seek out and interview Curtis. As Nicklaus made his way to the scorer's tent, I caught up with him and politely said, "Excuse me, Jack. After you've signed your card, can I have you for an interview?"

"Certainly," was Nicklaus's quick reply.

After I concluded my live interview with Nicklaus, I watched Summerall conduct a competent and civilized interview with Strange, who was obviously still stinging from his poor play. When he finished and we went off the air, I thanked Pat for letting me interview Nicklaus. When I began to remark favorably on Strange's apparent sportsmanship, Summerall halted me. "I approached Strange and said, "Curtis, we're in a difficult situation,'" Summerall explained. "I said, 'We've got a long fill and you and Jack are the last two on the golf course. Can I have you for an interview after you've signed your card?' He told me to get lost," Pat said.

Summerall was not a guy who would suffer that kind of demeaning treatment. So he said, "Okay, Curtis. I'm telling *you*...that after you've signed your scorecard, you will come out here and do an interview with me. If you don't, I'm coming in there, and I'm going to punch your head in." I then understood that it was something other than sportsmanship that compelled Strange to agree to the necessary interview.

I also understand that, to this day, even though Strange himself is working as a network television commentator, at times he can still be standoffish and petulant to the media. His competitive fires sometimes have overheated his internal furnace. After making double-bogey on the last hole while competing in the first round of the 1999 Players Championship, Strange, then also ABC's lead color-commentator, snubbed the media in a huff and refused to answer questions.

Summerall, a former professional football player and a man's man, was a big guy, and there have been occasions where he was very helpful in protecting me from the wrath of people I have offended with my commentary. Sitting at a bar in downtown Chicago, I was approached by a man who didn't like my accent and didn't care for the idea of having a Brit on an American golf telecast. He was really beginning to harass me when I finally asked, "Would you please, sir, leave me alone and go away?"

"I'll talk to you as much as I want. You're a public figure," he argued. "And you're not even an American!"

Summerall stepped in at that point and told the guy "He's asked you to leave him alone. Now get out of here."

"I don't need any bullshit from a washed-up football player, either..." were the last words out of the chap's mouth before Pat gave him a backhand with his forearm, with that metal plate in his arm due to a football injury. Summerall hit him in the neck and this guy flew across the room and smashed into the wall.

"Jesus, Pat, I think you might have killed him," I remarked. Pat apologized to the bartender and we left. Pat was very loyal. If anyone messed with his broadcast colleagues, they had to answer to Pat.

While players sometimes weren't impressed by my commentary, there were times when I wasn't impressed by their play. Once at the Kemper Open, the day's pace of play had dragged to an almost unbearable crawl. A dearth of rain delays didn't help matters, and when Chirkinian cut to a beauty shot of a family of ducks near a pond, I dryly and glumly chimed into the microphone: "Those were mere eggs when we started this morning." I'm sure the viewers could relate to how I felt because I've had many people mention that quip to me, especially people who have suffered five-hour-long golf rounds stuck behind slow-playing Nicklaus impersonators. Even Henry Longhurst might have liked that "eggs" reference.

Boredom played a key role in a story that is often told in Britain of an on-air misstep by none other than Longhurst and Peter Alliss. Perched in a tower behind the 18th hole during a women's tournament at Sunningdale, the day began to get long as the play began to slow down. Eventually, the minds of Alliss and Longhurst—no doubt sweetened by lunchtime beverages—began to wander. At some point, they ceased paying full attention to the television monitor that displays the shot that is being shown on the air. It is important for announcers to remember to work from the monitor and not from their vantage point, so that they can be sure to commentate on what the viewers are seeing. Alliss and Longhurst cast their gaze instead out onto the scenic vista up the 18th fairway in front of them.

The two were relaxed and taking in the scene, when the on-air monitor showed the very pretty Nancy Lopez standing over a putt. This camera shot was lost on Alliss and Longhurst, who were lazily transfixed by their view of the golf course and the horizon. As Lopez crouched over her putt on-screen, their commentary about the scenery was voiced-over:

"Ah, it's a wonderful view from where we sit, isn't it Henry?" Alliss waxed on the air.

"Yes, yes," Longhurst sighed affectionately, "it has always been one of the great sights in golf…"

Humor—sometimes intentional, sometimes not—was an asset in golf coverage, but it was mainly during rehearsal that the CBS golf broadcast team really let their hair down. Normally, Chirkinian would hold rehearsal an hour or two before the live telecast with all of the announcers in their positions, calling whatever action happened to be on the course at the time. Although the session was somewhat of a warm-up, Chirkinian took it very seriously because he would record our efforts as a "rain package." If inclement weather struck during the live telecast, CBS at least had some action to broadcast. Once Chirkinian had enough serious commentary on tape for the rain package, he'd let us know and we would turn wilder than March hares. The cameras would zoom in on gorgeous or funny-looking members of the gallery, and we would all have a good-natured laugh. The announcers would all tell dirty jokes, make ribald comments, and discuss our evening dinner plans. At Hilton Head, the blimp's camera zoomed in on the Harbour Town lighthouse as the sound technician added "dive-bomber" sound effects.

While broadcasting the PGA Championship at Bellerive, for some reason or another, Chirkinian rehearsed us very close to the time we were to take the air. I suddenly decided that, whether rehearsal was over or not, I just had to leave the tower to relieve myself before we actually went on the air. As quickly as possible, I came rushing back up the ladder of the tower and put my earphones on without realizing that in the time I was away, the rehearsal had ended and the broadcast had begun. I started joking on the air, thinking we were still in a lighthearted rehearsal.

"What the hell is going on here," Chirkinian shouted into my earphones. "Don't you realize we're on the air?"

"Nah, Frank," I giggled, "we're not on the air." This was, indeed, all going out *over* the air. Chirkinian blurted another insistent expletive into my earphones, and with that and his tone, I immediately sensed the error of my ways and snapped into my "on-air" mode. Thankfully, I didn't say anything too "lighthearted."

Our lighthearted rehearsals served as a chance to let off some steam and relax before the genuine, live telecast. Of course, anyone with a satellite dish at home and all of the affiliate television stations along the networks could tune in and watch the rehearsal feed, which I'm sure, at times, was more entertaining than the telecast. The ability of these people to see the feed is, in part, what eventually brought the rehearsal hijinks to an end. During a rehearsal for the Los Angeles Open, Corey Pavin was in camera range and was in the process of shooting a nice low round. A shot of Pavin walking up the fairway was shown. At the bottom of the picture, an official looking on-screen graphic read: *"Corey Pavin...the week's low Jew."*

Well, the brothers of B'nai Brith blew a fuse and protested to CBS Sports president Neal Pilson, who himself was Jewish and was equally offended. From then on, the broadcast team was asked to behave during rehearsal and the audio during the rehearsal feed was muted to ensure satellite viewers were prevented from listening in. Political correctness was not our strong suit during the rehearsals, but a tension release was vital before a live broadcast. The demands of a live broadcast, and the pressure to be 100% perfect in front of a live microphone, cannot be understated.

In 1978, I was traveling from London to Adelaide, South Australia to broadcast the West Lakes Classic, which was played at the Grange Golf Club. It was a nice tournament, and had the distinction of being the first event Greg Norman had ever won. It was also the location of the first event Wayne Grady had ever claimed victory at. Wayne Grady, in fact, had showed up in jeans and with no money. He had hitchhiked there from Brisbane, which is on the other side of the country, a month's walk north to south. Grady, a penniless assistant club professional, found a caddie and then borrowed money from the caddie to buy a sleeve of balls. He went on to win his first tournament. They let him play in jeans because he said he didn't have anything else to wear. Wayne and I have been tremendous pals ever since, and we used to always celebrate his birthday together at the Buick Open at Warwick Hills, where we'd get into the bubbly.

There were about three stops on my journey from London to Adelaide, and my plane developed undercarriage trouble. When we landed at Singapore, a tire blew, so the time just got later and later and later. I finally arrived at Adelaide Airport at 1:00 P.M. and was scheduled to be on the air at 2:00 P.M., with a broadcast that was to run until 6:00 P.M. I'd traveled halfway around the world and I was plainly exhausted.

Bob Tuohy, the tournament promoter, had instructed his wife to pick me up from the airport. Her first words to me in the baggage area were, "Ben, we've got about an hour before you're on the air for a four-hour stint, mate. We're going to have to hurry through Adelaide like grand prix racers." She was good to her word, because I have never been so scared in my life. Hairpin turns at what seemed like 80 miles per hour were completed with mere inches to spare. Adelaide was set out in squares by a British governor and I'll swear we went across diagonally, we were going so fast!

When we got to the club, I was catching my breath from this tour de force when all of the representatives of the club began attempting to welcome me. I said, "Ladies and gentlemen, there is no time. Let us wait until after six and I'll be glad to converse with you and maybe we'll have a cocktail. Right now, though, I've got to find out who is playing in this tournament before I go on the air." Fair enough.

I went to the press room and there was nobody there because most of the media were at the free lunch, or making their way out to the course. I spotted one chap. He reminded me of a gnome. He was tanned like a walnut and had a bald, brown head. With a cigarette dangling from the corner of his mouth, he was tapping away on an old, upright Underwood typewriter. I looked through the list of players and came to the name "N. Suzuki," which I knew was Norio Suzuki, the Japanese player. Directly below him on the list was a name with which I was unfamiliar: "Y. Suzuki." Quickly, I asked this fellow, who was busy typing, "Excuse me, mate. Do you happen to know what the 'Y.' in 'Y. Suzuki' stands for?"

Without stopping typing, and with a heavy Australian accent, he said "Yeah, mate. It's 'Yastartyamota, Norio's younger brother.'"

"What?" I asked. Would you mind spelling that?"

He says "Yeah. Y-a-s-t-a-r-t-y-a-m-o-t-a. Yastartyamota Suzuki."

So I wrote that down and went up to the tower, just a little confused that a man could have such a strange name, but, being exhausted, didn't put two and two together at all. My co-commentator was Graham Marsh, a formidable amateur golfer and eventual pro out of Perth, Western Australia who had been making a killing on the Japanese Tour. I'd seen him play many times, including his win over Peter Oosterhuis at the Scottish Open. He was a very cerebral guy, and this was our first time broadcasting together.

About 40 minutes into the broadcast, dammit, by Murphy's Law, "Y. Suzuki" comes into vision at the 14th hole. The guy was up with the leaders so the director cut to a shot of "Y. Suzuki" putting on the 14th green. I said on the air, "Graham, you know I'm familiar with the older of the two Suzuki brothers, Norio, but I have never, before this, set eyes on his younger brother, Yastartyamota Suzuki."

Marsh's eyes came out like organ stops and he started to cough and sputter. Puzzled, I covered for Marsh by saying, "Well, we're having trouble with Graham's equipment, but I'm sure he'll rejoin us soon when the technicians have sorted it out." Marsh thought I was making a poor attempt at humor, but I was totally in the dark. I then went on talking about Yastartyamota Suzuki and how he was playing so well. The coverage followed him in through the rest of the holes. He shot 68 and every time I would mention Yastartyamota, Marsh would go quiet and look at me with an expression both questioning and pleading. He took no part in the commentary, and I kept claiming to the viewers that he was having equipment difficulties.

The penny never dropped with me; I was so tired and so jet-lagged and so out of it.

Graham rejoined me for the rest of the show after Suzuki had left the course, and we finally went off the air at 6:00 P.M. As soon as the broadcast ended, Marsh grabbed my arm and said, "You pommie* son of a bitch, don't you ever play such a dirty trick on me again."

I said, "What dirty trick? I don't know what you're talking about, Graham."

He said "*Yastartyamota*, you stupid son of a bitch. 'You-start-your-motor Suzuki?' C'mon, his name is Yashinori! That's not funny, Ben!"

Finally, to my horror, the penny dropped. I was so tired and jet-lagged that I had not grabbed the gag that the bald Aussie in the press room had played on me. On our way to the clubhouse reception, I explained to Graham what transpired in the press room and that I had not done it on purpose. It was hard to convince him, and Graham warned me that I'd probably lose my job because he figured the Japanese would be phoning in droves to protest.

Once we reached the reception, where we were to mingle with all of the dignitaries, I got myself a glass of scotch. Neat. I was out of it big time. I started to shake so badly that the production people said, "Hey, you need to get to bed, and get some rest." I had been traveling for three days and three nights. They took me back to the hotel, and I collapsed. I don't think I've ever been any more tired in my entire life.

The only good news came when I was awakened for the next day's broadcast and learned that not one phone call was made in protest of my inadvertent Japanese slur. Otherwise, it may have been "Sayonara, Wright-san."

---

*Pommie is the Australian word for a British person. It's an ironic and insulting name meaning "Prisoner of His or Her Majesty." It's taken from "POHM" which was stenciled on the uniforms of the British prisoners who were shipped off to Australia. There's no love lost between Britain and Australia. The Australians call the Brits "Whinging Poms," and we call them "Dirty Diggers." If you call an Australian a dirty digger in a pub, there'll be a fight.

Another inadvertent Japanese slur I *didn't* get away with occurred at the 1991 Masters, during Saturday's broadcast. In those days, CBS had seven names on each graphic page of the leaderboard. The first seven in the tournament would be the first page, and so on down. Chirkinian had said in my earphones that going into the next commercial break he would scroll through seven pages of the leaderboard and I would narrate with commentary. That's 49 players, which is long. In preparation, I noticed that the first seven players were all of a different nationality.

Chirkinian finally cued me: "Okay, Ben, we're going into a commercial break. Go to it, lad." I began to describe the international aspect of the tournament and that it had never been more vividly exhibited than on the front page of the leaderboard, where there were seven different nationalities. I went through the first six names and nationalities, and was getting close to the last name when Chirkinian barked into my earphones: "We've got to abort the next six pages of the leaderboard and get out of here, Ben." He began a ten-second countdown. "In ten...nine...eight..." To be safe, I had to be out between two and one seconds. I had to quickly time my exit, and in order to cut short and conclude my thought about the seven nationalities, I said, "The last name is the Jap, Ozaki."

I had no idea that I had delivered a monumental racial slur in calling Jumbo Ozaki a "Jap." In Britain and Europe, that was an acceptable word for the Japanese. A Japanese slur in Europe is "slant-eyes" or "nips," but not "Jap." "Jap" would be akin to "Swede," "Brit" or "Scotty."

Frank Chirkinian's voice quickly and loudly filled my earphones during the commercial: "You dumb son of a bitch! You've done it again! Calling that poor guy a Jap! You aren't going to hear the end of this!"

Chirkinian was right. The phones were off the hook in bloody New York! All of the American-Japanese societies began protesting "the racist swine from England." Pilson, Chirkinian's boss, was very upset by this racial slur, which was totally unintentional. I spent most of the next month writing letters of apology. I had to have the letters approved by Pilson. At the end of each apology letter, I wrote, "*To give you an idea of how little significance I placed on calling the gentleman a 'Jap,' I have been known, in all my time at CBS, as a 'limey' and a 'Brit.' 'Limey' is a distinct insult, and 'Brit' isn't much better. Yours sincerely, Ben Wright.*

The day after the "Jap" miscue, Franz Klammer, the Olympic skier, was a guest of Peter Kostis. Kostis brought him into the CBS trailers where we were all sitting around waiting to begin the broadcast. Klammer said, "What is all of this bullshit about 'Jap Ozaki?' Why is Ben being pilloried for calling him a 'Jap?' Everyone in Europe calls a 'Jap' a 'Jap!'" Chirkinian's face fell into his boots because he had been madder than hell at me. Chirkinian took Klammer to the side and asked him if it was true that Europeans freely use the word 'Jap,' and Klammer confirmed it.

It didn't stop me from getting the "Racist of the Year Award" from *Golf Magazine*. It shows how you can inadvertently get into trouble on the air. You begin to realize how close you are to the edge all of the time. One wrong word, and you are history, as I well know. It may surprise you to know that I experienced this lesson very early in my career, when I almost lost my broadcasting livelihood in 1967. My broadcast debut for Britain's commercial network was at Pannal Golf Club in Harrogate, Yorkshire. The event was called the Sumrie Professional Foursomes Tournament, and it was a better-ball format. In the early years of the event, it was dominated totally by the teaming of Neil Coles and Bernard Hunt. Neil Coles is an elder statesman of British Golf and Bernard Hunt went on to become a Ryder Cup captain, so they were two formidable players. They'd won the tournament the four previous years.

In those days there was no videotape, so therefore we did a rehearsal and a dress rehearsal and then we went on the air live. I was positioned on the clubhouse roof, preening myself in my powder blue jacket and trying not to be nervous. The camera light went on, and I began: "...Good afternoon, ladies and gentlemen, from the clubhouse roof here at the Pannal Golf Club in Harrogate, Yorkshire. For the fifth year in a row in the final round of the Sumrie Professional Foursomes, Neil *Holes* and Bernard *Cunt* are strolling to victory...oh, dear me!" I stopped in mid-sentence.

It was unfortunate because even though it was a rehearsal, the feed went through all of the clubhouse and prestige tents on closed circuit. The crew had never worked with me and they thought I had said it on purpose as a joke. But the real truth is that it was an accident, a slip of the tongue. It absolutely, totally put me into a tailspin. With a short time to go before we actually went on the air, I knew we were going to concentrate our efforts on Coles and Hunt because they were running away with the tournament. It was really scary. Performing that broadcast was like tiptoeing through a minefield. I fully realized how difficult it can be once you get your mental wires crossed. I can joke about it now, but it was one of the most frightening things that had ever happened to me.

Jack Whitaker had told me of a race track announcer who lost his job while he was calling a big race at Belmont Raceway. The stretch run featured a glorious late charge by a horse named "Cunning Stunt." The announcer, screaming and shouting and all caught up in the excitement as the horses reached the top of the stretch, let his tongue get a little away from him and transposed the first letters of each word of the horses' names. As "Cunning Stunt" crossed the finish line with a victory, the announcer, for all to hear, referred in boisterous tone to the horse as... Well, you get the picture.

I knew my job was on the line, and for as many times as I had to mention Coles and Hunt, it's a miracle I made it through the broadcast without a fatal reprise. Whenever possible, I referred to them on the air as Neil and Bernard.

After the show, I received a message summoning me to the trailer of Major John Bywaters, who was Secretary of the British PGA. I thought, *Oh Christ, I'm going to be hauled over the coals here.* I thought I was in trouble. I presented myself after the show at his humble trailer. Bywaters looked up from his desk, invited me in, and told me to sit down.

"Scotch, gin or vodka?" he asked me.

"Scotch," I murmured.

He poured me a very sizeable scotch with one ice cube, in the British tradition due to ice rationing.

"I'm really proud that you managed to get through that show after what happened to you in dress rehearsal," Bywaters admitted.

"Everybody believes that I did it on purpose, you know."

"That's ridiculous, he said. "A gentleman like you wouldn't say those kinds of things knowing it was going through the clubhouse and pavilions. I knew it was a slip of the tongue, and it frightened me to such an extent that you might like to know that you'll never be faced with that problem again. Coles and Hunt will never be allowed to be teamed here again," he insisted. "I am not going to see a chap like you destroy his career with a slip of the tongue."

I wish I had the benefit of Major John Bywaters at my side 28 years later.

I was the first announcer into Wilmington, Delaware, as CBS prepared to broadcast live coverage of the 1995 LPGA Championship, sponsored by McDonald's, at the DuPont Country Club. CBS Sports was scheduled that season to provide coverage of the Sprint Championship and the McDonald's LPGA Championship.

I checked in at the CBS trailers between 10:00 and 11:00 in the morning on Thursday, May 11, where I found Chuck Will, our associate producer, being interviewed by a woman from a local newspaper. I could overhear that she was asking Will what sounded like loaded questions about women's golf: Why didn't we cover more of it? Why didn't the network cover as many women's tournaments as men's? I could hear that Will, God bless him, was tap dancing his way through this minefield, in his usually politically correct way, saying absolutely nothing, and taking a long time to do it, which he is wont to do. Will is very garrulous.

I walked through the trailer and settled in the producer's office to get some quiet after listening a bit. I was reading the local paper and preparing for the broadcast when Will came into the office and asked me if I would talk to the reporter. I agreed to speak to her, and was introduced to Valerie Helmbreck of the *Wilmington News Journal*.

I remember, very vividly, the first thing Helmbreck said to me: "Mr. Wright," she allowed, "I do not know one end of a golf club from another." Helmbreck was a television critic, apparently sent to the golf course to write about the CBS network coverage of one of Wilmington's biggest events. I told her that I understood her plight. I also offered to help her all I could with background information on the clear understanding that it was background information for her to use, but that I was not to be implicated by name. I am convinced that she agreed to use me only as an anonymous source. I knew I was taking a risk, in a sense, but I've trusted people all through my career. I've always had sympathy for writers, as that is where my career started. I have always tried to bend over backward to help.

As we talked, I got the impression that Helmbreck was struggling with her angle or the focus of her story. She seemed professional, but carried no tape recorder. I usually talk much too quickly for people to take coherent notes, so there was no way she could get it all verbatim.

"Why doesn't CBS cover more LPGA Tournaments on the network?" she asked me. "It's two against twenty-something." (Meaning: we covered way more PGA events.)

I pointed out to Helmbreck that, for that matter, CBS also only aired one senior golf tournament, but conceded her point and continued. "I know from my considerable experience," I answered, "that most of the occupants of most boardrooms of most major corporations likely to be sponsors of an LPGA event are male." I continued, "I have known that some corporate sponsors have shied away from the LPGA because of the lesbian element, which makes them uncomfortable." I said, "If you want me to put it in a nutshell, the situation is that there is too much blatant lesbianism on the LPGA Tour for the good of that tour in terms of sponsorship. Without sponsorships, LPGA tournaments are not going to get on network television, because you need a commercial sponsor to afford the huge price to be paid for television production costs."

Like it or not, the answer I gave her was based in fact, and everyone, including the LPGA, the sponsors, and the players, knows it.

I have, in fact, had corporate executives tell me that they were hesitant to get behind the LPGA financially due to the lesbian connotation it embodies. I had a very close relationship with the chief executive officer of one of the LPGA's greatest-ever benefactors. I knew this gentleman, an Englishman, very well. A very short time after he expressed these very concerns to me, his corporation moved their sponsorship money out of women's golf and into another sport. I had also talked to executives of two other major corporate sponsors, one of them a telephone service provider, both of whom expressed their misgivings about certain perceptions of women's golf. One LPGA tournament director had told me of his difficulty in obtaining corporate sponsorship dollars, and explained that he was, from time to time, confronted with questions from executives concerning lesbianism. This was not my *opinion*, but rather, knowledge gained from my experiences being associated with the types of people who become sponsors of LPGA events.

Helmbreck appeared to be scribbling fast, and asked me what percentage of LPGA players were lesbians. I told her that there was no way I could answer that question accurately. It wasn't a subject I really cared about.

Helmbreck continued her questioning by asking me about homosexuals on the men's PGA Tour. I answered her by saying that, "In all of my 41 years, traveling the world covering the golf scene, I have never been able to establish, to my satisfaction, any male golfers as a homosexual." Again, I wasn't saying there were no homosexuals on the regular Tour, just that if there are, they are very good at concealing their preferences.

That ended that part of the conversation very quickly. Helmbreck's questioning continued when she asked me why I thought men's golf was better to watch than women's golf.

I said, "Well, the women don't hit the ball as far as the men, for one thing." She asked why there was a difference between men's and women's performance on the golf course, and I answered by telling her a story that I've told many times and will retell here once and for all:

The best way I can tell you the difference between men's and women's golf at the highest level was told to me by JoAnne Carner after she'd won the Colgate-Palmolive Far Eastern Women's Open in the middle 1970s, at the Australian Golf Club in Kensington, Sydney. I was the host for the Channel 9 TV coverage of the event. JoAnne Carner's nickname has always been "Big Mama." She's a big, buxom, strawberry blonde golfer of Scandinavian extraction who is a lovely woman and has always been a good friend. I knew her as JoAnne Gunderson, when she won five U.S. Amateur Championship titles and went on to be a Hall of Fame professional.

After this event in Sydney—which Carner won by exploding the ball from a cavernous greenside bunker at the 18th to about one foot from the hole, to win by one shot—she was extremely happy. The tournament ended at about 20 minutes before five o'clock in the afternoon, and Channel 9 was committed to fill until five o'clock, when the network would take it away for the evening news. As the host, I was stuck there interviewing JoAnne Carner for the best part of 20 minutes, including the commercial breaks. With about five minutes to go, I had exhausted every topic of conversation I could think of with "Big Mama."

We went into the last commercial break before the last few minutes of the telecast, and the producer, Alex Baz, was in my earphones saying, "Okay, matey, three minutes to go before we're out of here. Make it sing!" We came out of the commercial break and I continued with the interview.

"JoAnne," I said, "we've talked about most everything, including what you had for breakfast. Now, what is the bottom line between men's and women's golf?"

Carner took a big drag on her cigarette, dropped it on the ground, stepped on it very carefully, and then answered, pointing to her chest, "These, honey. They don't call me 'Big Mama' for nothing."

The gallery that was gathered around us, and the director and technicians in my earphones all began giggling away. As I struggled to compose myself on camera, Baz called in my car "Go for your life mate, go for your life. I continued, "JoAnne, I suppose you'd better explain."

She said, "Of course. When I was a youngster, quite well-equipped in the lung area, I had to decide whether I was going to go over them or under them."

At that point, of course, people were roaring with laughter and I could hear through my earphones that the producers were very pleased. The Australians just love that kind of thing.

I said, "Well, JoAnne, which way did you go?"

Carner said, "I went under them! What I did was, I made sure I took a huge shoulder turn, and then I'd let those buggers fly!"

Again, everybody was on the ground, pounding the earth with raucous laughter. This was hilariously funny! The director finally said in my earphones, "Okay, Ben, you can wrap it up now." I took the cue and gave the ending spiel: "That, really, is all we need to know. Thank you very much, JoAnne, and congratulations on your famous victory. And for me, Ben Wright, we'll turn you back to the studio."

I had, as they say, "dined out on that story" for years. It is a funny and charming story. I told Valerie Helmbreck this entire story and explained that it was the most colorful illustration that I could give her of the difference between men's and women's golf.

At the end of the interview, Helmbreck departed and I thought I had made a serious attempt to give her the background information to enable her to write an informed piece.

I learned later that after her interviews with Will and me, Helmbreck had gone to several LPGA players and asked them to comment on my remarks about lesbians and breasts. Thankfully, most of the players refrained from comment, but I began to get scared. It was becoming obvious that Helmbreck was seeking to get reaction while attributing all of the statements to me.

After the rumblings made it back to Frank Chirkinian, who was not at the event, he came to me and asked me what had happened. I explained to Chirkinian that I had spoken to Helmbreck on background. Chirkinian, who was frustrated that I did so, took the bull by the horns and phoned Helmbreck at her desk at the newspaper. Chirkinian took a very aggressive attitude with her—the two exchanged unpleasant words—and Helmbreck, who hung up on Chirkinian, decided to publish and be damned.

At 5:00 the next morning, I got a call from Chirkinian to tell me that the story was splattered across the top of the front page of the *Wilmington News Journal* sports section, and that it was not good. The opening line of Helmbreck's article was a "quotation" from me: "Let's face facts here, lesbians in the sport hurt women's golf." In the published story, Helmbreck also put JoAnne Carner's words in my mouth—completely and utterly attributing everything to me. Suddenly, Carner's cute and charming story became a vile remark. It's not in my mouth to be saying those things about women! It wasn't that I said anything so outrageous, but it was the way it appeared that made it look so disgusting. That I would dare to talk that way about women's anatomy was considered sexist.

Later that day, Carner, who was playing in the tournament, confirmed to The Golf Channel that she had, indeed, made those comments to me 20 years previously, just as I had related in my telling of the story. Alas, the truth came too late and the damage had been done.

My comments about lesbianism and the LPGA Tour also appeared in Helmbreck's article, but they made it appear as if I was anti-lesbian and anti-LPGA Tour. Again, I had merely related what I had heard from corporate sponsors and executives.

I am not sexist. I am not anti-lesbian, and I'm certainly not anti-LPGA Tour.

In 1994, I organized and hosted a magnificent LPGA pro-am to benefit Crimestoppers at Kenmure Golf Club, in Flat Rock, North Carolina. Jim Nantz played in the winning foursome with Shelley Hamlin. I finished third with Janet Anderson. Pat Bradley, Colleen Walker, Missy Berteotti, and others participated. The LPGA could not have done a better job of showcasing their players. This was a top-class field of touring pros and we had a fine time. To say that I am anti-LPGA is rubbish.

Helmbreck's article also misquoted me as saying that the LPGA was "going to a butch game." The term "butch" is an Americanism that I do not use. Anyone who knows me knows I have never used that slur.

Chirkinian wondered if perhaps Helmbreck misunderstood my British accent or sense of humor. Anybody of reasonable intelligence also would know that I never would have been so outrageously outspoken on the record. I'm not that much of a madman that I would stick my neck out that far, even if I did believe and hold these statements as my own opinion.

Helmbreck's story containing "my comments" bumped O.J. Simpson off of the front pages of *The New York Daily News* and *The New York Post* with headlines like "Wright is Wrong," and "The Boob on the Tube." One of the writers who really played-up the story was Rudy Martzke, a television writer of dubious distinction who blasted the comments in *USA Today*.

Amidst all of the furor, I was summoned to CBS headquarters in New York. David Kenin, president of CBS Sports, was getting heat from network president Peter Lund. I was to take the train from Wilmington and would miss that day's scheduled rehearsal. I agreed to go to New York, but told Kenin that since the CBS attorneys would be there, I would have an attorney present as well. My agent, Bob Rosen, enlisted a high-powered attorney, Robert Stulberg, from Broach and Stulberg. Craig Foster, who was Bob Rosen's right-hand man, also attended the meeting, held at "Black Rock."

I had mixed emotions about going into New York. I was both frightened at the prospect of taking that elevator to the top floor to face what would surely be an unpleasant and intimidating inquisition by stony network executives. At the same time, I was eager to explain my side of the story, clear the air, and get busy with what surely would be our opportunity to explain to the public what really happened. I was looking forward to doing what I could to fix the situation.

When I arrived at the gleaming offices, and was greeted by unsmiling, tight-faced executives, my spirits fell as I got an ominous feeling in the pit of my stomach that, despite my hopes, we might be set on an adversarial course. The meeting lasted nearly seven hours, and it started off on a sour note.

David Jacobs, the CBS attorney, asked me, "How long have you been in this business?"

I asked, "What do you mean 'business'?"

"Journalism and television," he answered sharply.

"Forty-one years in journalism, twenty-something years with CBS, and a number of years with the BBC before that. I've worked Australia, South Africa, New Zealand...you name it."

Jacobs challenged, "Well, wasn't it rather naïve of you to trust a reporter?"

I said, "In your mind, it probably was. But I've been trusting reporters all through my career, and very seldom have I regretted that. Obviously, I regret it very bitterly in this case."

The tension was getting thick.

"Well, I find it impossible to believe that anybody can be so stupid as to think that their confidence is going to be respected by a reporter," Jacobs huffed.

"That's your opinion," I countered. "But I've done my best to help these people who have to fill their newspapers and magazines, and you can call it naïve if you choose."

"We can't possibly put that forward as an argument," Jacobs said.

"But it's the truth," I replied.

Rather than admit to saying what I said, and also explain the context, CBS's first priority was to hush the story up. The CBS executives and lawyers directed me not to speak to anyone concerning the incident. That was stupid of me to consent not to speak. I should have told the bloody world. But I must confess that I was very scared. My life's work, my defining existence, my way of life was suddenly in grave jeopardy. I had little choice but to follow along CBS's lead of silence, which allowed everybody to take potshots at me. I did get a chance to speak on the next day's golf telecast, but it was a defense directed by CBS and its attorneys, and a defense that had me looking into the camera and calling Helmbreck's story "not only totally inaccurate, but extremely distasteful."

While in truth we did have the opportunity to put down some of the things Helbreck wrote as misquotes, CBS expanded that opening to claim that I didn't make the comments attributed to me, and that I was gravely misquoted. The true story, that I had said these things off the record, was buried. That grieved me. I regarded myself as totally not guilty since I had uttered these comments in confidence.

That didn't hold up, according to Mr. Jacobs. In this age of American political correctness, the CBS brass felt that, on the record or off, they couldn't have me saying these kind of comments. They felt claiming the statements were made off the record was too naïve to be plausible, even though it was the truth.

CBS didn't tell me to lie, but they hid the truth by imposing a gag order on me. The idea was to create reasonable doubt. I protested that even on the record, the stories I told were attributable to other people, including JoAnne Carner. But no one would listen to me. My job was on the line, and I had little choice but to follow management directives. My participation in that meeting, at this point, was no longer relevant, and I had lost control. I could scarcely believe what was happening to me.

CBS then took over. It was in the hands of lawyers who would manage the statement, and I was allowed only to sign it. The lawyers went into their meeting and devised a statement.

Kenin and I had to go out front to quell the masses, under the bright television lights at a quarter to midnight, because a battery of news reporters—not simply the sports beat regulars, but scribes and television newshounds from all manner of media—were camped outside the CBS building. Out we went to deliver our noncommittal, one-line statement, which was to be read by Kenin. I couldn't see for the lights in my face when I came out of the front door of CBS headquarters. As I squinted from the lights and the camera flashes, I could hear the shouts of questions from the news reporters, who took on the appearance of a lynch mob. To me, it felt as if it were all a wild nightmare.

In the midst of the hubris, Kenin delivered the lawyerly statement: "I'm convinced that the offensive statements attributed to Mr. Wright were not made. Mr. Wright and CBS Sports have been done a grave injustice in this matter...."

Kenin and I then went back into the building and CBS had us smuggled out through the underground catacombs so that we emerged at 54th Street near the Rihga Royal Hotel. They had a man who looked like "Kojak," bald as a coot with a bloody gold earring, sweaty, taking us through these catacombs, some of which were evil smelling, through subterranean New York, and out a nondescript, almost hidden door opposite the Hotel. Kenin said good night and went home. I went to the seclusion of my room at the Rihga Royal, and couldn't even get a drink, which I badly needed.

I went to bed, but obviously not to sleep. I told CBS officials that, fearing more confrontation, I did not want to ride back to Wilmington alone on the train. Kenin, having faced the fury firsthand himself, surely understood, and told me to get myself a limo. The next morning I was driven back to Wilmington, where I delivered a prepared statement with Jim Nantz at the beginning of the CBS LPGA broadcast. The statement was written by CBS.

Once I got to my tower, Nancy Lopez joined me in the coverage and told me off the air that she had regarded Helmbreck with suspicion from the start. Lopez felt it was quite obvious that I was set up.

On Sunday morning, when I got to my tower there was a note for me clipped to the ladder. It was a letter from a high-ranking official at DuPont, the sponsor, who wrote: "Those of us who have pride in our community are desperately sorry that you should be so wounded in this way in Wilmington, but we know this lady. She's done it before, and no doubt she'll do it again, and you are just the victim." It was a letter of immense sympathy.

At this point, the furor began to quiet down, although there continued to be a great deal of sniping in the press, who delighted in the outrageous and inappropriate comments. I was totally on the gag order, though, and when I wouldn't talk, the media took potshots. Alas, the fourth estate would not let it die.

Even golf writer Dan Jenkins, whom in years previous I had escorted all over Europe in an effort to help him cover the European Tour, wouldn't let it go. At a party at the home of Jack and Nancy Whitaker on the eve of the 1995 U.S. Open at Shinnecock Hills, Jenkins and his wife June teased me endlessly. Jenkins and I were bosom buddies before that, but that night he badgered me to the point that I had to ask Nancy Whitaker to seat me at a different table. We've never spoken since.

I even discussed the situation with then LPGA Commissioner Charlie Mechem, who could have done more for me than he did, but I think he was scared. He tried to shy away from the controversy by giving me the benefit of the doubt. Mechem did a major fence-sitting act. Then new LPGA Commissioner Jim Ritts, without any knowledge of the facts, assumed I was guilty and was quoted as saying so. When he approached me two years ago at the Crosby in Winston-Salem, he tried to smooth his way in with me, and I told him, in no uncertain terms and even less gracious words, to "get lost." "Listen," I chided him, "you chose to condemn me without any knowledge of the facts. You were quite outspoken in your condemnation of me, and as far as I'm concerned, you can be left to you and your own." With that, I walked away. That's the first and last I've spoken to Jim Ritts, the now former LPGA Commissioner. I clearly was failing in my efforts not to be bitter.

In the autumn of 1995, five months after the Wilmington incident, with my contract about to expire, CBS and my agent Bob Rosen worked up a new four-year deal with built-in raises that would make me one of the highest-paid pure golf announcers in network television. I considered the four-year length of the contract a vote of confidence from the network. At nearly the same time, I enjoyed rave reviews at the grand opening of my newly designed Cliff's Valley Golf Club, in Traveler's Rest, South Carolina. It seemed that the controversy, once and for all, had been publicly laid to rest, although the embarrassment, befuddlement, and betrayal still lingered inside of me.

Months later, I was stupid enough to be caught on the phone, after an evening drinking, by Michael Bamberger of *Sports Illustrated*. Bamberger phoned me at some unearthly hour of the evening while I was in Sherwood, California for the Shark Shootout. It was late, and I was nearly asleep. Bamberger started the conversation by saying that he was doing a "pro Ben Wright" story, claiming that he was going to print my side of the story. I was later told that he'd used the same premise with others that he interviewed for the article.

I then did a stupid thing. I violated the gag order. I let my old tongue, which was alcohol sweetened, go free. I was drinking more heavily then. My marriage was getting to be a rocky ride due to stress. I shot my mouth off, and I said something that I bitterly regret. Someone had told me that this woman, Valerie Helmbreck, was getting divorced, was involved in a custody battle, and may be a lesbian. It was ill advised and very wrong of me to pass on that rumor to Bamberger. Helmbreck, in fact, was purported to be happily married. My conversation with Bamberger was very brief, but eventually lethal.

I hung up the phone thinking that Bamberger was going to write a nice piece about me, and once again, I was sliding down a slippery slope. Despite the fact that Bamberger's December 4, 1995 article was full of factual inaccuracy, it included the rumor I had related about Valerie Helmbreck, which was really inflammatory.

The *Sports Illustrated* article also quoted a caddie named Ken Doig, who claimed he was in the trailer during my interview with Helmbreck. Doig told *SI* that he had overheard me make the statements in question to Helmbreck. Of course he did, because, as I have said here, I did make them—off the record. There again, however, Doig could not have overheard enough of the conversation to realize those comments were not originally attributed to me.

Bamberger also quoted LPGA player Dottie Pepper as saying that she couldn't imagine me intending to say the things I was quoted as saying, but she was surprised to hear me quip about lesbians at the grand opening of my golf course at Cliff's Valley. British humor and American humor, apparently, sometimes do not mix. During the introduction, I mocked Jay Haas, who was playing in the opening exhibition, for his poor performance in the Ryder Cup and quipped that the mocking was a payback for him asking me about lesbians at dinner the evening before. This quip made me seem unrepentant.

Finally the article quoted my old friend Dan Jenkins, who, after pestering me at the Whitaker's aforementioned U.S. Open party, felt the need to volunteer the following less-than-gracious statement:

"I asked Ben, 'Did you say it?' and he said, 'Of course, I said it, but I was granted complete anonymity.' What I don't know is if he was joking. He'd had about two bottles of wine."

For his "exposé," Bamberger won a golf writing award. I lost my job.

The phone rang loudly through the house and when I answered it, Frank Chirkinian was on the line asking me if it was true that I had been suspended indefinitely. I hadn't yet heard the news, so I desperately phoned my agent, Rosen, asking him to contact CBS and find out what was going on. Kenin called me back at home and told me that he was sorry, but since I had brought shame on the network, I was suspended. The network would fully pay out my contract, but I was not going to broadcast for CBS again. Kenin seemed shaken and very upset. My contract with CBS expires in October of 1999, but since December of 1995, I have not broadcast one golf swing on the air for CBS.

The news prompted other members of the CBS announcing team to phone me. Jim Nantz was so unbelievably outspoken in my behalf that he put his own job at risk. He was constantly pleading for my restoration, and was immensely loyal, as was Chirkinian.

I remember the implications really hit me when I realized I was not going to be going to Pebble Beach for the first time in a quarter of a century. The AT&T Pebble Beach National Pro Am was always such a high time. It was our first tournament of the new season, and a normal time for the CBS team to gather in early February after our winter break. It always had a "reunion" feel. Not being a part of the "reunion" was a shattering blow. Any tournament would have been bad enough, but the fact that it was Pebble Beach made it just awful. We used to play golf at Cypress Point on Monday, Tuesday, and Wednesday before the event, and have a marvelous time. Now I would miss all of that. The prospect of not being there was an excuse for getting drunk again, probably every day of that week.

I tuned into the broadcast and saw that Bobby Clampett was broadcasting in my place. I thought to myself, *To hell with them. If they need Bobby Clampett at the seventeenth hole at Pebble Beach, they deserve all they get.* I was hurt and I was even lashing out at my former colleagues. Since that moment, I began to find CBS increasingly unwatchable. It hurt too much.

Hurt, embarrassment, humiliation, anger, self-doubt, self-pity, and booze became major players in my life that winter. The gradual demise of my marriage, health problems, and persistent hangovers were my daily fare. To add to my depression, my family and I were getting threatening phone calls from gay and lesbian groups.

On the morning of April 4, 1996, my 14-year-old daughter Margaret awakened me from bed, telling me that some people were in the house to see me. I was on a major hangover because I had been out drinking the night before. With my robe on, and in an awful condition, I emerged from my bedroom to find a sea of familiar faces standing in my living room, along with one man I didn't recognize.

It was an intervention. A very dark day in my life, indeed. Pat Summerall, who was on the board of the Betty Ford Clinic, was the prime mover of this event. In attendance were my best friend, vascular surgeon Buster Shealy, Jim Nantz, Frank Chirkinian, *Links Magazine* publisher Jack Purcell, my wife Kitty, and my daughter Margaret.

"What the hell is this?" I asked.

They had all gathered in secret the night before at an airport hotel, where they had coordinated the intervention. Each person, in turn, took turns reading a tale of woe they had written about me. Buster Shealy started the readings with warnings from the medical point of view. My wife and child wept mightily through their reading. It was a traumatic, god-awful experience. Just grueling.

At the end, I returned to my bedroom, showered, dressed, and left with a representative of the Betty Ford Clinic who had come to escort me to the desert enclave. The trip saved my life. We went to the airport and I confess that I drank my way across America. We flew from Asheville to Atlanta, where we connected to Los Angeles. The Betty Ford Clinic escort flew "in the back of the bus," while up in first class I was telling the flight attendant to keep the vodka coming all the way from Atlanta to Los Angeles.

When we landed in L.A. I was off the plane quickly and gave the escort the slip just for fun. I watched from behind a pillar as he went berserk looking for me. Eventually, I popped out from behind a pillar and said, "Boo!" I then said, "Well, my good man, this is where we part, because I have just purchased a one-way ticket to Jakarta, Indonesia."

"You haven't!" he replied.

With a twinkle in my eye, I said, "Yep."

"God, I need a cigarette," the escort admitted in a moan.

"You'll have to go to one of the airport smoking areas for that," I gleefully explained, "and while you do, I am going to the bar."

At the airport bar, I had a couple more snorts and then the escort and I boarded our flight to San Diego, whereupon he drove me the rest of the way to the Betty Ford Clinic and checked me in.

I was in the Betty Ford Clinic for 28 days: April 4 until May 2. It was from the clinic that I watched the terrible demise of Greg Norman in the final round of the 1996 Masters. I watched, and I cried. I realized that I was crying partly for him, and partly for myself. I felt it a parallel, and I felt my fall from grace was equally as spectacular as Greg's fall from the lead. I had broadcast 23 consecutive Masters tournaments, ending with Crenshaw's second green jacket victory in

1994. Now here I was, in the Betty Ford Clinic, not only separated from the Masters, but also torn away from the event while one of the most dramatic turnarounds in the history of the event was taking place. It hit me hard that I was watching the Masters on television from the Betty Ford Clinic.

I found the entire ordeal very difficult to put up with. I had a loathsome time in the clinic, but then again, one is not intended to have a good time at Betty Ford. Until that moment watching Sunday at the Masters on television, I had practiced denial at the clinic. I squared off daily against a tough little counselor named Rose.

"No, I'm not a drunk," I'd insist to her. "I'm not an alcoholic. You've got it all wrong."

"How many blackout experiences have you had?" she asked me.

I said, "I'm not quite sure what you mean by 'blackout.'"

"It's very simple," she said crossly. "The morning after drinking, you've no idea what happened. That's what we call a 'blackout.' If you've had more than six of those, then we regard you as a suitable case for treatment."

I said, "Well, I may have had six *hundred* of those."

"What?!!"

I explained that I was kidding, but admitted that I'd certainly had more than six blackouts by her definition. The treatment began.

The course is 28 days long. If the patient does everything instructed, they give the patient little medals along the way. It is very labor intensive. They gave me wake-ups each day at 6:00 A.M., and kept me on the go until midnight or 1:00 A.M. It's damned hard, and that's the way it's meant to be. They were chasing my ass around, making me finish all of my tasks.

I learned a great deal about alcohol at the Betty Ford Clinic. I watched, for instance, graphic film of bleeding esophagi and cirrhosis-ridden livers. I've seen film of a man tied to his bed in his last fit of delirium tremens before he dies. They showed me some damned frightening sights! I ran into some well-known people in the clinic as well. I encountered the owner of a professional sports franchise and a well-known female who was addicted to painkillers. Their names I must not reveal due to the secrecy oath the clinic insists upon.

I became a model pupil, and regard myself as terribly lucky to have gone through it because I was drinking so heavily before I went in that it was affecting all aspects of my life.

Unfortunately, while I was in there, I consumed enough food that it was way too much for me as well. I ate everything that was thrown at me. I absolutely ate three heavy square meals a day and got heavier and heavier. You're supposed to lose weight when you give up alcohol, but not when you eat like a bloody herd of cattle! There, then, was another challenge for me to overcome, which I am doing now with a regimen of exercise and diet.

While I may have had trouble passing the kitchen at the clinic, it was not difficult for me to be without drink. I wasn't and am not a person who needs to have a drink. I drink because I like it. I didn't like to drink in the morning, like some of my cohorts, and I didn't even like drinking at lunch. As I have mentioned, 5:42 is sufficient for me and there are plenty of times in which I don't even have one at that once-fabled hour of the day.

When it came time to leave the clinic, I was approached by a counselor who could get into terrible trouble if I mentioned his name, because he said to me: "I don't think you are an alcoholic. I think you are an abuser of alcohol."

"You have it absolutely correct," I agreed. "I enjoy drinking with my dinner, but I know so much more now about the evils of drink—and what it can do to you—that I am going to be very circumspect from now on."

The counselor nodded. "We get a pretty good percentage of people who leave here and don't go back to drinking, but like anything else, there are a few failures, too. I'm sure you'll go back to drinking," he said very straightfaced, "but if we've taught you one thing, and that is to drink like a gentleman, then we've accomplished something. That's not the company line," he said, "that's my line."

The Betty Ford Clinic did, indeed, teach me to drink like a gentleman. I know now that I have to avoid vodka for the rest of my life because it is my "mood altering" drink. Vodka made me very mean, sharp-tongued, and sarcastic in nature.

After extensive medical testing, I was released from the clinic and flew home, ready to begin dieting and putting my life back together. In the autumn, I traveled to Africa to broadcast the World Cup at Cape Town and the Sun City Million Dollar Challenge for the BBC. It was exhilarating to be in my tower, behind the microphone again, even in a freelance capacity. The high was short-lived, however, because I was faced with yet another personal challenge when I returned home from Africa to find that my wife Kitty had left me. That made me 0 for 4 in marriages, and it put me once again in a fierce battle with depression.

In the summer of 1996, my first golf season away from CBS was drawing to a close. Each year, at the World Series of Golf in Akron, Ohio, the CBS team would hold a large "end of the season" banquet at Anthe's Restaurant that would always be a memorable affair. A video called "CBS Lowlights"—a collection of all of the year's on-air gaffes and bloopers—would be shown, and the room would be filled with laughter and good-byes. Just as I had felt depressed about missing the season opener at Pebble Beach, and every tournament in between, for that matter, I was beginning to feel sorry about missing this affair. That is, until Jim Nantz phoned me and insisted that I come and join the crew as the "mystery guest."

I agreed, traveled to Akron alone, and appeared only at the banquet. To be back in the company of what really was my "extended family" provoked very emotional feelings. The warmth and affection and continued camaraderie I was given by everyone from the cameramen to my fellow announcers was staggering. To top it all off, Chirkinian rose in speech and said, "When Ben Wright left us, CBS lost 'the spirit of golf.'"

I could barely contain my tears.

After I returned home, I realized what a mistake it was for me to attend that party. It only served to make me more depressed than ever that I was no longer part of the team.

The sun also rises. I was in need of a break in the clouds. With my eyes clear, I thought I was beginning to see some rays of sunshine when NBC Sports president Dick Ebersol contacted my agent to inquire about using me on NBC's 1997 Ryder Cup telecast from Valderrama, Spain. The idea, which would have been a perfect use of my international experience, was unfortunately dropped when, as luck would have it, disgraced sportscaster Marv Albert came to trial on the Monday of that week. NBC's parent company, General Electric, admonished NBC Sports for its bad boy reputation and turned down Ebersol's Ryder Cup plan by apparently reminding him that

"NBC had been the sports network of O.J. Simpson, Marv Albert, and now, possibly, Ben Wright."

Damn, can you imagine, mentioned in the same breath as a suspected double-murderer and a reportedly kinky transvestite? I found the dreadful irony appalling! To be bracketed with those two people....

The following year, with Marv Albert's scandal far behind them, Ebersol and NBC made another overture to me during a clandestine meeting at the Omni Hotel in downtown Jacksonville during the 1998 Players Championship. The game plan was that I was to make my debut for NBC at the 1998 U.S. Open at the Olympic Club in June. We had lengthy, in-depth discussions during the five-hour meeting about how I might fit into the broadcast team. Ebersol rather cleverly asked me with whom I thought I could most enjoy a McCord-type relationship amongst their announcers. I had no hesitation in nominating, for the role of victim, Master Roger Maltbie, with whom I once made beer commercials for Michelob. We sampled plenty of the product as well. Ebersol intimated to my agent that he felt I could add a great deal to their broadcasts in terms of humor and quality of the language. NBC also planned to contact Valerie Helmbreck and make peace, as well. Ebersol had also apparently queried Arnold Palmer as to whether I should be restored to the booth, and the King had graciously and emphatically approved.

"But only," Palmer insisted, "if Ben's heart is still in it."

Alas, Ebersol was desperately hurt by the fact that—once again—although he had the blessing of "the King," he couldn't gain the approval of the executives, who apparently thought that not enough time had passed for me to return to the air.

Of course, the fact that Albert has already returned to the air for the Madison Square Garden Network is hurtful to me, and confounds any sense of fairness or logic. However, it is the reality of the medicine I gave myself.

I am constantly warmed by the support and encouragement I have received from people all over the world who express their wish to hear me announce golf tournaments again. They inquire as to whether enough time has passed and whether I have been able to put the incident behind me. When I view the entire situation, it is very unsettling to see all of the people who were affected by the wake of this titanic miscommunication and error in judgement. CBS Sports president David Kenin, CBS Television Network president David Lund, and head of production Rick Gentile have all, eventually, been removed from their various positions at CBS. Even Frank Chirkinian, the father of golf television, was removed, also just after receiving a magnificent contract that makes mine look like small change. Like most things, the attempted cover-up was far worse than the crime—a lesson learned and relearned by everyone from school children to corporate executives.

It was Lund who was most insistent that I never work for CBS again. Now that he's gone, who knows?

Valerie Helmbreck, of course, also suffered some indignity and professional loss. For what it's worth, I forgive Valerie Helmbreck without any qualifications. In the spring of 1998, I spoke to her by telephone for a story being written for *Sports Illustrated*. I think we sort of put things straight. We both bemoaned the fact that we were in curious and less than desirable professional situations. I was being paid without working, and she had in a job, but not the job that she wanted. She wanted to be an investigative reporter.

I found the telephone call to be desperately emotional, and it was nice to get it out of the way. We were entitled to our disagreements. We discussed our original meeting, and how we both got caught up in the heat of the moment. She may not have appreciated what I said that day in the trailer. She may not have understood the English way of putting it, for all I know. Either way, we buried a lot of business in this one-hour telephone conversation. We commiserated about how this thing had gotten far too big for both of us. There was a lot of sympathy for me in her, and I certainly wish I had not said remarks that were hurtful to her.

As far as I'm concerned, that chapter is over...and so is this one—but not before I offer an apology to anyone who was truly offended by my statements. I never meant to hurt anyone, and never imagined it possible that as a gentleman, and a mere observer of the game of golf, I could be embroiled in such a controversy.

If You Ever Go Across
the Sea to Ireland...

Though the Irish are given to weepy sentiment and poetic humor, I am one Brit who will shamelessly wax eloquent with total abandon when pub talk turns to the Emerald Isle. Let me count the ways...

If the truth be known—and this will be considered heresy—I actually prefer the golf in Ireland to the golf in Scotland. While admitting that the Scots fathered the game, and recognizing that there are monuments of windswept history resting between Glasgow and Edinburgh, Scotland also maintains an awful "class system" element that is totally absent from the Irish psyche. It is far more enjoyable to play golf in Ireland, and I have presented myself throughout that land since I was a wee lad. Hospitality abounds, and I feel quite certain that no Brit in Celtic history has received better treatment than I.

In fact, many times an Ulsterman on the next stool has questioned whether I had some Irish blood in me. My suspicion is that the Irish accuse me of being one of them because I behave like one of them...an irresponsible lunatic! It's a wonderful compliment, and totally accurate.

I remember visiting the Waterville Golf Club at the glorious tip of the Ring of Kerry. The Waterville Club has the distinction of being the longest golf course in the British Isles, and the head golf professional there, Liam Higgins, appropriately, is a perennial long-drive champion. It was Higgins who personally took me out to play and show me the course on the day I visited, and though the weather wasn't fit for man nor beast, Higgins, in an amazing show of hospitality, gamely played on through the horizontal sheets of blinding rain. His spirit was warm, and after the first three holes of this madness, Higgins must have guessed that I was trying to be accommodating by listening to his pride-filled tour of the course. Until this point, neither of us had even mentioned the weather.

"Mr. Wright," Higgins finally queried as he squinted from under his hood, "do you really want to continue on playing through this?"

We "played" the next 15 holes by the fire in the cozy upstairs bar at the Waterville Clubhouse. The spectacular view of the rugged links from the window had us conceding every putt and tapping in every pint.

The Irish, although utterly welcoming, can, at appropriate times, dispense a directness. I cite the darling woman behind the bar in Dingle, who expressed relief when I mentioned that I had an early tee time at Tralee the following morning, because, as this very proper lady unabashedly let loose, "We're bound to be getting pissed on later in the day."

On my first visit to Royal Portrush, my caddie surely bit his lip and withheld comment through the first two holes. The lad watched as I unleashed unruly blows on holes that plainly demanded accuracy. I sprayed my tee shots wildly into the heather that he then silently trudged through in grim pursuit. My card read 5-7 against par of 4-5 as we marched on to the third tee. As I surveyed the hole, the caddie finally spoke:

"Mr. Wright, you'll not bring that driver out again, otherwise you'll be carrying your own bag." Only an Irish caddie could pull that off and make it sound charming. Of course, his advice or, rather, threat, rescued my score and made for a much more pleasant trip around.

Royal Portrush, a 100-year-old club and an H.S. Colt design in Northern Ireland, is the site of the only British Open played in Ireland. Max Faulkner won that 1951 Open, and, amazingly, it took 18 years for another British player—Tony Jacklin—to become "champion golfer for the year." Also amazing is the fact that at one of Royal Portrush's other major events, the 1995 British Senior Open, the winner was Brian Barnes—Faulkner's son-in-law.

In my opinion, Royal Portrush, which has also hosted the British Amateur, would be a suitable site for another British Open. The only knock on Royal Portrush is the clubhouse, which is totally inadequate for such an important event. But the golf course itself is one of the greatest in the world. Royal Portrush demands a full range of shots and offers a full range of conditions, in an inspiring and natural setting.

Fifteen years after my initial visit to Portrush, I returned in 1996 with a travel group to once again face Royal Portrush's Dunluce Links. When I walked into the pro shop, the golf professional peered at me from behind the counter and uttered, in something between a growl and a whine, "Why have you been so fookin' long in returning? I can't believe that you'd stay away so long." It was the first thing he said to me before we'd even said hello, and it made the hairs on the back of my neck stand up. It was an eerie moment, and I was totally flattered by his warmth. The Irish can be both mystical and funny in their delivery of such sentiment.

I was also totally flattered when, upon my arrival at Ballybunion a few days later, I was greeted by the Minister of Tourism for the whole of Ireland, who came out to meet me and the rest of my travel group. Imagine the pomposity with which I was able to carry myself after that formal greeting. When I think further of the fact that the directors of Ballybunion have seen fit to list my name in their yardage guide as a prominent visitor, it damned well makes me consider the depth of Irish hospitality bottomless.

Ballybunion, in County Kerry, has to be seen to be believed. I am ill-advised to attempt to use words to describe the misty, seaside experience that is Ballybunion. The spectacular links were forged by nature and sculpted by wind and sea.

While Ballybunion is an absolute gem, I just wish Tom Watson hadn't been allowed to monkey with the design in 1995. Watson called the subtle changes "adding definition," but I see no good reason for that to have happened. Making visible the 18th green, which was previously a bit of a blind-shot relic, was, to me, unacceptable. Ballybunion is a course that has stood a relative test of time, so why the hell mess with it? I'm reminded of the sage sentiment of Alister MacKenzie, who was known to feel that just because one is a great player, that doesn't give him the right to be handed an architectural badge to mess with greatness.

I was pro-Ireland in my writing before it became fashionable. I realized I was against the majority when I ignited controversy by advocating in the *Financial Times* in the 1970s that the British Open be contested at Portmarnock. It is generally considered heresy that the Open Championship should be held in the Republic of Ireland, but I received correspondence from readers who agreed with the idea, citing the contributions the Irish have made to the Ryder Cup.

I also received a letter from Portmarnock, advising me that they would be pleased to host the Ryder Cup matches, but not if it takes a financial payoff to do so. Finally, a Ryder Cup was scheduled to be played in the land of players like Padraig Harrington, Paul McGinley, Christy O'Connor Sr. and Jr., David Feherty, and Darren Clarke. The two courses in the running were Portmarnock and the K Club.

Portmarnock, which proved its mettle by hosting the 1960 World Cup and the 1991 Walker Cup matches, is situated just outside Dublin. It was founded in 1894, and it's a course you won't depart without an adequate coating of sea spray. Portmarnock is a hearty dunes course that thoroughly embodies all of the elements of Irish golf.

The K Club at the Kildare Hotel and Country Club, on the other hand, is a parkland course in County Kildare that was opened in 1991. Unlike the fearsome and natural Arnold Palmer/Ed Seay design at Tralee, the K Club was completely manufactured and is in no way comparable to the wild linksland courses on the coasts. It is elegant and lush, with man-made water hazards and an opulent clubhouse and hotel.

Sadly, the K Club and all of its money won out in Ireland's Ryder Cup bid. Money is the reason the Ryder Cup was awarded to the terrible Belfry in the first place, and now, again, we see the dollar talking.

I have been fortunate to enjoy the ultimate show of hospitality—an honorary membership—from the most traditional of Irish links clubs: Lahinch. Commonly called "the St. Andrews of Ireland," Lahinch sits on the grassy bluffs overlooking the Atlantic Ocean just south of the breathtaking Cliffs of Moher in County Clare. To take a trip 'round Lahinch, founded in 1893, is to walk in the footsteps of Old Tom Morris and Dr. Alister MacKenzie, who are credited with the design and redesign, however quirky it may be. Immaculate, untouched living history is glorious Lahinch. The blind shots presented at the famed Klondyke and Dell holes would be assumed to be conceived by a madman had they been designed in the modern age. White stones placed on hilltops provide the only visual direction for the player, who can summarily lose his depth perception in the swirling and blowing grasses. Fortunately, when MacKenzie was given the charge to redesign Lahinch in the 1920s, his impeccable sense led him to leave the Klondyke and Dell holes as they were—in effect maintaining two antique relics that live on to this day.

To play at Lahinch is to be transported.

I was named an honorary member of Lahinch for writing about the resident goats, which graze freely on the course and proudly adorn the whimsical club logo. I have recounted many times my initial visit to Lahinch and my first experience with the goats.

As I inspected the clubhouse area waiting to tee off, I noticed, as many have, a barometer hanging on the stoop that was missing the telling hands. The words "see goats," were scrawled on a card pinned to the face of the otherwise obsolete, glassless barometer. When we presented ourselves to the club secretary, I politely asked the genial chap if he knew the meaning of the scrawl. I struggled to understand the explanation through his animated brogue.

"Well, lad," he replied, "a wee herd of goats roam our course, and we've no need for a barometer, because the goats, they warn us well when to make our retreat from the links."

It seems that when the goats were headed toward the clubhouse, the members knew to follow because the goats possessed a sense that guided them to shelter when unplayable weather was drawing near. The goats, to this day, position themselves on the porch in time to beat the weather. Which is more than can be said for some of the stubborn golfers, because rugged weather in a place like Lahinch cannot be judged by the normal climatological standards. After our short chat, the secretary then sent me away to the tee with another memorable sentiment and Gaelic hair-raiser.

"Enjoy your round, newfound friend."

I have always been a huge fanatic about golf course design; it gives one the chance to be an architect of nature. In my early days at the *Financial Times*, I would take every possible opportunity to write about course architecture. I had a real bee in my bonnet about modern designers creating "obstacle courses" that were no fun to play. An example is Jack Nicklaus building layouts where unless you can hit a high, left-to-right, floating, 215-yard 2-iron that would stop on a dime, your ball bounced sideways into oblivion. It struck me very early that golf courses were being built—particularly in America—that were vastly too difficult for the people who were playing them. Let's face it: 80 to 90% of the golfers in the world aren't very good. They enjoy the game, and its spirit, but certainly can't break 80 consistently. Therefore, to me, it is quite ludicrous for a golf course to have 100 sand bunkers that the ordinary golfer not only can't get out of, but is scared to death of when he or she gets in them—which is why they can't get out.

It's always been my attitude that the great golden era of course design—aside from the Scots, who did all of the very early layouts in the 19th century—was the time when standouts such as Donald Ross, Dr. Alister MacKenzie, and Charles Blair Macdonald were in full form. The "Golden Era," then, was the early days of this century up until the stock market crash of 1929.

I feel it is very important that a golf course be built on MacKenzie's premise that it must give the maximum enjoyment to the maximum number of people. This includes scratch golfers, low handicap golfers, *and* high handicap golfers. High handicap golfers are perfectly entitled to play, and should be given a course where—although they may score 120 on it—they can say they've had a good day and leave without feeling that they've been beaten to a pulp. Half the new courses that are being built these days beat you to death. I find this quite ridiculous.

I also believe that because there's so much more earthmoving equipment available today—equipment that wasn't available to the great early architects—people move dirt just for the sake of moving dirt. I can't tell you the number of courses that I've been to where the people have plowed up all of the trees, and then had to *replant* them, just because they've got this damned earthmoving equipment. My whole attitude on golf design is that you must not remove a single tree that you don't have to. Now, I'm also of the opinion that evergreens (perennials with low branches) shouldn't be used on a golf course if you have to crawl on your knees beneath them to play a shot. You have to select the right trees. There's a right tree, and there's a wrong tree.

Over time, I became obsessed by the design business and really embraced the minimalist style of the early days of this century. This was a period when courses were built mostly with mules and primitive equipment—before bulldozers came along. I think the architects working at that time made the most beautiful courses because they *followed* the contours of the land instead of *reworking* them. One day in the late 1960s, some businessmen in England came to me and said, "We'd like you to set up with a designer because we like what you write about. We'd like you to do some golf courses on the line that you often propose in your columns." I thought this would be wonderful, so a company was formed in London called "Golf Services International, Ltd." I became their designer, and we started in 1970 to try and get work.

Eventually, I got a contract from the Scottish & Newcastle Breweries to design 27 holes in the southwest corner of France. The course was to be built in a little village of St. Cyprien, very close to the Mediterranean and in the shadows of the Pyrenees, which were mostly snowcapped, even in the summertime. The area was called Languedoc-Roussillion, and it was quite beautiful. Unfortunately, the 27 holes I designed were built under the worst circumstances because the French proved to be impossible to do business with. Every time I returned to London, for example, they'd start doing things their own way—even though they knew nothing about golf. The "Frogs" and I had all kinds of differences of opinion, and I found them impossible. I had an engineer on the site named Barry Huchinson. He was a great guy and a great worker, and somehow we got the job finished. God knows how. To tell you the truth, though, I don't even know if the course is still in existence. I'd love to go and find out. I was pretty happy with it when we finally got done, but the French have probably changed it and turned it around backwards.

One of the holes I designed, a long par-four, featured the tee right on the edge of the beach. This was rather disconcerting to the golfers, apparently, because there were a lot of topless bathers on that beach. Not surprisingly, play seemed to slow down here. Basically, though, you aimed away from the Mediterranean and the point of the drive was to avoid a large salt lake up ahead. We had a bit of trouble with that lake and had to do a lot of soil washing to get the salt out so the grass near it would grow. In addition, the course was built on a rubbish tip, so it wasn't exactly what you'd call prime land. Anyway, if you were successful in missing the salt lake with your drive, you aimed your second shot at a snowcapped peak in the Pyrenees. It was quite a dramatic hole. I wonder if it's still there.

Following the debacle in France, I was commissioned to build courses on the stately home parks of Lord Bathurst and the Earl of Warwick. It appeared we were now going to do some serious business. The course I planned for the Earl of Warwick included a short par-four that ran down a slender island located within the moat that encircled Warwick Castle. The castle is in the Midlands, close to Birmingham, and it's been there since the 12th century. Because of the castle and the moat, I was sure that my 290-yard par-four would have been stunning.

Sadly, the gas crunch came along in October of 1973, and just like that...we were gone. Nobody wanted to build a golf course anymore. The Earl eventually sold his castle to Madame Tussaud's, the well-known waxworks tourist attraction. Lord Bathurst decided not to do his course as well, choosing to go the polo route because Princess Anne was a frequent visitor. It's not to put too fine a point on it, but our company went belly up because of the cancellations. I, however, continued to be obsessed with golf course design.

I truly believe that I got more satisfaction out of designing a golf course than from any other facet of the game—bar none. For me, it far exceeded the excitement of commentating at the Masters. The creative urge and the charge you get from beautifying a piece of land, and the responsibility to not screw it up, is such that it really is enthralling.

Twenty years later, out of the blue, I was hired to do the voice-over on a promotional videotape for a golf course called The Cliffs at Glassy Mountain in South Carolina. The layout was designed by Tom Jackson, an architect with offices in Atlanta and Greenville, South Carolina, and it is really beautiful. The course runs along the very edge of Glassy Mountain, the last sizable mountain at the southern end of the Appalachian chain. As the name implies, the golf course is at 3,000 feet above sea level and players can literally look down on a clear day and see all of South Carolina. It's an utterly magnificent spot for a golf course, but it's also very modern and very difficult— far too difficult, in fact, for a lot of the people who play there. *Golf Digest*, though, rated it as the fourth most aesthetically pleasing golf course in the United States, after Cypress Point, Pebble Beach, and Augusta National. That is *damned* heady company.

Anyhow, I did the voice-over for the videotape on the golf course. Afterward, I was invited by the advertising people to have lunch at The Cliffs with its developer. There's a three-mile climb from the gatehouse to the clubhouse, and I was told that it cost $3 million to put the road in. The place is mind-boggling. At lunch I met Jim Antony, the developer, a local man. If you saw him, you would not believe he has two pennies to rub together. He almost always has old clothes on and dirt on his boots, and he'll jump on a bulldozer at the drop of a hat. He has an incredible love for the land, and is very keen to preserve as much as he can of the character of this beautiful area. I was very impressed by this country boy from the moment I met him. He said to me, "I was born here and I don't intend to leave." That told me he was not a fly-by-night developer who comes in, does his damage, and then runs for his life to avoid being arrested. Jim is a very different kind of cat.

During our conversation at lunch, Antony said, "I've just purchased a piece of property on Highway 25 leading from Greenville, South Carolina to Hendersonville, North Carolina." I was aware of the property he was referring to, an area called Highland Farms. There had been plans to put a retirement home on the land, but the previous developer couldn't get it together, so Antony bought it after it had been for sale for ages. I had looked at the property once and thought it was perfect for a golf course. I had hoped that I could build one there, but my group of developers couldn't put it together, either. Jim came along and bought it for a song.

After he told me about his new property, Jim said, "You're the golf expert, what would you do with it?"

I said, "Having seen the layout you have here, I'd make sure I did a course that was as totally different from the existing one as possible. It would be of the minimalist style. Minimum movement of dirt, and old, classic Scottish-American design principals. I'd also make it a heck of a lot easier than The Cliffs, because there are going to be a lot of people who can't play this one, either because they're elderly or simply not very good at the game."

"That's an interesting concept," Jim said. "Would you be interested in actually designing such a course?"

"Yes, I would," I answered. "If the price is right."

He then asked me if I wanted to go into partnership, but I declined. I was already involved in a lawsuit against my former partners in a development called Kenmure in Flat Rock, North Carolina that was very acrimonious. I told Antony I would design the course for a fee and for a percentage of the real estate sales. He said he would get back to me, but I never expected him to, since I had no track record as a designer here. Why would he give a design job to a fellow who doesn't have anything to show him? I couldn't show him the course in France because I didn't even know whether it was still there.

To my surprise, Jim Antony's proposal actually came. I accepted it, and away we went.

Former PGA Tour player Dave Hill, who was once criticized for calling a U.S. Open site "a cow pasture," would have been proud of me because the property we were to build on had actually been a cattle farm. When we announced that we were going to build a golf course there, we had a reception on the property under a tent on a very cold day in March of 1994. Several of us got there very early and found that some of the cows had taken refuge in our tent because it was so cold and windy. We shooed the cows down to the pasture, which now contains the first, second, and ninth holes.

I walked that property until I was blue in the face, thinking about how I would lay out the course. I was very familiar with it, but it took me a while to put together a routing plan. Once I had a plan together, I had to see if it worked on the ground. I had all kinds of problems with certain holes, but the real problems started later. Two guys involved with the engineering and construction were Tony Monger and Leon Allison, and I just loved them to death. They had the most hellish job because when we started to build North Carolina experienced unbelievable flooding and it was absolutely terrifying. I had moved 300,000 cubic yards of dirt—a minimal amount—but once it was done the course was washed away on a regular basis. It was terribly soul-destroying for the guys because usually they worked from 7:00 in the morning until 4:00 in the afternoon. As soon as they were finished, the heavens would open up with thunder-bumpers. Damn me if we didn't get to the point where we were sprigging the golf course, and the sprig would just wash away. Naturally, it's not just the rain that falls and goes into the gages. The course was built in a valley (it's called Cliff's Valley), so all that water rushed off of the hillsides as well. It was hellish. I have a photograph of me standing in mud up to the tops of my knee-high Wellington boots. We quintupled the original budget in terms of drainage, but the great thing is now we have a course that can withstand the most brutal weather.

Building Cliff's Valley was like being a petulant child. I would think of a perfect place to put a green, get started trying to build it, and then I would decide that it wasn't the right place after all. Half the business is really on the ground, shaping the course all the time. I couldn't find the right place for the second green and eventually had the brilliant idea that the point of the golfer's aim should be a huge pine tree in back. It worked very well. The second and tenth greens, however, are the most severely sloped because they suffered the most washout. They really did have rivers running in them on a regular basis. Unfortunately, we never did build them back up to my original designs. I have to take responsibility if people curse me for four-putting those greens, which they do.

Part of the golf course's charm is that it features two creeks. At the north end, Terry Creek comes down off Panther Mountain. At the south end of the course, Beaver Dam Creek comes from totally the opposite direction. These two creeks combine into one in front of the 15th green and then go out through the property. It was natural for me to build the golf course around those two creeks. I was also blessed with two man-made lakes that were separated by a dike.

Generally speaking, the process was a joy, and the most exciting thing I've ever done. While the project in France was built on a rubbish tip, this was a beautiful piece of property. I figured I couldn't do much harm when I was building on a rubbish tip. It could, after all, be returned to being a rubbish tip if I made a mess of it. If I ruined *this* gorgeous piece of property, though, I deserved to be jailed.

Fortunately, I think the proof of the pudding is there for all to see. Cliff's Valley has become a very popular course.

Gary McCord has not seen my course yet. He's likely, however, to make pronouncements about something he hasn't seen. I'm sure he assumes that I've built a "puny" golf course to suit my own "puny" game, which is generally left-to-right. If Gary would bother to come and play Cliff's Valley, he'd soon learn that most of the trouble on the inward half is on the right-hand side. "All the way to the barn," as we golf commentators are wont to intone, there's a creek on your right.

I was extremely nervous when it came time for the grand opening of Cliff's Valley. I had persuaded four good friends—Paul Azinger, Jay Haas, Jim Colbert, and Bob Murphy—to come and help open the course by playing an exhibition match. They were wonderful about donating their services. The date for the opening was October 2, 1995.

The night before, we'd held a dinner in Greenville and all four of the players and their wives attended. During the festivities, I sort of provoked the Senior Tour players (Colbert and Murphy) into a real match against the PGA Tour players (Azinger and Haas). I said to the older guys, "You can play from the white tees and the young guys can play from the blues."

"Bullshit!" Colbert and Murphy replied. "We'll play from the same tees as the those guys and we will beat their asses!"

The battle was on.

The next day, the temperature was 80 degrees and there wasn't a cloud in the sky. When the players arrived at the first tee, some real money was laid on the line. Murphy produced two $100 bills, gently placed them on the ground, and dramatically stuck a tee through them. The other players followed suit and put up $200 of their own money. The invited guests in attendance loved it.

In hopes of adding some additional fun to the event, I walked along with the players and provided commentary on a sound system. On the first hole, the three thousand people who were watching were delighted when Azinger holed his second shot on the par-four. The old guys hit back on the par-three second hole, however, when both Colbert and Murphy sank their putts for 2's. The best ball for the four players after two holes was four—which is pretty strong. Jim Colbert then made an eagle 3 at the first par-five. We were off and running, and it was a wonderful exhibition.

After fifteen holes, the match was dead even. What had started out as a happy, joke-filled affair, however, had now become a very quiet, very serious situation. *Now* it was a matter of pride. Consequently, with money *and* bragging rights on the line, Azinger and Haas won the sixteenth and seventeenth holes to secure the match. The teams bet another $100 on the 18th but, to Colbert's and Murphy's annoyance, the young guys won that hole, too.

All four golfers played the course from the back tees, which are just about 7,100 yards in length. Azinger and Murphy each shot 68, and Haas and Colbert finished with 71's. Not only was it the first time *they* had played the golf course, it was the first time *anyone* had played Cliff's Valley. It made for a wonderful kickoff.

Afterward, we adjourned to the house I'd built just across the lake at the fourth hole. My best friends from England, the Cooper family, were staying with me in the house. P.J., the father, had brought with him a case of Pimms #1, so we had quite a party to celebrate the opening of Cliff's Valley.

Some time later, I got a note from Bob Murphy. It read:

Dear Ben,

You did good! In reply to your question about what I would change: don't change a thing!

When it comes to golf course design, conversation often turns to the Old Course at St. Andrews in Scotland. It was golf's first course, designed wholly by nature. Those, like PGA Tour player Scott Hoch, who called the course "the worst piece of mess I've ever seen," are just ignorant. I'm not saying that you have to like a place like St. Andrews immediately. Goodness knows, Bobby Jones had a delayed appreciation of it, and he was more cerebral than probably any golfer who ever lived. What you have to do is realize that a lot of the old courses are anachronisms. Yes, some of them have hidden hazards. But that doesn't make them any less wonderful. There are a lot of courses in Ireland where you have a blind shot at a par-three, Lahinch being the great case in point, where they place a white stone on the top of a hill to give you a direction marker to the flagstick. Imagine that! A totally blind par-three where you have to aim over a rock each day! Courses like that are a part of golf history, simply because in the old days they didn't have the necessary equipment to move a hill.

Anybody who calls St. Andrews "a mess" is misguided. A great player named Eric Brown, a Ryder Cup captain on two occasions, once referred to St. Andrews as "a goat track." This comment did not endear him to his countrymen. There's always someone dumb enough to make remarks like these about the great old monuments to the game. To change St. Andrews radically, to eliminate the hidden hazards, would be like painting a mustache on the face of the Mona Lisa. It's a relic, and it should be respected as such. The same is true for courses like St. Andrews. You may not enjoy it, but you *should* respect it.

I've always regarded St. Andrews as a wonderful, wonderful old golf course because of its hallowed history. The first seven holes lead down to the corner of the peninsula where eight through eleven play, and the remaining holes head back to the town. If the wind is blowing left to right going out, you're going to have the opposite wind coming back—which is the way golf really should be played, because it becomes a full examination of your abilities. This is perfect, really, although it's been fashionable for many years to build golf courses with a ninth hole that finishes back at the clubhouse.

Golf in Britain is different because you can easily encounter the weather of all four seasons in a single day. If a golfer doesn't like to get wet or blown about, then okay, go somewhere else and play. But don't knock the game's most historic course. Just say, "I'm going to take my ball and clubs and go elsewhere." Then go and play on a bloody course that's probably akin to a dartboard, where you can pitch the ball and it lands softly in a pile of pudding that's supposedly a putting green.

In my opinion, the PGA Tour plays a stereotype game at Tournament Players courses. They're all the same, basically. They've all got spectator mounds around all of the greens, so you're playing the same kinds of shots all of the time. The pitch-and-run is virtually nonexistent in America. It's only because of the fact that the Americans play so few shots of different kinds that the Europeans and the rest of the world have been able to catch up. The game of the U.S. Tour is such a limited game compared to some of the golf on the European Tour and in other parts of the world, where the courses are not perfectly groomed. Every course that is used on the PGA Tour is just about perfect. There's not a blade of grass out of place, which means you can throw darts at every green. It's a different game, but it's not a great game in terms of variety.

The wonderful thing about golf is that it's not a fair game: at one point or another, it's *unfair* to everybody. But you know what? There's nothing wrong with having a game that's unfair. You win some and you lose some.

Just as in life, sometimes you get good bounces...sometimes you get bad lies.

All the World Is a Golf Course...And All of Us Its Players

It was indeed a somewhat surreal moment. Joined by a small group of friends one summer evening in 1996, I had driven from my home in Flat Rock, North Carolina, into Asheville and onto a commercialized strip of road. I passed fast food outlets and a collection of brand-name motels on my way to the Biltmore Square Mall. Inside the mall, somewhere between the up-market apparel stores and high-end boutiques was a decidedly unglamorous movie theater where my friends and I purchased tickets. We were then seated in a jerry-built cinema to watch my first-ever appearance on the silver screen.

Due to a prior commitment, I was unable to attend the Los Angeles premiere of the film "Tin Cup." Since I was no longer a part of the CBS broadcast team, I was also not present at the special premiere that took place at the PGA Championship in Louisville, Kentucky. I found some irony in being relegated to the Biltmore Square Mall Cinema, where I was just another paying customer, with no fanfare or glamour. Certainly none of the other moviegoers that day even had any inkling that one of the on-screen performers was indeed seated in the audience. As I considered my surroundings and waited to see my film debut, I began to think about the incredibly charmed life I had led. Untold numbers of people had seen me on worldwide television, heard my voice over the radio, and read my newspaper columns and magazine articles. Now, I would appear on the big screen with the likes of Kevin Costner, Renee Russo, Don Johnson, and even Cheech Marin.

Without question, my life had contained highs and lows—good bounces and bad bounces, if you will—but equally beyond doubt was the fact that I had been to places I'd never dreamed of going. I have enjoyed the comfort of luxury, the wealth of experience, and the company of some of the most fascinating people ever to exist. Movie stars, heads of state, captains of industry, the great golf scribes and yes, even the golfers, have proven to be vibrant and memorable acquaintances.

Vibrant, for instance, is a term that describes Gary Player quite adequately. Player is, pound for pound, probably the fittest man ever to play the game of golf. Player is like his idol Hogan in the respect that he has achieved tremendous accomplishments with less natural physical talent than his competitors. His impish sense of humor and ability to charm the media, along with his diminutive size, cast him in the role of the underdog when, in fact, he had the fierceness and fight of a pit bull.

I first met a 19-year-old Player in 1955 during his first visit to England. It was, for him, the most trying of circumstances since he had just missed the cut at Royal Liverpool, one of several consecutive cuts he had failed to make. I was walking to the railway station at Hoylake with Player and Hugh Lewis, then the club professional at Altrincham Municipal in Cheshire, England. A gale bearing sheets of rain stung our eyes and skin, and Player, who had no raincoat, sheltered as best he could beneath our umbrellas.

Lewis, an occasional tournament aspirant who was also ousted after 36 holes, was on his way home to perform his shop tasks.

The 5-foot-7-inch, 140-pound Player turned his big brown eyes up at the burly Lewis, who stood well over 6 feet tall, and asked "How can I possibly improve myself, Hughie, quickly, before I'm totally broke and have to go home?"

Lewis, in typically dour North Country tones, replied in a booming voice, "Gary, lad, why don't you use whatever money you have left to buy yourself a one-way ticket on a banana boat sailing for Johannesburg and find yourself an honest job? You've no business being out here."

Player was plainly crushed. But in all truth, at the time he had an ugly, flat swing and apparently little aptitude for the game. This moment, along with the mocking he regularly received from other British players, served as the motivation that drove Player to a regimen of endless hours of practice. It was shortly afterward that he started to show his wares.

Player was hardly fancied as a competitor when he arrived at Muirfield ten days before the 1959 British Open, planning to diligently prepare for the event. The club secretary, Colonel Evans-Lombe, informed Player that he was welcome to use the practice fairway, chip, and putt, but he could not play the course.

"I know that you are preparing the club for the Open Championship," Player pleaded with Evans-Lombe, "and I have flown thousands of miles to do just the same, sir. As I stand here, though, I can see people playing on the golf course."

"Yes, there are people playing on the golf course," Evans-Lombe retorted, "but they are members."

Incredulous, Player phoned his sponsor, George Blumberg, who was the unofficial "father of South African golf," who backed Player. Blumberg was in London, and upon hearing Player's plight, set the wheels in motion by involving Lord Brabazon of Tara, president of the British PGA, to sort out the impasse. Eventually, Evans-Lombe relented, and Player was allowed to play the course, but only once a day. One day, Player ventured out for an extra nine holes, and the following morning learned that, as punishment, his caddie had been banished. This time, it was the club captain who had to intervene in Player's favor.

Such arrant nonsense hardly helped Player, but it probably strengthened his will to win. He was further emotionally encouraged when his wife, Vivienne, arrived with Jennifer, their two-month-old first-born child, whom Gary had never seen.

The first and second rounds of the tournament were played on Wednesday and Thursday, with the cut coming on Thursday evening. The final two rounds were played on Friday, with a blind draw determining when the players would tee off. The leaders were not sent off last as they are now, but rather were randomly scattered throughout the field. And so it was that Player's draw meant that he would play very early in the morning and in the afternoon. Player's week of preparation at Muirfield yielded the desirable results, with opening rounds of 75 and 71, and his solid morning round of 70 on Friday left him in position to make a run at the championship.

Player entered the final round declaring that it would be "66 or bust"—and so it should have been. Birdies at the 10th and 12th were followed by 2's at the par-three 13th and 16th holes. Although Player went through the 17th green and chipped back weakly, he made a 20-foot putt for his 4. Now, Player needed only a par 4 for that 66 he'd targeted and so coveted. Instead, he drove into the left-hand bunker, advanced the ball only 100 yards with a 6-iron, hit the same club to the front of the green, then took three putts for a sorry 6.

Player was devastated, feeling that he had thrown away the championship, even though the other leaders still had nine holes to play. It took his wife 15 minutes to sufficiently console him at the scorer's hut, where he slumped over and wept in utter despair before eventually signing his card.

The aforementioned Blumberg, Player's great friend and mentor, persuaded him to have a stiff drink after taking a cold bath on returning to the Marine Hotel in North Berwick during the agonizing wait to learn his fate. Countryman Harold Henning, who had bet heavily on his compatriot, telephoned from the golf course at regular intervals with finishing scores. Englishman Fred Bullock finished two shots behind, and then eventually only Flory van Donck of Belgium was left with a chance to make a par-4 to tie. Ironically, he drove into the same bunker that Player had, then failed to make a 40-foot putt to force a playoff.

The flustered championship committeemen hurried to find Player, awaken him, and get him back to the golf course to present him with the Claret Jug. Player, as if literally awakened from a nightmare, was informed that he'd won his first Open Championship.

My association with Player continued the following year when I covered the 1960 Canada Cup at Portmarnock in Ireland. Player was scheduled to play with Bobby Locke when he was overcome with an asthma attack. The tournament committee held back Player's starting time because he was hampered enough to be stretched out flat on his back on the benches around the snooker table in the clubhouse.

I dashed back into Dublin to retrieve some medicine that I carried with me in case of a recurrence of the asthma that plagued me as a child. I presented Player with the pills, which he swallowed before recovering sufficiently to go out and shoot 65, a Portmarnock record.

In 1972, Player was at the height of his powers. That year, I stood only a few paces from Player when he hit the shot that won him the PGA Championship at Oakland Hills in Birmingham, Michigan.

Like at the British Open 13 years previous, Player was sure he'd blown his chance to win the PGA Championship near the end of the final round. The 15th hole at Oakland Hills has a bunker in the middle of the fairway. Because of his adrenaline, Player, who normally drove short of the bunker, drove right into it. He strove mightily to get the ball out and onto the green, but sent the ball from bunker to bunker. As was his wont, Player then crafted an absolutely magnificent bunker shot to nearly one foot from the hole. Inexplicably, he then missed the putt.

I walked near Player as he muttered his way to the 16th tee. Apparently struggling to erase the previous hole from his conscience with a mighty swipe, Player came off his drive at 16 so badly that the ball steered a monstrous distance right of the fairway. The look on his face was now that of a man suffocating.

When Player reached his ball, he found that its position was so far off-line that the ball rested on the stamped-down grass of heavy gallery traffic. Despite the fortune of a therefore improved lie, Player snapped into sharp focus when he began to examine the grim reality of his position in relation to the green. He would need the loft of a 9-iron to get the ball over the tops of the trees standing guard. If the ball did not get high enough, it would not clear the wall of willow that screened the green. At the same time, if Player's high shot was not 150 yards long, it would fall into the pond that nearly surrounded the green and laid openly in wait for the ball. Finally, would he even be able to avoid the sand by stopping the ball on the green from its lie in the rough? His position looked like certain doom, and the situation called for the type of shot that only the most imaginative player could even visualize. To try it and miss it, however, is to expose oneself as foolish in a desperate attempt.

Clad in the trademark black clothing and white cap that served as his version of Superman's cape, Player looked the shot over and then took a measured swipe at the ball in the grass. As the shot rose up barely over the trees, Player ran sideways toward the fairway, breathlessly straining to see the unpredictable result of his handiwork. The crowds shifted and mumbled, and then exploded in glee. Against all odds, the ball hit and stopped just about four feet from the hole. If I had not witnessed this with my own eyes, I would not have believed it possible.

A reinvigorated Player made the putt for birdie and thereby pulled his head from the noose. When the portly young Jim Jamieson bogeyed 17, and then missed a two-foot putt to bogey the last, Player had rescued his second PGA Championship title.

Though Gary was an emotional player, his instinct and pride never allowed him to give up. With customary sincere bravado, Player even irrationally declared to superagent Mark McCormack that he would come from seven shots behind Hubert Green on the final day to win the 1978 Masters. To Player, the possibility that he could actually do that was not farfetched. To the slack-jawed amazement of McCormack, Player backed up his outrageous claim by blistering the inward half in 30 shots to card a record-tying 64. Green, Rod Funseth, and Tom Watson all finished one shot short of the 277 Player set as clubhouse lead, as Green's day finished with a missed shot at the last hole. After Player's victory, Green went back to the hole to try the shot for a second time—he missed.

Player doggedly traveled all over the world in search of victory after tireless victory, giving maximum effort to any sized tournament. Take, for instance, the following sequence of events. In 1974, I witnessed Player win his sixth Australian Open, propelled largely by a third-round 63 over the difficult Lake Karrinyup course in Perth, made even more difficult on this occasion by wind and rain. The plane in Perth was held for us following the tournament, and Player and I boarded, bound for London.

During the long flight, Player slept and read Churchill, who was another of his idols. Both Player and I were merely laying over in London for a few hours before catching connecting flights to a golf tournament in Spain. Player accepted an invitation to breakfast at my home in Epsom, Surrey, between flights, especially when he learned that my house was located near the farm of local racehorse trainer Brian Swift.

Somewhat bleary-eyed, we enjoyed a breakfast prepared by my mother, and Player visited Swift long enough to purchase a four-year-old mare named "Look Lively." It was then back to Heathrow for our flight to Spain. Our grueling trip was made longer still when our flight to Madrid was delayed due to fog.

We finally arrived in Madrid, connected to Murcia, and drove on to the La Manga Campo de Golf resort on Spain's Costa Blanca. Words cannot describe how exhausted I was by the time I got into my hotel room. The last sight I saw out the window as I drew the drapes to get some well-needed sleep was Player, alone on the practice range, hitting balls. I'm not certain how long I slept, but I know that when I awakened and opened my drapes, I once again set my eyes on the incredible sight of Player, who'd by then returned to the range to hit more practice shots.

The La Manga Campo de Golf resort was staging a pro-am played over 72 holes. The novel format found the professionals not recording their individual scores separately, but rather including their amateur team's best ball score. The tournament host, Greg Peters, who also owned the resort, was hoping to foster camaraderie between the professionals and the amateurs, and each team played with a different professional each round.

My team drew Gary Player for the vital third round. So determined was Player to record a good score and make the three of us play to the best of our abilities that he ran from amateur to amateur coaching us on each and every shot. The 53 he shepherded us to in Spain, and Player's subsequent victory in that event, was little noticed and long forgotten by the golf world. However, it surely resounds in the memories of we amateurs that experienced his enthusiasm, and surely counts among the worldwide and unequaled victory total that Player touts.

In the days and weeks following his victory in Spain, Player went on to win the Brazilian Open by shooting a 59 at Gavea. In fact, he won on six continents in consecutive weeks, and now beats his drum on the Senior Tour.

Sometimes, I long for what seemed like the "happy-go-lucky" days of old. I think the Senior PGA Tour is a wonderful place to see some of the more colorful, relaxed players that were the stars of a rich and more jovial era.

I covered only one Senior Tour event during my time with CBS, which was the Ameritech Senior Open—once in Traverse City, Michigan and once in Chicago. I'll admit, it was huge fun for me because the senior players are really my contemporaries. It was very relaxed, and the players, grateful for this "second chance," were much warmer and more cooperative, generally speaking, than the young guys on the regular Tour. Public relations is very important to the Senior Tour, and the players there have a better reputation for corporate entertaining, attending sponsor cocktail parties, and being accessible to the fans.

There is still some element of the long-gone glamour of the regular Tour amongst the seniors. On the regular Tour, the days of players going out for beers and telling stories are history. Players these days are off fast-fooding with their young families. The modern tournament professional has become a like a mini-corporation, attempting at every chance to "brand" their very name and likeness. In the mid-1970s, I began to see this disheartening evolution take place. Players began toting their briefcases around, and taking meetings with their managers and agents in the locker room. As players hit balls on the practice tee, their swing coaches, their media representatives, and their accountants surround them. The charming image of seeing Jackie Burke Jr. giving Ben Hogan a putting lesson on the practice green is now totally foreign to the modern player, who must exist in a real "dog-eat-dog" environment due to the pressures of the financial concerns involved.

For better or worse, professional golf has become big business and virtually all motivation is financial. Perhaps the most nausea-inducing example is that certain players either refuse or are contractually unable to sign autographs on golf balls that are not the brand they are paid to use and endorse. Tiger Woods recently refused such an autograph request—even though the signature ball was to be used for Billy Andrade's and Brad Faxon's charity event. I don't think Arnold Palmer has ever charged or turned down a request—and others should listen as he is "the King."

Professional golf is now a glamour circuit, although it seems very few of the players practice what would be deemed a glamorous lifestyle, especially by the standards of camaraderie and panache established by their predecessors. On the European Tour, some of the players were simply too poor to do anything but sleep in their automobiles in the car park of exclusive golf resorts. On the U.S. PGA Tour, there were simply players known for their frugality, like Curtis Strange and Mark O'Meara, who perhaps were fearful that if they ever lost their game they'd never earn another check.

In my experience, though, the Senior Tour is refreshingly somewhat of a throwback to what the Tour used to be like, both on and off the course. The players are more at ease, enjoy fine wines, gourmet dinners, and quality time spent with their fellows and their wives. The "old school" players, who remember what the Tour was like in days gone by, maintain this special flavor. While I am heartened by the opportunity these senior players get to relive their golden days of frivolity and enjoying the finer things, it goes without saying that golf fans of all ages also enjoy the chance to see the greats in action on the course.

I think that it behooves Player, Palmer, and Nicklaus to support the Senior Tour, but to pick their time to get out. Palmer is no longer able to play up to his own high standards, and the sight of Nicklaus creeping around is dispiriting to those, like me, who remember the Golden Bear at the height of his powers. Physically, Nicklaus's body has taken a beating. One must remember that if Nicklaus is hurting like hell, it would hurt a normal person far more. Jack is a real tough guy, but I don't think even a fit Jack Nicklaus would beat the likes of Kite, Watson, and Zoeller too often on the Senior Tour. Nicklaus is spread way too thin and has aged too much to be the competitive force he was on the regular Tour. I love the guy to death for thinking that he can still win, but the trouble with Nicklaus is that he has such an ego that he thinks he can do it all. How can he possibly be the greatest golfer, the greatest designer, *and* the greatest businessman of all time? Especially when he's surrounded by "yes men"?

The only man I've ever seen stand up to Nicklaus was the irascible Pittsburgh sportswriter Bob Drum. Nicklaus had won the 1972 Masters and the 1972 U.S. Open at Pebble Beach, but in the British Open at Muirfield, Nicklaus played conservatively and lost to Lee Trevino by one shot. His bid for the Grand Slam ruined, Nicklaus played another year without a major championship victory before Drum finally ripped into him at a reception at the Marine Hotel following the 1973 British Open, which was won by Tom Weiskopf.

Long into the night, Drum suddenly turned on Nicklaus with his gravelly voice. "You're a damned coward, Jack," Drum pronounced within earshot of me and the others gathered. "Do you wanna know why you lost last year? You know why you only finished fourth here? Because you pussyfoot around with a 3-wood and a 1-iron when you're the finest driver of the ball in the world! You can never catch up! Just take your driver, your wedge, and putt as well as you always do and you'll win everything!"

Jack was well speechless, angry, and embarrassed. One month later, though, making full employ of his driver, Nicklaus stormed to a four-shot victory over Bruce Crampton in the PGA Championship at Canterbury Golf Club near Cleveland, Ohio. Not long after, Drum received a photo in the mail of Nicklaus holding his driver, sent and signed by the Golden Bear himself.

I marvel at all of the times I have watched Nicklaus, in full control of his game, hole putts when he had to hole them. He had the power to make things happen when he needed them to happen most. He was supernatural, and he had what no one else had—the seeming ability to will things to happen. In my career, I was fortunate to witness Nicklaus's entire longevity, first casting eyes on him at the 1959 Walker Cup at Muirfield, when he was an 18-year-old wonderchild. He was a big, fat, blond, obnoxious youngster with a crew cut. In his earlier years, the galleries could be very spiteful toward Nicklaus, as he was in position to dethrone the beloved Palmer. I can remember seeing patrons who'd positioned themselves behind bunkers, holding up handmade bull's-eye signs that read, "Hit it here, Jack."

One of my funniest recollections of Nicklaus occurred at his home in Columbus, Ohio in 1968, when the rift occurred that forced the touring professional golfers to split away from the PGA of America and found the Tournament Players Division, which was then renamed the PGA Tour in 1975. British golf writer Pat Ward Thomas and I sat across the coffee table from Nicklaus in his living room, where he anxiously awaited the outcome of the negotiation, but he was forever darting out of the room to take phone calls. The rebellion was in full swing and Nicklaus had aligned himself with Gardner Dickinson and Dan Sykes in leading the revolt. Nicklaus was getting beat up and criticized over this move, and was very frazzled.

It was teatime that afternoon, and in an attempt to calm everyone down, Nicklaus's wife Barbara had baked a great tray of cupcakes. Thomas and I drank tea and ate a few of these lovely little cakes, while Nicklaus, very much in a dither and in a totally stressed condition, ate 26 of those cakes! One right after another in front of us, Jack inhaled 26 of them. After Ward Thomas and I accounted for all of them, we no longer wondered why Nicklaus had the unfortunate nickname "Fat Jack."

Much is made of Nicklaus's invincible victory record. But for all of his competitive fire, I also marvel at the way he has faced defeat.

Nicklaus was lurking, in fact, at the 1963 Open Championship, which is remembered for the playoff between Phil Rodgers and eventual champion Bob Charles. The British galleries also remember, unfavorably, the way the American Rodgers placed his porkpie hat over the hole after holing out. This showy gesture was considered thoughtless by the British, since they considered it to be an attempt to distract the South African Charles, who needed his putt on the 72nd hole to tie Rodgers.

Nicklaus, though, had a strong chance to win that 1963 British Open. To his detriment, he had yet to learn the manner in which increased adrenaline flow can betray the golf swing. I followed him around the course as he hit the ball through the green and into difficult lies on two of his last four holes at Royal Lytham. I watched the young and highly competitive Nicklaus, having dropped two strokes to par on those last four holes, shed real tears of frustration upon the unsuccessful completion of his round.

I could understand and even almost empathize with his rare tears because I had seen the intensity of his emotions only days earlier. I was recording a BBC radio interview with Nicklaus on a makeshift recording set in the dusty storeroom above Eddie Musty's golf shop at Lytham. Jack and I sat across from each other on opposite sides of a card table. On top of the card table sat the radio microphones, wired into the tape recording unit and electronic equipment.

I made my way through the interview, probing the 23-year-old with questions about his strategy and technique. His penetrating eyes stared intently into mine as he listened to each question. His answers, one by one, were just as pointed and direct as his glare.

When the subject came to motivation, I inquired as to what motivated the young Nicklaus, and what his immediate and realistic goals were.

His hard stare remained on me for a beat, and then his answer came at me with the force of a hurricane gale. "Motivation and goals?" he replied loudly, his shrill voice rising. The audio meters on the recorder began to bounce into the red as Nicklaus, his fist clenched, began to pound repeatedly on the card table as he continued.

"I"... *BANG!* ..."am going to be"... *BANG!* ..."the best... *BANG!* ..."there ever was!" *BANG!*

Suddenly, the card table between us collapsed from the intensity of the pounding.

"Christ!" I shouted.

Then, just as suddenly, with the recording equipment lying in shambles at our feet, we began to laugh like hell. At the same time, the hairs stood up on the back of my neck.

My God, I thought. *If this guy is for real, he'll actually do it.*

Jack's emotions were once more on display four years later at Hoylake, when he was the Open runner-up. Broadcasting the event for the BBC, lead announcer Henry Longhurst, in the only British Open I would have the pleasure of broadcasting with my mentor, dispatched me to interview anyone I could as the tournament came to a finale. Nicklaus had finished, and was waiting to see whether Roberto de Vicenzo, playing in the final group behind him, would overcome his clubhouse lead. De Vicenzo, the 45-year-old beloved Argentinian, had narrowly failed to win the Open championship throughout 20 years of valiant striving. He'd been third to Henry Cotton at Muirfield in 1948, third to Bobby Locke at Royal St. George's, Sandwich, in 1949, and second to Locke in 1950 at Troon. He was sixth to Ben Hogan at Carnoustie in 1953, third to Peter Thomson at Hoylake in 1956, third to Kel Nagle at St. Andrews in 1960, third to Tony Lema at St. Andrews in 1964, and fourth to Thomson at Royal Birkdale in 1965. In almost each case, de Vicenzo's putting had betrayed him under pressure.

Fourteen years previously, de Vicenzo had admitted that he had wept before his final round of the British Open at Carnoustie. It wasn't because he had played poorly in the morning's third round—far from it. De Vicenzo had scored 71 and was tied for the lead with Hogan at lunchtime. He had cried because he was faced with the deep realization and inner fear that his putting was not going to hold up under the pressure of the final round. His ghosts did, indeed, catch up with him that afternoon. De Vicenzo shot a 73, five strokes worse than winner Hogan.

Now it appeared that he had his last chance. Only Old Tom Morris at 46 and Harry Vardon at 44 had won the Open at such an advanced age—Morris in the last century, Vardon in 1914. De Vicenzo, who had won nearly 150 tournaments and 30 national championships around the world, but never a major, nevertheless had a good feeling when I found him before his final round, characteristically, in the caddie shack rather than the locker room.

"I feel like many peoples are with me," he said in his pidgin English, which Roberto loved to jokingly call his "PGA English." And of course, de Vicenzo was correct. The British held Nicklaus in awe, but the British public had yet to bestow their affection upon him. Gary Player was admired for his work ethic, but not for his cliché-ridden, rather pompous and often ridiculously pious public utterances. How the British loved Roberto, though. They respected his powerful talent, but they adored him for his gentlemanly humility, his self-effacing humor, and his unfailing politeness even when obviously distressed, most often by his putting.

Now, de Vicenzo needed to play the final three holes in 1-over-par to fend off Nicklaus, Player, and Clive Clark.

De Vicenzo's 3-wood into the teeth of the wind at the 16th caught the middle of the green—birdie. A superb tee shot at the dangerous 418-yard 17th set up a 9-iron approach. He two-putted for par. Another perfect drive at 18 allowed him to safely hit the green with the same club and begin the march up the 18th that he had always dreamed of.

While this was going on, I began to interview Nicklaus live. As we spoke, it became apparent that de Vicenzo was indeed going to break through and achieve the victory of his lifetime. As de Vicenzo made his way through the bleachers up the 18th fairway, he received a huge and warm ovation from the large gallery.

Interrupting the interview, I suggested to Jack that we pause and savor the moment for our mutual friend. Actually, we had little choice, since the cheering and applause was so thunderous that our voices would not have been audible over the microphone. Jack whole-heartily agreed.

As we viewed the scene in silence, my glance turned to Nicklaus, who was shedding tears of joy at the heartwarming sight of Roberto putting out to claim his championship—at Jack's expense. It was a magical moment that caused me to fight back my own tears. Instead, I quickly motioned to my cameraman to film Nicklaus and capture this incredibly unselfish and sincere display of class.

He is magically compelling—in victory as well as defeat.

As I mentioned earlier, I saw Brian Barnes defeat Nicklaus twice in one day during the 1975 Ryder Cup matches at Laurel Valley. That double defeat was very hard for Jack to take, but he was an absolutely impeccable sportsman after it happened. Nicklaus was a cold-eyed killer, but if you got the best of him, he was the first to recognize it.

I remember seeing the Bear at the conclusion of the 1977 British Open, when he walked off of the 18th green at Turnberry, having just undergone an incredible shoot-out with Tom Watson. Jack shot 65-

66 in the final rounds, and Watson shot 65-65 to get the best of Nicklaus by one shot. These two rivals were playing their own contest, 10 shots clear of their nearest competitor, Hubert Green. As Nicklaus and the champion Watson walked past me off the final green, Jack put his arm around Watson and congratulated him.

Although Nicklaus is so obstinate in so many ways, I revere him because he is able to temper his competitive fires enough to be more gracious in defeat than in victory. Make no mistake, though—his competitive fires burn constantly.

I had the opportunity to feel the intensity normally reserved for his competition when I got the chance to play nine holes with Nicklaus near his home at Lost Tree Village in Palm Beach, Florida. Jack and I negotiated strokes, and he gave me four over the nine holes. Fair enough.

It was a fine afternoon as the greatest golfer of all time and I casually made our way around the links, chatting and enjoying the round.

After five holes, however, I had Nicklaus 1-down. Suddenly, the chitchat ceased, and Nicklaus grew quiet. Instead of this continuing as a social outing, it became like the bloody championship of the world! All of a sudden, all of the fun was switched off and Nicklaus was all business. From that point on, he thumped my ass into the dirt and beat me 2-up. I have to admire a guy with such competitive instincts. The incident, however, also provided me a little insight into Nicklaus's career. I believe he may have lost as many championships as he won by forcing himself to play catch-up after handicapping himself with poor early rounds. When he was on, Nicklaus was head and shoulders above anybody I ever saw. One can speak of Hogan's technique or Palmer's incredible charisma, but no one was equal to Nicklaus when put against his combined talent and longevity.

No one had a more intense knowledge of Nicklaus's longevity than his frequent opponent Tom Weiskopf. Tom has been eternally linked to Nicklaus, not only because of their clashes on the golf course, but also due to the fact that they were both very talented products of Ohio State University.

I observed Weiskopf at Royal Montreal Golf Club at Ile Bizard, Quebec in 1975 when he won the Canadian Open by triumphing over Nicklaus in a sudden death playoff. Weiskopf was exuberant and emotional about his win.

"Tom," I said, "when you won the tournament, you went totally ape over beating Nicklaus!"

"Ben," Weiskopf replied, "everybody assumes that because Nicklaus and I have the same Ohio State background that we are big buddies. Everybody assumes that we are colleagues and friends. Well, I hate Jack Nicklaus more than I hate anybody in the world. I think he probably despises me, too, because he has been able to absolutely *stomp* on my ass. It makes me sick when people infer that Jack and I grew up as buddies. When I hear that, I want to throw up. I hate Jack Nicklaus with a passion," Weiskopf said. I hate him because he has always been able to beat me. Why *wouldn't* I hate him?"

I felt a cold shudder at the seriousness with which he told me this.

Weiskopf could never come out of Nicklaus's shadow, and with an attitude like that, one can see how the intensity of their rivalry was mentally unhealthy for Weiskopf, who may have been obsessed with the haunting presence of Nicklaus. Of course, I think Weiskopf is correct in that Nicklaus loved beating him and made sure that he kept beating him to keep him down. Nicklaus was definitely that way—he wanted to *own* his opponents.

Weiskopf, to his detriment, was oftentimes his own worst enemy. Tom is truly a genius—but a wayward one. When I think of the genius of Weiskopf, I am reminded of people like artist Vincent van Gogh and English comedian Spike Milligan, in that they had enormous talent but were three parts mad!

Weiskopf was nuttier than a fruitcake. Many people don't realize that the reason Weiskopf's record is so spotty is that there were times when he didn't know how to put the brakes on his partying. He would then end up sleeping in a hedge the night before a final round while in contention to win a tournament. He didn't earn the sobriquet "Terrible Tom" for nothing.

In 1968, I was a guest of National Airlines at the Country Club of Miami, where I was to play in the pro-am portion of their golf tournament. Included in my group were the mayor of Miami and Weiskopf. Tom had come down to South Florida from his home in the snows of Ohio, where he had just been forced to complete a comprehensive and compulsory period of Army reserve training. His game, therefore, was not up to the level of skill he had become accustomed to. My game, however, was quite good, as I played then to a 4 handicap.

Weiskopf's frustration with his game in this very public setting, with an attentive gallery, coupled with the fact that I was actually keeping up with him, began to wear on his nerves. The mayor, late for his tee time, had been drinking, and was beginning to get under Weiskopf's skin.

On the eighth green, Weiskopf's ball was 20 feet from the hole. My ball, a scant five feet from the cup, was on Weiskopf's line.

"Why don't you putt your damned ball and get the hell out of the way," an annoyed and curt Weiskopf hissed at me. I was startled enough to then three-putt, and my game fell apart. Weiskopf and I didn't speak for the rest of the round.

The mayor and I repaired to the clubhouse bar following the round, where he began to tell me about the swank barbecue reception he was throwing at his home later that evening. When Weiskopf passed by on his way to the locker room, the mayor stopped him to shake his hand and invite him to the exclusive evening soirée.

"Why the hell would I want to go there?" asked Weiskopf, shaking his head and walking away.

I had little choice but to write about Weiskopf's abhorrent behavior and the incident in the *Financial Times* and *Golf World* magazine (UK), both of which I was regularly writing for. For the five subsequent years, "Terrible Tom" maintained a stony silence and never exchanged a word with me.

At the 1973 British Open, Weiskopf battled Johnny Miller in the rain down the stretch. It was a magical match featuring the two tall, elegant players. I followed Weiskopf every step of the way through that final round, making sure he knew I was there behind the ropes. Even his wife Jeannie expressed dismay about our feud as I walked with her through the scrambling galleries.

To Weiskopf's eternal credit, after his triumph, he apologized for the cold shoulder he'd dispensed to me by inviting me to his victory party at the Marine Hotel that evening. We buried the hatchet and celebrated his victory in uproarious fashion. Weiskopf drank his drinks and his wife's drinks too, as the party degenerated into a real scene, with Weiskopf and Nicklaus—the usually bitter rivals—red-faced, singing along with a Scottish baritone in full highland dress. It was the worst rendition of "Amazing Grace" I have ever heard.

To his everlasting credit, Weiskopf has proved to be a very fine golf course designer, and it is in the area of design that I believe his true—albeit maddening—genius has become evident.

Though Weiskopf surely regarded Nicklaus as his chief rival, there's no doubt that it was by supplanting Palmer that Nicklaus truly got the world's attention. While "the King" and "the Bear" have engaged in spirited competition on the golf course and in business, Nicklaus— though he succeeded Palmer as golf's top player in the mid-1960s— will never unseat Palmer in the category of charisma. Palmer single-handedly rescued the British Open from obscurity, and with television as his vehicle made golf available to the masses in America, where it had been viewed as a minor elitist sport. The sight of a charging, macho Palmer, showing off his chest hair and tossing aside his cigarette, eventually made golf a sport suitable for television. Hell, there was a day when Arnold would smoke three cigarettes on a par 3!

Again, I've been fortunate to enjoy a pleasant relationship with Palmer, whom I have watched play all over the world.

In 1970, Palmer, Tony Jacklin, and I were together at the Dunlop tournament in Canberra, Australia. Canberra, a nice enough city, is a boring place when compared to Sydney, Perth, and even Adelaide. One evening of the tournament, we were all invited to a reception at the mansion of Lord Kerr, the governor general. Palmer, still a young man, was loathe to attend the reception because he theorized that "it would be full of blue hairs."

"Arnold," I reminded him, "you—and Tony, for that matter—are here under contract to Dunlop. I don't think it would be cricket for you two to skip the reception."

Arnold reluctantly agreed, and, along with Jacklin, we took a limousine ride to the governor's mansion, planning to make an appearance and leave the dinner as early as possible. When we walked into the room, I grimaced because Arnold's worst fears were confirmed. There was not a person under 70 years old in the room—"blue hairs" *and* "white hairs" as far as the eye could see. Palmer and Jacklin did the best they could, smiling tightly and mingling, though always keeping one eye on the door for the chance to make a quick getaway.

Suddenly, in the midst of all the tedium, the doors flew open and a vision of loveliness entered. She had long, blonde hair flowing down her back and she perfectly filled in the lovely strapless dress she was wearing. The woman, who entered by herself, was a stunning whiff of classic beauty.

"Who is *that?*" Palmer asked, his eyes wide. Jacklin's jaw was on the floor as we were told that she was the wife of the army minister, who was out of town.

Jacklin and Palmer, excited to have a youthful and beautiful presence to talk with, began chatting her up as we were called to dinner. We were then seated at a long table for an elegant and elaborate dinner, served by white-gloved waiters at each chair. It was a very, very formal dining experience, as one might expect at a reception thrown by a governor general.

Throughout the dinner, Palmer, Jacklin, and I, captivated, were vying for the attention of this glamorous beauty. We had the lovely lady sufficiently cornered, and Palmer and Jacklin were no longer desperate to leave the party early.

When the plates were cleared away at the end of dinner, the governor general rose and gave a well-spoken toast to Her Majesty. A popular announcement was then made: "Ladies and gentlemen, you may now smoke."

Almost immediately, the lady of our affection, in her revealing dress and eye-catching splendor, broke into our conversation with her Australian accent. "Excuse me, fellas, but I've gotta let one go."

To our amazement, she then rose two inches off of her chair and let out a majestic, seam-splitting fart!

Jacklin quickly turned to me, and in his British accent, exclaimed, "Ben! Did you *hear* that?"

My wide-eyed look told Tony that I had.

"I don't know about you," he said, "but that just dampened my bloomin' ardor!"

Indeed, the lady's mystique had, shall we say, definitely dissipated.

Of course, Australia is a place with an attitude all its own, and a significant amount of the body of my broadcasting work has been spent there each winter, enjoying its people and their individual quirks. Five-time British Open winner Peter Thomson has been as gracious a host to me as Australia has to offer. On one occasion in the late 1960s, he not only set me up with "Ms. Australia," Pam Tudor, but also leant me, indefinitely, the keys to his prized E-Type Jaguar, and arranged tickets for us to attend the Melbourne Cup, Australia's major social and sporting event. It is a horse race watched by everyone, as businesses closed to afford all the chance to watch.

Ms. Tudor and I gathered at a private box in the exclusive club at the racetrack for the event, when the man in charge of the party announced, "Okay, welcome all. Now sheilas, bugger off. Sheilas at this end of the bar, and the men at this end."

With that announcement, the men split up with their wives and dates for the remainder of the event. The women were allowed to rejoin us only at the end of the event, and only for one drink. That was how the chauvinistic Australians unabashedly still treated their women in the 1960s.

New Zealanders and South Africans also display an unassuming candor that admittedly I find refreshing. Also in the late 1960s, I watched South African Simon Hobday play a lousy round in a tournament at Crans-sur-Sierre in Switzerland, which is a magnificent and luxurious ski resort and golf club three hours outside Geneva. The clubhouse bar—fittingly casual during the day—converted into a nightclub for resort guests each evening at 6:00, when prices became nightclub prices and patrons were expected to dress accordingly.

As I mentioned, "Hobbers" played a terrible round, missed the cut, and went immediately from the course in search of a beer in consolation, crawling into the nightclub. Hobday, by the way, is never one you'd want to model clothes for you. He looks like an unmade bed even when he is dressed to go out. Shortly after he entered this nightclub, the snobby French barman denied him a drink.

"Sir, we cannot serve you in those filthy clothes," the barman insisted. "You must go away and get yourself into formal clothes or you cannot drink here."

"Whatever are you talking about?" asked a puzzled and put off Hobday. "Here I am playing in the ridiculous Swiss Open and all I want is a beer."

"No, no, monsieur. You must get into a different outfit."

Hobbers, dumbfounded and no less thirsty, left the nightclub to change his outfit. He returned not long after, and presented himself again to the barman.

"Alright, you little French joker," he pronounced as he bellied up to the bar, "how about this for an outfit?"

Hobday stood before the barman, in all of his hairy nakedness, with his underpants stretched over his head. I will never forget the sight of Hobday sashaying across the bar, and the disruption it caused in the nightclub. Hobday was wild, mad, and totally away with the fairies. Like many of the Australians, he was, and is, a bold and entertaining man.

Hobday was reported to the British PGA, which was not amused, and levied a 1,000-pound fine—its largest ever at the time—for player misconduct.

Without bias, I must admit that covering professional golf and playing the game in Europe and the United Kingdom was an immensely entertaining experience. In order to lodge in proximity to the Open Championship, for instance, I would rent stately homes near the championship venues along with other fourth-estate colleagues, including Dan Jenkins.

The obvious culture and class clashes were sometimes inevitable. In 1978 I was ensconced in a stately home near St. Andrews owned by Lord Jamie Elphinstone, nephew to Her Majesty Queen Elizabeth.

Elphinstone, a man of great sophistication, made certain that we were spoiled by the finest fare possible, indulging us in meals and drink. The first night, our group went through nine bottles of rich Port, the second night seven, and the third night five.

On the fourth morning, Lord Elphinstone and I were engaged in our daily conference concerning what to serve for dinner, when golf writer Dan Jenkins overheard our discussion and offered the following immortal remark:

"Ben, for Christ's sake, don't give us anymore of that goddamned orange fish," referring to the exquisite smoked salmon so prevalent in Scotland.

I could tell Lord Elphinstone was taken aback when he raised his eyebrows at me and whispered in his British accent, "Ben, you really do have some extraordinary friends."

Of course, the Jenkins culture clash was also well-illustrated when I took him to the French Open one year. I showed him around the elaborate Palace Biarritz, a hotel that was at one time a residence of Napoleon. We made our way up to the top of the indoor atrium via the beautiful spiral staircase, where we had a view of the lobby below. Jenkins then surprised me by dropping a soccer ball down over the staircase, which bounced around the baroque lobby, sending the formal frock-coated doormen scurrying around in their tails and covering their heads!

I once rented a stately home 27 miles south of Turnberry called Cairnryan. I also imported a wonderful female Cordon Bleu chef from London who prepared a sumptuous dinner each evening. Jenkins lodged with me there as well, and asked one day if I would mind if he invited Tom and Linda Watson over to join us for one of our dinners.

"Well, if you must," I said.

Watson, who had a late starting time the following day, consented to join us, and made the 27-mile drive with his wife on the Friday night of the championship. The chef on this particular evening produced some gorgeously rich chocolate éclairs for dessert. They were sinfully rich, smothered with ice cream. Much in the same way I had seen Nicklaus make his way through the tray of cupcakes on his couch in Columbus, I watched Watson eat over 20 of these éclairs! I don't know if nervousness played any role in his intake, but Tom went mad for these things, and I felt it necessary to pull his wife Linda aside and apologize.

"Linda, I can only hope I haven't put your husband out of the Open Championship," I said. "I don't know how any man could not be weighed down by having such a massive amount of these delicacies in his belly."

As we now know, Watson, perhaps *fueled* by the éclairs, went out and shot 65 in each of the last two rounds and enjoyed a memorable victory over Nicklaus.

I had my own bit of history at the famed Turnberry Hotel and golf course. I had driven up from London in the company of a certain fashion model to play in a celebrity tournament. On the morning of the second and final round, I was enjoying a blissful morning in my suite, occupied in bed with my companion. The lady and I were engaged in, as Gary Player would call it, a little "rumpy-pump."

It was the height of passion, cooled by the summer breezes blowing from the sea, presumably over the Alisa Craig and through the open windows. Suddenly, along with the soothing breezes, into the room came the sound of the public address system, over which I heard the announcer introduce my group to the first tee. Of course, I had lost all track of time in full attention to my morning duties!

I leapt from the bed, whipped on my clothing, and stumbled down all of the famed 126 stone steps of the Turnberry Hotel, trying to tie my shoes along the way. Making it to the tee in the nick of time, I was greeted with a sigh of relief by my playing partner, Peter Tupling, a former Walker Cup player, who is now a professional. Despite my ill-prepared condition, Tupling and I teamed up to birdie the last five holes and finish second in the event with a low round of 61.

I have enjoyed the many pro-am and celebrity tournaments I have been invited to play in over the years in Europe and the United Kingdom, even though my pro-am career was perhaps most memorable for its inauspicious debut.

My first pro-am partner was Bobby Locke—one of the greatest putters ever—in the Bowmaker tournament at Sunningdale, England. To prepare, I arrived hours ahead of my starting time and was told that my caddie was known as "One Tooth Jock." I wasn't sure what to think when "One Tooth Jock" emerged from the caddie shed to make his appearance. He was a hulking, malodorous Scotsman, dressed in a long military green coat and boots, with a solitary fang hanging over his lower lip. We proceeded to the driving range, where he watched me slap at the ball for nearly an hour without a single word of comment. Trying to break the ice, I offered him a five-pound note with which he could get himself some lunch before our tee time. He grinned and nodded in what I assumed was appreciation. I took my putter and a few balls to go practice putting with, and instructed him to meet me on the first tee at 12:25, seven minutes ahead of our 12:32 starting time.

Nervous to begin with, and eager to get started, I soon realized that "One Tooth Jock" was nowhere to be found at the appointed time. The starter resorted to summoning him over the public address system, but to no avail. Pacing and waiting, my mindset was shattered when I was forced to face the fact that Jock and my clubs were absent without leave, and that I would have to make my pro-am debut with a set of brand-new Hogan clubs borrowed from Sunningdale club professional Arthur Lees.

Walking up the hill toward the seventh green, I heard the horrible sound of wheezy singing. I then spotted Jock heaving over the horizon toward us, stumbling and struggling with my golf clubs strapped across his chest, singing "Glasgow Belongs to Me."

"Jock, where the bloody hell have you been?" I asked sternly.

He grinned, and I realized his only lunch had surely come from a bottle. "Sir," he said drunkenly, "I set off from Number 1 with a group of players, and after we had gone seven holes and nobody asked me for a club, I realized I was with the wrong foursome and came looking for you."

My travels, packed with similarly curious and entertaining experiences, led me from the ridiculous to the sublime. It was in Spain at La Manga in 1975 that I was introduced to the teenaged younger brother of a European Tour player. His family name was well known in Spain, and it was proposed to me that I face the young kid in a nine-hole match and have a look at his promising game. It was also further proposed that we wager 20 pounds per stroke, and that to keep it sporting the young man would play each of his shots from his knees.

I regarded this as typical Spanish bravado, and, assuming that they underestimated my ability, knew with absolute certainty that I could never lose a gimmick match like this. When the slender unknown junior teed his ball and knocked it 240 yards down the fairway from off of his knees, though, I had the feeling I was seeing something special. The feeling of excitement I got from watching the young man play replaced the growing and overwhelming feeling that I had been had. I shot 43 over those nine holes, and the kid shot 38! I lost 100 pounds to the young Spaniard, who spoke no English. His brother, the European Tour player, was named Manuel, and the young prodigy was called by the name of Seve.

Of course, Seve was not to be the last of the young golf prodigies to whom I would be introduced. At CBS, I was assigned to do a feature on a 16-year-old amateur golfer named Eldrick, who was beginning to get a reputation under the name of "Tiger."

I first chauffeured Sam Snead—one of the most prolific winners in golf history—out to the driving range in a golf cart to analyze Woods's young swing and get his perspective on Woods's potential. Snead's commentary was concise.

"With these kids, you can never tell if they're going to be any good," said Snead. "A player like this might actually be past his peak. Some players can peak early and burn out."

I was astounded that Snead would infer that Woods could actually be past his best at the age of 16. Golf demands a star system, and it was in a boring period. Woods was about to rescue it. Snead's point is well taken in that Woods is very thin, and one begins to wonder how long his body can stand up to the kind of torque he generates. Woods gives it such a ride from the tee, I wonder how many shots he has in him before everything starts to crack up.

At present day, I don't think Woods is a spent force. But he's certainly not the force we were led to believe he would be, either. The media and those that endorsed him created that image. My sense is that Woods will be forgotten in a shorter time rather than a longer time. It is very difficult for any man to be paid so much and keep his desire. The desire will be blunted by the remuneration. Only the single-minded concentration of a Nicklaus could allow focus in the midst of all those riches. Woods is a young man and has lots of things he could be doing at his age, and lots of means to do them. Distractions will naturally abound, and time will reveal both his physical wear and motivation.

After my first interview with the young Woods, I must say that I was impressed with his charisma. He looked me right in the eye and gave me a nice interview. He then emerged starry-eyed from the bright lights of the network television interview just in time for his father Earl to provide a dose of perspective.

"Back to the real world of cheeseburgers, Tiger," he said. "You've got homework to do tonight." As much as I admired Earl Woods for that kind of direction at that time, I fear eventually he became the tail that was wagging the dog.

I was also excited by young John Daly, who I first observed, like everyone else, at the 1991 PGA Championship at Crooked Stick Golf Club in Carmel, Indiana. Lightning struck for Daly that week, and lightning struck literally when an electrical storm claimed the life of a gallery patron. From my vantage, I witnessed the lightning bolt striking down from the ominous sky. During the storm, I was paralyzed with fear on the wooden floor of the metal scaffold tower in which I was positioned. It was not a very intelligent place to ride out the storm, but I was admittedly too scared to climb down and make the quarter of a mile dash to the safety of the clubhouse.

Daly's story, on the brighter side, was one of the most dramatic fairy tales I have ever witnessed. It was a wonderful story that made Daly appear to be a blue-collar successor to Palmer himself. Daly, a man of minimal education with a challenging background, was the last alternate, and drove straight through the night from Memphis when he learned that, against all likely odds, a position in the championship field had opened for him. In fact, I understand he drove straight to the golf course, and, without even a practice round, won the PGA Championship. It was a heroic effort made more exciting by the way he simply blew the ball by Bruce Lietzke, his nearest competitor.

When he gave $30,000 of his winnings to the family of the lightning victim, I knew that the Daly persona would become something special. I also learned then, after a little checking, that Daly had a drinking problem. Tour player and neighbor Tommy Tolles explained to me that he had roomed with Daly while playing in South Africa, and that Daly had trashed the room. According to Tolles, Daly was fine if he stuck to beer, but wild on whiskey.

I shot a feature with Daly for CBS in which I visited him in his home. He played the guitar for me, and was splendidly candid. Daly seemed to trust me.

Not long after the PGA Championship, though, Daly started to get into very public trouble. Perhaps the success was too much too soon, as marital, financial, and psychological problems descended upon him. His battles with alcoholism are well-documented, and just when everyone seemed ready to count him out, he won the 1995 British Open at St. Andrews. No one will ever be able to take the glow of those victories away from Daly, and who knows if and when he will strike again.

Tour jokester Fuzzy Zoeller, a two-time major championship winner as well, has become Daly's mentor and sponsor in his fight against the bottle. Zoeller is the greatest guy, but if I wanted someone to look after Daly, I wouldn't pick Fuzzy. I have lifted my right elbow with him on many occasions all over America.

Zoeller and I have enjoyed a jolly relationship over the years, and he once afforded me a gracious and generous gesture that I will never forget. With a chance to develop a golf resort at a place called Avery's Creek in Asheville, North Carolina, our group signed Zoeller to a letter of intent for an exclusive 10-year, $1 million endorsement deal through which he would represent the resort. Later, when the banks pulled the plug on our financing, I was delegated to go and break the news to Zoeller in the hopes that he might "commute our sentence."

I went to Zoeller's home in Floyd's Knobs, Indiana, and nervously explained our plight. "No worries," Fuzzy said, smiling as always. He retrieved the contract, literally tore it in half, and tossed the pieces into the fireplace.

The big-hearted Zoeller—aside from his two major championship victories—has endeared himself to golf fans by gaining a reputation as a comedian among the PGA Tour players. As a very young man working in Manchester, England, in 1955, I happened across a few other renowned funnymen one evening. I was in a nightclub called "The Cabin Club," and I joined in conversation with four guys who were referring to themselves as "goons." Their names were Harry Seccombe, Michael Bentine, Spike Milligan, and Peter Sellers.

These four guys were total madmen, each with a very sharp British sense of humor. Seccombe, a Welshman, was a world class singer as well as a comedian. Bentine, from Peru, was Etonian, and nuttier than a fruitcake. Milligan regularly spent time in an asylum "getting readjusted." As for Sellers, he went at 100 miles per hour all through the night. As we drank, Sellers realized that I was pretty good at imitating dialects, so he and I began assuming any number of various characters carrying on conversations. A crowd gathered around to watch, listen, and laugh as Sellers and I went at this until 8:00 A.M., never once using our own genuine voices. When I think about us finally leaving the "Cabin Club" in the bright daylight of the morning, I realize what utter madness this was for Sellers to abuse himself in this fashion. He'd been warned and warned that he had a serious heart problem, and yet I have never met anyone who had such an accelerated death wish as Sellers. That was how he lived, and he could never see his way to taking it easy. He was always on the edge, and every time I saw him after that night he was no different. We always trotted out our various dialogues, but I could never keep up with him, particularly when he would steal the show and break me up by doing his beloved "Inspector Clouseau" character.

A few years later, I did some work for Granada Television, which was one of the independent British television networks. I served as a producer on a daily, half-hour, live television magazine show each evening called "Scene at 6:30." One day each week, the show would feature a different musical act. The acts varied from baritone singers to traditional bagpipers, some well-known and some newcomers. One morning, I got the call that the act scheduled for that evening would be unable to appear. I was in a real pinch, and wracked my brain for a suitable alternative that might be available on short notice. As a last resort, my associate producer, Dick "Tricky Dicky" Fontaine, offered a little-known group that was appearing from time to time at a grungy nightclub in Liverpool called "The Cabin."

Fontaine phoned the lads, and the quartet was indeed available for a nominal fee. They were also grateful for the exposure that the telecast would provide. When the four lads arrived at the studio, however, I was aghast.

"These boys are not going on the air until they clean up," I insisted, as I gave Fontaine the money to take them down the street and get their hair cut and washed. I did my best to make "The Beatles" presentable. Against my better judgment, they went on the show that evening and performed what seemed to me to be dreadful music, but at least I had solved my problem and filled the airtime with which I was stuck.

Then the phones started ringing, and the response was overwhelming. Young girls turned up outside the studio doors, hoping to get a firsthand look at the scruffy but well-mannered boys. Our viewers were over the moon about "The Beatles," but I just couldn't see, or hear, their talent.

Five or six weeks later, when scheduling upcoming shows, I instructed Fontaine to rebook the Beatles for a return appearance.

"We'd better get those boys back in here," I said. Each of the two times we brought them back, the crowds outside grew larger. Fifteen thousand people gathered in the street on the third encore appearance, and crowd control measures were employed to keep the crush out of the television studio.

When my young female secretary was forbidden from going into the studio to see the Beatles, she wept buckets and beat upon my chest with both fists.

Our fourth attempt to feature the Beatles on "Scene at 6:30" was blunted by the Beatles' new manager, Brian Epstein. He had priced them out of our range. The Beatles were on their way to the big time.

The "Fab Four" would later become rock and roll royalty—but my career also took me into the rarefied air of *genuine* royalty.

In 1973, I was taking a flight in the first class cabin of a jet traveling from London's Heathrow Airport to Malaga, Spain. I was on my way to the 1973 World Cup, and His Royal Highness, Charles, the Prince of Wales, then the world's most eligible bachelor, was on his way to call on the Duke of Wellington's daughter at their family estate. Prince Charles, traveling with his aide, was obviously elegantly dressed, and pure blue of eyes. Upon landing, as we taxied down the tarmac, it was evident that a media mob had assembled at the bottom of the stairway. Charles stood and offered to break protocol and allow all of his fellow passengers to leave the plane and descend the stairs before he did. This would allow us to easily pass through the crowd and get to the terminal before the media throng blocked our exit. I thought this was a rather classy and thoughtful gesture by the future King of England.

The Prince's aunt, Her Royal Highness the Princess Margaret, was to do the prize giving at the Aga Khan's regatta, at which I was in attendance because I was playing golf as a guest of the Aga Khan at nearby Pevero on the island of Sardinia. The Princess was relieved of her duties when she turned up at the reception intoxicated, dressed in a peasant-like outfit with stains on it. She was not even allowed to speak, and someone else was quickly recruited to fill her role as she sat and observed.

It was becoming known at that time that the Princess Margaret was having trouble in her marriage with her husband Tony Armstrong Jones. It was whispered in certain circles that Jones preferred the company of men.

After the awards, the gathered adjourned for a reception. Armstrong Jones made a beeline for my then third wife Judy, asking her to sit with him.

"Let's go and sit at a table so I can get away from that blousy bitch," he pleaded.

At the same time, the Princess suggested to me that I join her in conversation at a table. I tried to make pleasant small talk and explain that I had met the Queen as a boy when my father received the Order of the British Empire, but the Princess was only interested in prattling on about "that tick of a husband" of hers.

After the reception, my wife and I got a laugh out of comparing notes and relating the vicious manner in which they complained about each other.

I did encounter the Princess Margaret on another occasion when I was stringing for the *Sunday Times*. Armstrong Jones contributed to the newspaper as a photographer, and late one afternoon as I was leaving for the day, I was startled to find the Princess Margaret in the lobby.

"Hello," she growled, "have you seen that miserable weasel of a husband of mine?"

Embarrassed for her, I answered "No ma'am," and skipped out quickly.

P rior to the 1978 elections in Great Britain, I attended a political reception, again with my wife Judy, who served as chair of the local Conservative Party. I was introduced there to the candidate expected to become Prime Minister of England, and enjoyed a great conversation with Mrs. Margaret Thatcher, with whom I was wholly impressed.

"What about you?" she pointedly asked me. "Why are you wasting your time? How about you standing for Parliament? With your gift of gab, you might very well be groomed for stardom in the party."

Mrs. Thatcher was making a subtle reference to the fact that my mentor, Henry Longhurst, who actually served a term in Parliament, was thought to be an attractive candidate for prime minister due to his tremendous professional oratory skills.

When I thought about Thatcher's suggestion that I stand for Parliament—a suggestion which I suppose many would find flattering—I found that it only opened the old wounds of the most puzzling disappointment of my life. As a boy of 13—and as a man standing with Margaret Thatcher—I was never able to understand how the electorate rejected Winston Churchill after the war when the first elections came along in 1945. I simply could not understand how—after the willful and strong way he led the kingdom so flawlessly through its darkest hour—the electorate could have the temerity to throw out my hero in favor of a little man named Clement Attlee, who looked like a bank clerk at best.

I idolized Churchill until his dying day. He was a horrible man in lots of ways, and far from perfect, but he had the true gift of oratory skills and firm leadership. He was just what Great Britain needed at the time.

I could not forgive my fellow men for having done this, and it was a big raging torment inside of me. It was Churchill, by the way, who uttered these words to describe the game of golf: "A curious sport whose object is to put a very small ball in a very small hole with implements ill designed for the purpose."

Rather than burden Mrs. Thatcher with a Churchillian diatribe on my lifelong disappointment with the voters, I simply reverted back to Longhurst's reason for only serving one term in Parliament, and demurred to Mrs. Thatcher with the same philosophy.

"Mrs. Thatcher," I answered with a twinkle, "I duly appreciate the compliment. But I am having far too much fun out on the golf tours to consider standing for Parliament or, God forbid, being elected Prime Minister."

While I never again met "the Iron Lady," I was in the company of her husband Dennis Thatcher at the grand opening of the Lake Nona Golf Club near Orlando, Florida. Thatcher was to be honored and would serve as the keynote speaker. Seated at great round tables in the large banquet room, we all enjoyed a full dinner with wine, and then listened to various club officials rise to make little speeches as the microphone was passed around from table to table by an emcee.

Once everyone had congratulated each other and themselves by saying their piece, the emcee launched into a full introduction of the honored guest, while making his way with the wireless microphone toward Mr. Thatcher's table.

Upon completion of the welcoming introduction, he placed the microphone down in front of Thatcher. The entire room was then treated to the sound of heavy snoring through the public address system, for Thatcher had fallen blissfully asleep.

At another dignified sports banquet, I was seated with Lord Westwood, a splendid old gentleman who was the owner of the Newcastle United Football team, and the evening's featured speaker.

The banquet crowd, comprised of rugged footballers and soccer writers, drank their way through dinner and were boisterously carrying on. As the time for Westwood's speech grew near, I asked His Lordship how he possibly thought he might be able to quiet the raucous crowd and keep their attention through his scheduled speech.

Westwood nodded knowingly and told me of his tried and tested strategy. "Ben, early in the speech, I will say something totally outrageous, and mark my words, suddenly these asses will look at each other in disbelief and henceforth keep serenely quiet."

As the crowd restlessly shifted in their seats, Lord Westwood, aware of their impatience, was called to the microphone and made his way to the podium with his speech in hand. He then looked over the crowd, and began his speech by uttering:

"Well, well, that is not the first time today I've climbed off a warm seat with a piece of paper in my hand!"

I must admit that I laughed loudly at this proper gentleman's tawdry reference to "the throne." Ah, daring British humor never fails.

I know that there are those who question—as I did with Churchill—how the American electorate could have seen fit to vote President George Bush out of office in 1992 in favor of the far less experienced Bill Clinton. The vote was even more puzzling after the way Bush handled the Gulf War, with the nearly unilateral support of every other nation in the world. I take their point, and have a huge admiration for the gentleman George Bush and the manner in which he conducted himself.

Once again my charmed life in golf allowed me the ability to become acquainted with Bush after playing with him at Cy Laughter's famed "Bogey Busters" golf tournament at the National Cash Register Club in Dayton, Ohio. Bush was vice president at the time, and we had such an enjoyable game that he asked to play with me again the following year. Years later, he presented me with a pair of impressive cuff links, replete with the Seal of the President and his autograph, which I prize and cherish to this day. But that day as Vice President Bush gave me his calling card, which would prove to be an even more valuable gift because it included a private telephone number to access him, was a truly special day.

"If you're ever in a jam, here I am," he said as he handed it to me. I kept the card, never expecting actually to use it.

A few years later, though, I was experiencing great difficulty in renewing my green card, which allowed me to continue earning my living with CBS Television after my permanent move to the United States. The administrative red tape was getting thick, I was having little luck pleading my case, and had actually hired lawyers to do the same. After much internal second-guessing as to whether it was appropriate, I decided I had no choice but to dial the telephone number on George Bush's calling card. The lawyers were making no progress, and I was getting desperate.

Skeptical that the humorless and official-sounding man who answered would actually connect me to Bush, I meekly gave him my name and explained that the vice president had given me his card. The next voice I heard was that of Bush. He greeted me warmly, then listened as I explained my plight.

"Ben, I want you to hold the line," Bush said. "I am going to put you on right now with one of my aides, and you can rest assured he will make your problem go away."

I was relieved that my green card would indeed be secured, amazed by the genuine sincerity of Bush, and somewhat chagrined by the level to which I had to go over the heads of the administrators at the Department of Immigration and Naturalization. "All this for a bloody golf announcer?" the administrators must have thought.

When Bush became president, I was assigned by CBS to put together a piece on Bush's affinity for the game of golf, which would air on the "CBS Evening News." With Bush's approval, I flew up to his summer home in Kennebunkport, Maine with a camera crew. The president and I played a round at his home course, the Cape Arundel Golf Club, and I interviewed club professional Ken Raynor before returning with Bush to his lovely seaside home on Walker's Point.

In the piece, I was gentle in analyzing Bush's swing, which I found to be quick and in need of work. I also detailed Bush's impressive golf pedigree, which included his maternal grandfather Herbert Walker, who bears no less distinction than Samuel Ryder, as he was the donor of the Walker Cup, and a USGA president. His father carried on the tradition as a USGA vice president.

Later that year, the president told me that he enjoyed the piece. The occasion was when I introduced Bush while serving as the master of ceremonies for the "Ambassador of Golf" honors in conjunction with the World Series of Golf at Firestone Country Club in Akron,

Ohio. After the ceremony, the president invited me to the cottage he was occupying just off of the 16th hole for drinks. We laughed as I regaled him with the tale of a time I played golf with another president: Ferdinand Marcos of the Philippines.

M arcos and I were teamed in a foursome during the pro-am portion of the Colgate Palmolive Far Eastern Women's Open in Manila. My playing partner was JoAnne Carner, and President Marcos had personally chosen the beautiful young Jan Stephenson as his partner. Marcos, though, had a terrible round because he could not help himself from being distracted.

It was plainly obvious by the way Marcos gawked and flirted that he had a complete crush on Stephenson. At first nervous as a schoolboy in her presence, he began to relax, and before the round was over, he could not keep his hands off of his playing partner. I'm certain it was very uncomfortable for Stephenson. Although she was bothered by the cad, Stephenson managed the 18 holes of diplomatic challenge with admirable aplomb.

Unlike Marcos, a president with real dignity and class was Gerald Ford. I played in the President Gerald Ford Pro-Am Tournament for ten years. For each of those ten years, the "pro" in my group was Gary McCord—which meant that, in effect, we were the only group without a pro. Ford's golf game, which was much maligned by the press, was better than it was portrayed. He is a big man who hits the ball far but crooked. His and his wife Betty's generosity and graciousness are supreme.

To my astonishment, the Fords invited my fourth wife Kitty and me to be seated at their table during the awards dinner one year. When Mrs. Ford learned that my young daughter Margaret was also present at the hotel, she insisted that we all slide together and that a chair be pulled up so that Margaret could join us.

I'm not sure if the significance was lost on young Margaret, but it was a heady experience for me as I looked across the table at the former President and Mrs. Ford, Bob and Dolores Hope, Jim and Laurie Nantz, and basketball star John Havlicek.

At that time, I knew that Mrs. Ford was a recovering alcoholic, but Mrs. Hope, far more animated than her husband, kept nudging me and proclaiming proudly, "It's martini time!" I sheepishly slipped down drinks with Mrs. Hope, trying to avoid the eye of Mrs. Ford.

I immensely enjoyed my access to presidents and royalty. Even "the King and I" once flew across the Atlantic together. From 1972 until 1978, when I was commuting back and forth from England for my CBS broadcasts, I would take a flight out of Heathrow known as "the Pan-Am Lunch Flight." Passengers would begin the flight seated in the first-class cabin, and after takeoff they were ushered upstairs for fine dining with linen tablecloths, china, and silverware. It was a properly mellow and civilized way to travel, and one never knew with whom one might be seated, as the flight was generally made up of top-drawer people.

I mention "the King and I" because my lunch and travel companion on two of those flights was Yul Brynner. He was a fascinating conversationalist, and the many drinks he and I enjoyed over the six-hour flight ensured that we would eventually get through New York's JFK Airport upon landing with a minimal amount of pain.

I first met "The Man Who Would Be King"—Sean Connery—at the previously mentioned Bowmaker Tournament at Sunningdale. Toward the end of the day, Connery, Peter Alliss, Dave Thomas, and I somehow found ourselves the last players left on the practice putting green. Boys will be boys, and our small talk led to an improvised 18-hole putting match. Thomas and I putted against Alliss and Connery in a 10-pounds-per-hole wager.

During the course of the putting match, an elderly official-looking chap with a club crest on his jacket emerged from the clubhouse and approached Connery on the green.

"Sean," the man interrupted, "can I request that you autograph this scorecard to my daughter before we leave for the day? She's waiting in the clubhouse."

Connery, who had applied for membership at Sunningdale, was sure to reply politely but firmly in his authoritative Scottish brogue: "I'll be glad to sign anything for you later, sir. I'm occupied right now in a bit of putting and wagering, so I'll see you when I am finished."

We resumed our merry and competitive putting match, but it was not long before the elderly member, eager to leave in the waning twilight, emerged again from the clubhouse and approached Connery on the putting green to ask again for the autograph.

This time, an enraged Connery grabbed the man by his decorated lapels.

"I told you once that I would do it when I am finished. Now bugger off!"

Regardless, Connery's genuine charm and status won him a membership at Sunningdale, where I also once played a round with Rita Hayworth.

I was in Connery's company again when I played in the Sean Connery Pro-Am, which he threw in his home territory at Royal Troon in 1973. It seemed all of Glasgow was there to follow my group, which featured Gary Player as our professional, and Geoff Lewis, the Queen's jockey who had won the English Derby on Mill Reef. Due to the teeming galleries and the large number of celebrity amateur players, the pace of play that day was very slow, and by the time we finished our six-hour round tied for the lead most everyone had gone home and the clubhouse bar was nearly empty. Lewis and I, however, stopped in for one drink.

To say Lewis was diminutive would be an understatement. The little jockey was knee-high to a bullfrog, but he was like a miniature Jack Nicklaus in that he could hit the ball 200 yards straight down the middle.

At the conclusion of my drink, I bid Lewis good-night, and explained that I was going to take room service and get some rest due to our early starting time in the second round the following morning. Lewis claimed he would shortly implement a similar dinner plan, but I could see the light of battle in his eyes. He claimed he was going to bed, but I knew my teammate would be out drinking instead.

My fears were confirmed the following morning, when Player, Lewis, and I reconvened at the first tee, with a large gallery again there to follow us. Lewis arrived just in time, and after being formally introduced to the crowd by the tee announcer, he strode onto the tee box for all to see. Bending to stick his tee into the ground, the dizzy Lewis tumbled through a full somersault, and landed flat on his back, looking up at the sky and laughing hysterically. Still drunk from the night before, Lewis barely got the ball airborne for the rest of that day, and our team, much to my chagrin, faded into fourth place.

I would very often also see Connery each year when the CBS crew would go to Los Angeles to broadcast the L.A. Open. I had many magical nights camped out at Bel Air Country Club, seated at a round Hollywood table with the likes of Connery, comic actor Bob Newhart, singer Howard Keel, songwriter Mac Davis, actors James Garner and Richard Crenna, and others. It was a period when the PGA Tour was becoming indelibly linked to celebrities, and in most cases, the celebrities were all too happy to party with the CBS TV announcers and participate in our broadcasts.

I played a round of golf in L.A. with "Goodfella" Joe Pesci. Imagine the hilarious and bold Pesci, translating my British comments into his version of "Brooklynese" over all 18 holes—because that is exactly what he did!

From 1971 until 1983, country singer Glen Campbell was the celebrity spokesperson for the L.A. Open, which was then called "The Glen Campbell Los Angeles Open." Campbell, perhaps best known for his tune "By the Time I Get to Phoenix," has now totally gone to God, but at the time he was heavy into drugs and drink. Sadly, there were times when Campbell either wouldn't show up for our broadcasts or was simply too incoherent for Chirkinian or Campbell's agent to consider allowing him to go on the air.

For 20 years, the San Diego tournament at Torrey Pines Golf Club bore the name of singer Andy Williams. When his tournament ran late one year, Williams offered to let me ride with him in his helicopter to Los Angeles so that I could still catch the day's only flight back to London. Apparently distracted by his teenage lovely, he reneged and left me behind, stranded in California for a wasted day.

Ever more thoughtful was Sammy Davis Jr., who presided over the Greater Hartford Open for 15 years, beginning in 1973. Davis, himself a tiny bag of bones, had a real affinity for the little people, so each tournament week he would stage an elaborate lobster and steak dinner for all of the real CBS TV working crew. The cable pullers, stage managers, production assistants, and the workers who constructed the scaffolds were treated to Davis's generosity and a performance by "The Candy Man" himself.

Davis did a great Ben Wright impersonation, even topping Ben Crenshaw, whose impression of me, though he thought it was good, always made me sound like I was from Texas.

In 1980, Davis's tournament went to a sudden death playoff between Howard Twitty and Jim Simons. CBS, never wanting to preempt "60 Minutes," went off the air. In the 18th tower, Davis could hear the angry shouts of the crowd, some of whom were protesting because they had been viewing the action on portable televisions and on monitors in the hospitality tents. Davis—who'd been indulging in his Dubonnet aperitif and popping God knows how many pills—leaned out of the tower to incite and antagonize the crowd.

"You know what your first name is?" he yelled. "It's 'mother!'... And you *know* what your last name is!"

Now the crowd, already ugly, was ready to turn on its very host. Both amused and enraged by the little man's taunts, the gallery now recognized that it was open season for shouting and hooting, which they did with evil enthusiasm as Sammy gestured at them from the booth above.

I only hoped he wouldn't need to use the pearl-handled, snubnosed revolver I saw sticking out of his pocket.

Bob Hope is the only celebrity that has maintained a celebrity tournament on the PGA Tour, with his Bob Hope Chrysler Classic still thriving. Ed McMahon hosted the Quad Cities Open in Coal Valley, Illinois. Dean Martin and Joe Garagiola each took their turn presiding over the Tucson Open. Actor Danny Thomas, who worked tirelessly for charity, was devastated when, after 14 years of hosting the Memphis Classic, his name was unceremoniously dumped from the title for that of Federal Express.

Jackie Gleason was desperately hurt when, in 1981, the PGA Tour took the Jackie Gleason Inverrary Classic tournament away from him, even accusing him of having been drunk on the telecast. "The Great One," who was cheered by galleries all over the golf course, threw some terrific parties at his huge Tudor home on the eighth hole of Inverrary's West Course. Gleason, a large man who was indeed larger than life, invited me into his elaborate pool table room, which featured a magnificent sunken bar. Behind the bar was a life-sized mechanical gorilla that was designed to serve scotch.

PGA Tour Commissioner Deane Beman did away with the celebrity tournaments by successfully commercializing the tour. Although purses were elevated, some of the history of the Tour was certainly

erased when venerable tournaments like the Westchester Classic
became known only as the "Buick Classic," and the Heritage Classic
became the "MCI Classic." Are fans really expected to instantly be
able to differentiate between the Buick Open, Buick Classic and the
Buick Invitational? The Los Angeles Open is now only the "Nissan
Open," and Tucson, which has hosted a tournament since 1945, became known as the Nortel Open in 1996, the Tucson Chrysler Classic
in 1997 and 1998, and the Nortel Open again in 1998!

N o celebrity tournament better displayed the era of commercial-
ization than the Bing Crosby National Pro-Am. The tournament
at Pebble Beach, founded by Crosby in 1937 and lovingly referred to
as "the clambake," fell into the hands of sponsor AT&T in 1986. AT&T
squelched the intimacy of the event by turning it into a wholly corporate, customer-client endeavor. With der Bingle no longer alive to
protect his clambake, Mrs. Crosby realized that the event had lost its
soul and forbade AT&T from using her husband's name.

During Bing's heyday, the Crosby tournament was absolutely
splendid. A major quality of celebrities came out of respect to Bing.

Pebble Beach was, and to some extent still is, a hangout for the
stars—one-time stomping grounds, if you will, for Elizabeth Taylor,
Randolph Scott, Clark Gable, Rita Hayworth, and in the modern age,
Clint Eastwood, Michael Jordan, Bill Murray, James Garner, and Jack
Lemmon.

Crosby was such a wonderful host. His loyal decision to put his
showbiz pal Phil Harris in the tower at the 18th hole and make him
part of the CBS telecast was classic Bing, but it drove Mrs. Crosby
nuts. She was straight-laced, and she surely didn't like this raunchy
old bugger. Harris was one of the funniest, most irreverent men I
have ever met.

On one of the telecasts, Chirkinian put up a camera shot of a
beautiful 90-foot yacht making its way along the coast behind the
17th green.

"Here we have another full load of pure Colombian making its
way into town," piped Harris in his deep gravelly voice.

Each year, Harris smuggled three bottles of "Old No. 7" into the
tower at 18 to last him through the weekend's telecast while Summerall
looked the other way. When the live camera shot once inadvertently

caught Harris swallowing a sip of the sauce, Summerall had no choice but to make light of Harris's sin and give him a chance to talk his way out of it.

"A little top-off of your favorite, Phil?" asked Summerall glibly.

"Ahh...my friend Jack Daniels," Harris replied. "You're gonna need permission from the Atomic Energy Commission to bury me because my liver is gonna cause a world of environmental trouble."

Harris was incorrigible, but I, having been accused of being like-minded, enjoyed Harris's sense of humor. I bloody well needed the laughs, because most of the time I was suffering extreme cold manning my tower position behind the 17th green. I would sneer down at the sea otters, floating happily on their backs in the bay below, grinning and cracking oysters on their chests.

The back of the high tower faced the ocean, and had to remain open to allow the howling ocean winds to safely pass through. On one occasion the wind was so strong that I remember witnessing all of the contents of the broadcast position blow out of the tower and into the bunker behind the 17th green below.

I suffered the agonies of the damned up there above 17, and usually left the tower after each broadcast with sea salt all over my back. There was nothing I could do to adequately battle the elements up on that windy perch. I had battery-powered heated socks, and once even took up the bedspread from the hotel room in the lodge. The dastardly Chirkinian, in a display of his wicked sense of humor, once put me on camera in that condition. I was mortified to see myself on the monitor because I looked like a chattering old woman wrapped in a shawl.

Upon seeing the poor sight of frigid Ben Wright on television, the deputy manager of the lodge at Pebble Beach came to my tower at 17 just before the next day's rehearsal. He expressed his dismay at seeing me so cold up in the booth, and presented me with an electric blanket to take up the ladder with me. I thanked him profusely, and understood his concern that potential tourists all over America were viewing me wrapped in apparel that looked as if I were on an Arctic expedition.

Once in the tower, I crouched near the outlets to plug in the electric blanket.

"Ben," said my cameraman, Ricky Blaine, with a halting yet sympathetic tone in his voice, "Uh, just a minute, Ben. I don't think the remote electric circuit can stand an electric blanket."

He could see the plaintive look on my face at hearing the news.

"Alright, let's give it a try," he mercifully acquiesced, "at least through the rehearsal."

I plugged the blanket in, wrapped it around my lap, settled into my seat, and turned it on the highest setting—and fused the entire neighborhood! My monitors went dark, Blaine's camera went black, and my treasured blanket knocked CBS off-line until the engineers could re-fuse the electrical system.

I spent lots of time at "Club 19," the subterranean bar in the lodge at Pebble Beach, drinking with celebrities like Charley Pride and Jack Lemmon. One sunny afternoon I was having a splendid lunch on the patio with Chirkinian and a few of the other announcers. Phil Harris bumbled in, and sat down alone at another table. Chirkinian dispatched me to ask him to join us, which I did.

"Thank the guys, but I can't," Harris conceded. "I'm supposed to meet a friend here, and he's bringing a girlfriend that I wouldn't want to bring to your table."

I must have looked puzzled because Harris then explained, "Ben, she's so fat that if anybody ever cried 'haul ass,' she'd have to make three trips!"

Laughing and shaking my head is dismay, I returned to my table and repeated Harris's crass joke to compatriots. Sure enough, when Harris's friend eventually entered the patio with his girlfriend, Harris stood right up, waved to get our attention, pointed directly at the woman, and shouted, "See what I mean?"

So wicked.

I did encounter Crosby away from the splendor and joy of his Pebble Beach tournament when I played a practice round with him at Turnberry, Scotland. Knowing Bing's love for the game and that he would certainly appreciate the setting, I was also convinced that this would be a special occasion when I learned that his sons Nathaniel and Harry would be joining us. It was agreed that Bing and I would team up in a friendly match over the famed links against the youthful boys.

Unfortunately, the round was not memorable in the way that I'd hoped it would be. What I remember is the viciously mean way Crosby treated his sons. The boys didn't play well, and Bing poured scorn on them to a cruel degree. Crosby berated them about their lousy shots, and, in my opinion, embarrassed himself but was unashamed of his behavior. Bing never showed this infamous side during his Monterey Peninsula happening.

Happily, "the clambake" has resettled as a charitable pro-am run by Kathryn Crosby each year at Bermuda Run Golf and Country Club in Winston-Salem, North Carolina. The event maintains a better flavor of Bing's tournament, and the presence and memory of the great entertainer is honored with trophies and his familiar silhouette sporting the Trilby hat and pipe. The fact that I am invited yearly to participate as a celebrity reminds me of the special status, deserved or not, that I have enjoyed throughout my career. Certainly the most important yield is the wonderful relationships that I have been exposed to and have maintained.

Stories like those I've just told you were rushing through my mind as I sat in the dark in the cinema at the Biltmore Square Mall waiting to watch "Tin Cup."

The genesis of my involvement in the movie occurred when filmmaker Ron Shelton, who directed such memorable sports films as "Bull Durham," "Cobb," and "White Men Can't Jump," contacted CBS. He inquired about an arrangement whereby he and actor Kevin Costner could join the CBS crew in observing PGA Tour events. Along the way, Costner took golf lessons from McCord, who had the job of teaching him how to authentically mimic the swing of a genuine PGA Tour golfer. It was a perfect job for McCord, since he himself had spent his entire golf career trying to impersonate a genuine PGA Tour player. McCord served as technical director on the film, which, I suppose, is why the movie only grossed $66 million. Without him, I suppose the studio could have counted on at least $100 million.

After months of observation, Shelton and Costner were ready to begin shooting, and wished to make the CBS team a big part of the film, which was the story of a driving range pro contesting for the U.S. Open Championship. My part was small, and by film standards my pay was small, as I was compensated $9,000 per day and flown to Houston for only a day or two of shooting.

I met with Costner, a very pleasant family man who was devoted each evening to his children; Cheech Marin, who only had to move for me to start laughing; and Don Johnson, who was pleasant enough, but always maintained what I thought was a wild look about him.

Crew call the first day was at 6:00 A.M. on a brand new golf course in Houston, Texas that Shelton had leased as a location before a ball had ever been struck on it. Bleachers, skyboxes, and scoreboards were erected to make the setting look authentic. In their attempt to make my part as a network golf announcer authentic, the producers went a little over the top. I was presented with a script full of clichéd English pomposity, complete with four- and five-syllable words that would never sound natural.

I protested to Costner and Shelton, and they agreed to allow me to ad-lib my part based on the on-course action I would be witnessing in the story line. Costner sat at my feet below the desk, describing the action that I was ostensibly witnessing from the television tower. They seemed amazed by my ability to ad-lib, until I explained to them that I ad-libbed for a living on live television, and was used to working in an environment where yelling "cut" and stopping and doing it again was not a luxury. My work had to be perfect the first time, because there were no second chances on live television. I think they appreciated that kind of professionalism. The irony is that while I ad-libbed my lines for a key scene, I had to synch up my commentary while Kevin, on camera, tried to bank a chip shot off of a port-a-john and onto a green. I referred to the port-a-john in British parlance as a "water closet," and the scene turned out to be very entertaining. What the viewers around me in the Biltmore Square Mall Cinema didn't realize is that it took no less than 86 takes for Costner to perfectly bank that shot and have the ball roll right up to the lens. It was a camera shot that would last all of 10 seconds.

For each and every one of his 86 takes, all day long, I had to provide live, ad-libbed commentary.

Hey, there's no business like show business.